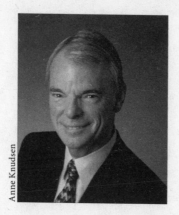

Anne Knudsen

MICHAEL SPENCE is a professor of economics at the Stern School of Business at New York University, a senior fellow at the Hoover Institution, and a former chairman of the independent Commission on Growth and Development. A recipient of the 2001 Nobel Prize in Economic Sciences, he lives in California and Italy.

Also by Michael Spence

Market Signaling: Informational Transfer in Hiring and Related Screening Processes

Industrial Organization in an Open Economy (with R. E. Caves and M. E. Porter)

Competitive Structure in Investment Banking (with Samuel Hayes and David Marks)

THE NEXT CONVERGENCE

The Future of Economic Growth
in a Multispeed World

MICHAEL SPENCE

PICADOR

FARRAR, STRAUS AND GIROUX
NEW YORK

THE NEXT CONVERGENCE. Copyright © 2011 by Michael Spence. All rights reserved. Printed in the United States of America. For information, address Picador, 175 Fifth Avenue, New York, N.Y. 10010.

www.picadorusa.com
www.twitter.com/picadorusa • www.facebook.com/picadorusa

Picador® is a U.S. registered trademark and is used by Farrar, Straus and Giroux under license from Pan Books Limited.

For book club information, please visit www.facebook.com/picadorbookclub or e-mail marketing@picadorusa.com.

Grateful acknowledgment is made to the following for permission to reprint previously published material: World Bank Group, from *The Growth Report* © 2008 and *Economic Growth in the 1990s* © 2005; International Monetary Fund, from the *World Economic Outlook* © 2010 and *China's Changing Trade Elasticities* © 2007; The Economist Newspaper Limited, London, from the May 27, 2010, print edition of *The Economist;* Sir Andrew Crockett, from *China's Role in the World Economy: Looking Forward to the 12th 5-Year Plan* © 2010.

Designed by Abby Kagan

The Library of Congress has cataloged the Farrar, Straus and Giroux edition as follows:

Spence, Michael, 1943–
    The next convergence : the future of economic growth in a multispeed world / Michael Spence. —1st ed.
      p. cm.
    ISBN 978-0-374-15975-7
    1. Economic development.   2. Sustainable development—Developing countries.
    3. Financial crises—History—21st century.   4. International cooperation.   I. Title.
    HD82.S694 2011
    338.9—dc22

2010047716

Picador ISBN 978-1-250-00770-4

First published in the United States by Farrar, Straus and Giroux

First Picador Edition: August 2012

10 9 8 7 6 5 4 3 2 1

For Giuliana

A man only becomes wise when he begins to calculate the approximate depth of his ignorance.

—Gian Carlo Menotti

Those who cannot change their minds cannot change anything.

—George Bernard Shaw

My belief is that every good cause is worth some inefficiency.

—Paul Samuelson

Contents

Preface

In 1999, I completed nine years as Dean of the Graduate School of Business of Stanford University, ending fifteen years of academic administration, the preceding six as the Dean of the Faculty of Arts and Sciences at Harvard. It was a wonderful period in my professional life, one I would not have given up, even with the knowledge that hindsight brings of the rewards, challenges, and petty tribulations. I learned a great deal about management and implementation, about organizations, incentives, and motivation. Though this was not the purpose, I think it has made me a better "older" economist.

But the truth is that fifteen years is a long time, long enough to drift fairly far away from the day-to-day debates in economics. Some colleagues have referred to me as a former economist, causing me to wince a little, even if there was an element of truth in it.

Prior to academic administration, I would have been described as an applied microeconomic theorist, with an interest in the details of market structure and performance and a special interest in the information structures in markets—markets where there are informational gaps and asymmetries that affect market performance. Market functioning and performance in the presence of informational gaps had been the focus of my doctoral work. The work on market signaling was an attempt to assess how markets would try to close informational gaps, and it was recognized by the Nobel Prize in Economics in 2001, in the excellent company of George Akerlof and Joseph Stiglitz. One can think of market signaling as being an attempt to understand how sellers of high-quality products send credible signals to potential buyers in a market environment in which the buyers do not have the quality information separate from the functioning of the market and the embedded signaling.

In 1999, when I stepped back from academic administration, Internet mania was in full bloom. The potential of the Internet and the World Wide Web to have a major impact on markets, industries, and indeed whole economies was starting to come into focus. The Internet bubble in the stock markets and in venture capital was under way and inflating rapidly. Companies were being formed and financed in some cases without even a hint of where the revenues, let alone profits, were going to come from. Venture capital flowed like water from a decapitated fire hydrant. Companies went public early in their life cycle and traded at values determined largely by day traders, many of whom could not describe the business of the company or its products except in the vaguest of terms. It was uncharted territory with little historical data to constrain the expectations and enthusiasm, at least for a while. Then reality set in, revenues and profits in many cases did not materialize, and of course the period of overvaluation came to an end, as so often happens, with startling rapidity.

The fact that there was a bubble and then a burst bubble led some to conclude that there was nothing there in the first place. That was not and is not right. Overvaluation does not imply the absence of fundamental change. Often it is associated with an overestimate of the speed of change. It seems clear that in this case, the principal mistake lay not in forecasting huge impacts on economic systems and processes, but rather in overestimating the pace of adoption.

This gap between the potential of an innovation and its widespread adoption is one of those lessons that we learn and then tend to forget, or we don't learn it because of inattention to history and its lessons about human and organizational behavior.

As I thought about the potential uses of the Internet, it started to become clear that the informational structures in markets, supply chains, and transaction systems—indeed, the whole global economy—were set for a fundamental and permanent shift. With a background in this part of economics, I decided to set out to try to make sense of what all this meant for the functioning of markets and economies. I talk about that in Part IV. Information technology is one of the most powerful forces now affecting growth and the distribution of economic activity in the global economy.

The information layer that surrounds, organizes, and governs the real economy and all its parts is gravitating to the Internet; that is, to networks of computers and people. Time and distance and cost are compressed in the information layer. Many of the costs associated with being remote, from markets and head offices, were expected to decline with this new technology, and in fact they are declining rapidly.

I asked myself the question, "Where is the largest long-run impact of the technology surrounding the Internet likely to occur?" Once you note that time and distance and related costs are compressed, and that remoteness loses some of its significance, the answer seems obvious: the big impact is likely to be in international markets, global supply chains, in access to information and services in places that have been remote from them—in short, in the global economy, and especially in the developing countries.

As I embarked on this line of inquiry, an unexpected call came from the World Bank asking if I would deliver a keynote lecture in 2005 at the principal annual conference held by the Poverty Reduction and Economic Management Network in the Bank. The proposed subject was growth in the developing world. Now, I thought to myself, it is true that, in light of the route just outlined, I am interested in this. But giving a lecture on the subject in an institution with several thousand of the world's most knowledgeable people on the subject of development struck me as slightly risky. I voiced this doubt. The response I got was that new views from outsiders are sometimes useful, that I had a background in microeconomics and some experience with investment, and that growth as an essential enabler of poverty reduction and progress had experienced a period of underemphasis.

I wasn't entirely persuaded, but resorting to my past, I thought if it goes badly, it will be a useful signal and I can move on. And if it doesn't go badly, that signal will be useful too.

I enjoyed it, seemed not to bomb, and, to cut a long story short, after some discussion in partnership with the World Bank and a number of other sponsors, we decided to ask a group of distinguished political and policy leaders from developing countries to join a commission focused on growth: on learning from their experience and that of others in multiple countries and from academic research. The goal was to deliver the results of this learning process over the past fifteen years back in a form that provided useful guidance to their counterparts, leaders in developing countries, and to the next generation of leadership.

Forming the commission would itself be a screening device. If the distinguished leaders whom we asked said no, we planned to conclude it was probably not a useful exercise at this stage and to drop the project. But they didn't say no, and we launched the Commission on Growth and Development (CGD) in the spring of 2006. Its work concluded in June of 2010. The written work product can be found on the archived website of the CGD.

Interacting with these developing-country leaders, their colleagues, and literally hundreds of my academic colleagues was the experience of a lifetime—for me, a high-speed learning process that was, to say the least, exhilarating and humbling. I learned about growth and development, about complexity, pragmatism, and persistence, and about leadership. For an economist trained in an advanced economy, it was startling to see how incomplete and imperfect were the frameworks and models available to guide policy choices in developing countries. It was even more startling to see how effectively the developing countries navigated this sea of complexity and uncertainty. I came to see the process as akin to a long sea voyage undertaken with incomplete and sometimes contradictory charts, not unlike the early explorers who set out to discover, explore, and map the contours of the planet and to exploit its resources.

In doing this work over four years, I visited the commissioners in their home countries and talked with their colleagues, as well as with business, labor, and civil-society leaders. While an outsider can never achieve the level of institutional knowledge that insiders possess, I made some progress in seeing the world through their eyes; not through the lens of a Western business or policy agenda item, but from within the framework of the hopes, aspirations, and goals embedded in their own growth and development agendas.

In the course of my own voyage of discovery, I realized that the pattern of growth and poverty reduction in the developing world was spreading and accelerating, and along with it a growing sense of optimism. It also dawned on me, later in the process, that the high dependence on the advanced economies has started to decline, especially in the last ten years, and that the developing world is becoming a large and increasingly important part of the global economy, with all the opportunities and challenges that go along with this growth. The largely separate worlds of the advanced and developing countries are converging. As a consequence, the growth of the developing world will increasingly be part of the lives of everyone, regardless of where they live and work.

A year or so ago I described to my oldest friend—we grew up together—a plan to write a book about the high-speed growth in the developing world and the rapidly changing profile of the global economy. His advice was to make sure that the book "is about me as well"—meaning him, and his children and grandchildren, those who live in the advanced countries. I thought a lot about that. He wanted the book to include an assessment of what the growth of the developing world meant for his offspring and their children. I think it has come out that way. The huge asymmetries between advanced and developing countries have not disappeared, but they are declining, and the pattern for the first time in 250 years is convergence rather than divergence.

This is a world in which vast numbers of people look with greater optimism at their own future and that of the next generation. But it is also a world facing large new challenges that are a consequence of the expanding prosperity. The real story of the future of growth is how well the coming generations understand our evolving interdependence, its positives and negatives, and then creatively find ways to manage and govern it.

In writing this, I have relied on the energy, insight, and generosity of spirit of a large number of people whom I admire. Prominent among them are the members of the Commission on Growth and Development who have helped lead the economic, political, and social transformations of their countries. My colleagues in universities and research institutions have been extraordinarily generous in sharing their research and insights with practitioners. The high quality of the interaction between these two groups during a set of workshops on growth and development was for me one of the most rewarding parts of the past four years.

Roberto Zagha at the World Bank was secretary to the commission. I owe him a great debt for his breadth of vision in guiding the work of the CGD, for guiding me through the learning process, and for his ideas and idealism. Mohamed El-Erian, now the CEO and co-CIO of Pimco, is a friend and teacher—about investment, the global economy, the global financial system. We have discussed the issues and written about them together. I have included in Part IV of this book adaptations of two of our joint efforts on global governance and on the sustainability of emerging economy growth post crisis. Bob Solow, the creator of modern growth theory, was the other academic on the growth commission, and the most important one. It is not possible (no matter how many superlatives one uses) to overstate the impact he had on my thinking and that of all of us. It was, in many ways, a microcosm of the enormous influence he has had on the concepts and values that form the foundation of modern economics.

Andrew Wylie and Scott Moyers encouraged me to try to write this book and guided me through the unfamiliar process of writing for a non-academic audience. Andrew has done this for many authors with diverse backgrounds. He is a master at it.

I am very grateful to Eric Chinski and his colleagues at Farrar, Straus and Giroux for their help and support in getting the manuscript into good shape, and for their editorial insight and support.

My wife, Giuliana, and my family were incredibly supportive as I logged vast numbers of miles in the air, as part of the work of the CGD and in the writing of this book. That plus a large dose of encouragement and enthusiasm made it possible to complete the work.

I finished the editing of the manuscript in Bonassola, a small town on the coast of Liguria in Italy. I am grateful to the very kind folks at the Gelateria Delle Rose for letting me work at their bar close enough to the wi-fi access point. It became *il mio ufficio* for part of the summer.

THE NEXT CONVERGENCE

Introduction

This book is about the third century of the Industrial Revolution, the one we are now living in. As best we can tell from limited data and painstaking scholarly work, for several hundred years up until about 1750, economic growth was negligible everywhere. By our standards, people were poor for the most part (there were elites that were rich), and in some places there was a small, commercially oriented middle class. Being rich and being in power were closely associated. In a no-growth world, the game is zero-sum. It is not therefore surprising that power and wealth were highly correlated. This picture was true pretty much for the entire world.

Then, around 1750, England started on a new course, of industrial revolution. Per capita incomes started to rise. Growth accelerated and was sustained for the first time in recent history. The pattern spread fairly rapidly in the nineteenth century to continental Europe and then to the United States and Canada, and Australia and New Zealand, the last four being what the distinguished scholar Angus Madison refers to as the European offshoots. And it continued for two hundred years, up through World War II. Some of it spilled over to parts of Latin America, but in a less complete form.

By 1950, the average incomes of people living in these countries had risen twenty times, from about $500 per year to over $10,000 per year, and in the case of many industrialized countries much more than that. This new growth was driven by the application of science and technology to production, logistics and communication, management and institutional innovation, and changes in governance and the way in which politics and government interacted with the economy—in short, to every aspect of the modern economy. (We will come back to all of this in the course of the book.)

The dramatic shift in the pattern of growth was confined to what we now call the advanced or industrialized (or, sometimes, mature) countries. It affected the lives of roughly 15 percent of the world's population. Outside of that group, the pattern of the preceding several hundred years simply continued; there was very little growth. People remained poor. Colonialism took what wealth was generated and allocated it to the industrialized imperial powers. There were of course some changes. Trains, and eventually automobiles and electricity and telephones, showed up but had little impact on the vast majority of people. The global pattern was therefore one of rapid divergence between the (then developing) advanced countries and the rest.

The snapshot picture of the world economy in 1950 was the result of that remarkable 200 years of economic history: a breakout period for a minority of the world's population, with some 750 million people living in industrializing countries and the remaining 4-plus billion left behind. The world had never before seen differentials of this magnitude.

Starting after World War II, the pattern shifted again, though it was difficult at the start to see it as a mega-trend. The countries in the developing world started to grow. At first it was relatively slow and in isolated countries. Then it began to spread and accelerate.

That was the start of a century-long journey in the global economy. The end point is likely to be a world in which perhaps 75 percent or more of the world's people live in advanced countries with all that entails: increasing income levels, with likewise increasing patterns of consumption and energy use. In addition to the spreading pattern of growth, the remarkable feature of the postwar modern era is the speed. In the high-growth developing countries, there have been sustained periods (a quarter of a century or more) of growth at 7 percent and more. To put this in perspective, high-speed growth in the *first* 200 years of the Industrial Revolution would have been between 2 and 2.5 percent.

This book is about the 100-plus years that began in 1945 and will run to the middle of the twenty-first century. Since we are slightly over halfway along, we can think of it as a midterm report. It is about two parallel and interacting revolutions: the continuation of the Industrial Revolution in the advanced countries, and the sudden and dramatic spreading pattern of growth in the developing world. One could call the second revolution the Inclusiveness Revolution. After two centuries of high-speed divergence, a pattern of convergence has taken over.

The return of convergence combined with growth has wide-ranging and deep implications, ones we are slowly becoming aware of and starting to wrestle with. My main aim in this book is to try to make this very rapid change and shifting pattern of economic activity and power a little more comprehensible to the interested and engaged reader.

What happened to cause an additional 60 percent of the world to begin the process of joining the world of affluence, or to be well on the way? How is growth at rates approaching 10 percent a year possible when the previous high-water mark was probably 3 percent? How long does it take for a poor country to make the full transition to advanced-country status? How long can it last—or indeed can it last? Is there a speed limit? Are there natural "brakes" that will inevitably slow the process down, or even stop it? Is there something wrong with the advanced countries if they do not or cannot grow at these new high rates? What drives or causes growth in the advanced countries, and is it the same set of forces in the developing countries? How can income differentials of twenty to forty times persist over extended periods of time?

Can we learn over time to manage something as complex as the emerging and evolving global economy, with its rising interdependencies and complexity? Or is the present global financial and economic crisis a precursor to a pattern of more destructive instability, eventually leading to disillusionment and abandonment of the enterprise? What will happen to populations, incomes, natural resources, and the environment? Can the environment withstand a fourfold increase in the ranks of the relatively wealthy? Can we produce enough food and energy to support this kind of growth? Is it possible for this to continue, or is there a massive multidimensional "adding up" problem in which what was possible for the "few" will not be possible for the "many"? Is the management and governance of the global economy that was in place for the last quarter century going to work in the future, or is it going to need fundamental change?

I have organized the narrative into four parts. Part I deals with the rapidly shifting characteristics of the postwar global economy. It is, in effect, a picture of what the global economy looks like and how it got there in the last fifty years. Part II is devoted to sustained high growth and poverty reduction in the developing world: where it is occurring, how it happens, and where it is not occurring, with some attempt to analyze the reasons for the much slower growth in lagging regions.

We shall see (or at least I will argue) that both the high growth and the low growth cannot be explained by strictly economic factors alone. Leadership, politics, governance structures, and the effectiveness of government have crucial parts to play in the drama.

Part III turns to the short- and longer-term impacts of the global economic and financial crisis that gripped the world starting in 2008. What impacts did this have on the developing countries, and via which transmission channels? The crisis has brought many lessons about the fine texture of interdependence. How well did developing countries respond to the crisis, and what is the medium- and longer-term outlook for them in a world in which developed countries struggle with deleveraging, fiscal stability, a shortfall in demand, stubbornly high unemployment, and low growth? What lessons have the emerging economies absorbed, and how will those lessons impact financial and economic globalization, growth strategies, and dynamics? Are there lessons in what the developing countries have learned that are relevant in the more advanced economies?

Part IV turns to the future and a set of issues, forces, and trends that have to do with whether this pattern of spreading high growth in incomes and wealth can be sustained. There are economic, governance, natural resource, and environmental braking mechanisms that may slow the process down or cause it to stop altogether. In looking at these, we will encounter a variety of different versions of what are sometimes called "adding-up" problems.

Perhaps the availability and cost of energy will cause a slowdown in growth. If all or a large fraction of the developing countries try to supply labor-intensive goods and services to the global economy, the global market, large as it is, may not be able to absorb them. That may mean that the poorer and less competitive economies will not find a way to enter the global economy, an essential prerequisite for growth. The increasing interconnectedness in the global economy and financial system is running ahead of the system of governance. The latter is still dominated mainly by nations and their priorities. Perhaps there are limits to globalization without a parallel process of change in global governance?

My main goal is to make the dynamics of developing-country growth more understandable and that growth's relationship to and interdependencies with the global economy more visible and easier to understand. I do this for two reasons. First, for many of us who live in OECD countries (countries with membership in the Organisation for Economic Co-operation and Development), developing-nation conditions and growth are relatively outside the range of our day-to-day experience. The impact of that growth on the global economy and the advanced countries is a complex and interesting dynamic process, and one that is still imperfectly (though better) understood. Yet the consequences of that growth are of enormous importance and will be felt by the vast majority of the world's population for years to come.

I also think that in order to meet the substantial future challenges of sustaining global economic prosperity in an inclusive kind of way, it is helpful and perhaps even essential to have a basic knowledge of the evolution of this increasingly large and important part of the world. The reactions of developing countries to international issues are conditioned by their growth experience and prospects. We need to see the world through their eyes, just as they will need to be able to see through ours. That two-way understanding is likely to be an essential underpinning of our future capacity to manage global interdependence. Without it, progress on a host of issues—climate change, the WTO, regulating the global financial system, global governance, rebalancing the global economy, and maintaining stability—will be much harder to achieve. We are at the very early stages of learning how to do this.

Growth in the developing world has made the major emerging economies systemically important. Their choices and paths have significant effects on one another, and on the advanced countries. This is new. It is a function of the growth, the increasing size and, significantly, the increasing incomes of the major developing countries. The old system in which the advanced countries under the G7 umbrella took responsibility for avoiding collectively the suboptimal outcomes that might arise from narrow, nationally focused policies, and in which the developing countries focused on domestic growth and development agendas, worked as long as the systemic external effects of the latter's behavior were not large enough to destabilize the system or create major imbalances. That world is gone.

The crisis of 2008 nearly caused a second Great Depression. Rapid and effective action by governments and central banks averted that outcome.

The emerging economies have rebounded from the crisis surprisingly quickly. They are now the main engine of global growth. The advanced countries have fared less well. They face slow growth, high unemployment, fiscal distress, and a lengthy period of unwinding the high levels of debt accumulated before the crisis. In that complex environment, nations are trying to work together to stabilize and rebalance the global economy and to restore conditions that will permit a return to sustained growth.

In the postwar period up to the crisis, the priorities guiding international cooperation were set by the G7, representing the advanced countries. Post crisis, the baton has been passed from the G7 to the G20. The latter represents the advanced countries plus the major large, high-growth emerging countries. Given the size and growth of the latter, it is a natural transition, though certainly one accelerated by the crisis.

The central question before us now is whether the G20 can do this job effectively. Keeping the global economy open, restoring demand, reregulating the financial system, preventing a destructive deflationary cycle, and creating effective international mechanisms for responding to future shocks are among the critical items on the agenda. We do not yet know how this will come out. Much is at stake, and much will depend on the ability of the advanced and the major developing countries to work together in a cooperative way.

PART ONE

The Global Economy and Developing
Countries

1. 1950: The Start of a Remarkable Century

I was born in 1943, during World War II. It was near the end of a turbulent half century, militarily and economically, a violent period with a Great Depression sandwiched between two great wars, a nightmare for many. It was the end of an era and the start of something quite revolutionary and new.

The Industrial Revolution started in Britain at the end of the eighteenth century. It had been under way for two hundred years by World War II. Before that, growth, by modern standards, had been negligible for a thousand years all over the world. But then Britain, and in sequence continental Europe, North America (the United States and Canada), and Australia and New Zealand, began a growth acceleration. It was not breathtakingly fast by postwar standards, on the order of 1 to 2 percent a year. Over a long period of time (a century or two), however, that growth (and its scientific and technological underpinnings) caused huge differences in incomes between what we now called the industrialized countries and the rest or the world.

You can see this inflection point and sudden change in direction in a famous chart produced by the distinguished economic historian and Nobel laureate Robert Fogel (see page 12). It is a picture of population growth with the underpinnings being the rapidly expanding productive capability of the growing economies.

The beneficiaries of this growth were the populations of those few countries. They represented then and still do now about 15 percent of the world's population. The remaining 85 percent experienced little or no

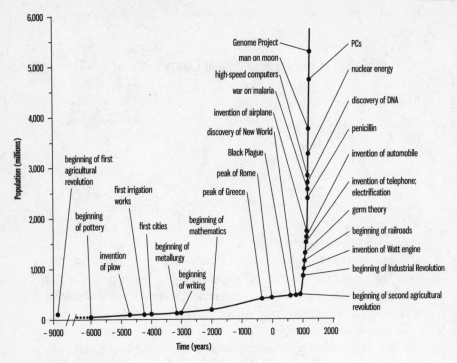

Source: Robert Fogel, "Catching Up with the Economy," *American Economic Review* 89(1) (March 1999): 1–21.

Note: There is usually a lag between the invention of a process or a machine and its general application to production. "Beginning" means the earliest stage of this diffusion process.

change in circumstances. Parts of Latin America were something of an exception, a fact that we will return to later. The rest of the world, including all of Africa and Asia (East and South), was poor. Incomes were typically about a dollar a day, sometimes less. The vast majority of people were rural, engaged in subsistence farming and closely related activities.

Before 1750, most of the world was like the 85 percent in 1950. They were poor and lived in an environment that was technologically and economically largely stagnant. There were a few wealthy people, those who owned land or other assets or who had political, economic, and military power. Intercountry differences were not large. Continental Europe and China did not differ much in economic terms: indeed, around the time of the Ming dynasty (1600), China's income per person is believed by scholars to have exceeded those in Europe—though, by today's standards, not by much.

Even though Germany and Japan had expansionist aims in the twentieth century, one in the industrialized world and the other with a more colonial flavor in a preindustrial part of the world, those were thwarted by defeat in the war. Everywhere else, the dismantling of the colonial structures was already under way. Colonial empires were dissolved completely after World War II, creating scores of new states of varying sizes and shapes, each beginning a sometimes bumpy and difficult journey as a new nation. From a purely economic standpoint, some of them should have been parts of larger states. But designing for economic viability probably was not a feasible program as the colonial period ended. Colonial history and geography and tribal differences had much more to do with the outcomes than economic rationality or common sense. The legacy is a world with over two hundred countries, many of which have little economic viability. In addition, in many there was no sense of nationhood or citizenship. Building the essential foundation of national identity and unity has proved challenging.

After the war, the international agenda included rebuilding war-ravaged industrialized economies, building the governance and the economies of a raft of new countries that had been former colonies, and, finally, creating multinational institutions to manage and invest in this fluid multinational landscape, in the hope of a less violent, more stable world.

War, bloodshed, and the inability to manage or prevent conflict were not an invention of the twentieth century. The scale, efficiency, and extensiveness of the damage were. Postwar leaders and citizens alike strove to fashion a new, cooperative, and less zero-sum approach to the international architecture that determined, or at least influenced, how countries interacted with each other. The driving force behind the spreading Industrial Revolution was science and rapidly advancing technology. It made incomes rise and war more dangerous.

A generation of postwar leaders saw this potential for destruction and understood the potential for further conflict in a world characterized by struggling postwar industrial economies, a battle for access to scarce natural resources (especially energy), huge differences in incomes and opportunity across the world, and deep political and ideological differences. Without knowing the final destination—no one did—they set out to change the trajectory of the global economy. Looking back, one can see that they largely succeeded.

Japan had joined the industrializing group in the nineteenth century. It began a lengthy process of modernization and opening with the Meiji Restoration in 1861. By 1940 it was a partially industrialized country and the only non-Western colonial power in Asia. By 1945 it was a defeated nation with an uncertain future. But it was about to become the first sustained high-growth country in the postwar period—indeed in recorded history. Its growth, and the underlying strategies and policies, became an example that was emulated all over Asia and eventually more broadly. Looking back, one finds it hard to overstate the importance of the example that the Japanese case set. Among other things, it grew at unprecedented rates armed with almost no natural resource wealth of the conventional kind, and in so doing upset much of the conventional economic thinking about the sources of wealth and growth in the developing world.

China fared worse. Battered by external interventions its per capita income actually declined in the nineteenth century, a relatively uncommon occurrence in economic history outside of periods of plague. The two thousand years of dynastic rule collapsed in the early part of the twentieth century, replaced by a republic that presided through a Japanese occupation and the Second World War. The Republic never really had a chance to succeed. By 1949, when the Communists took control, China was one of the poorest countries in the world, and thirty years later, under central planning and collectivized production and agriculture, it had made little visible progress.

2. Static Views of a Changing World

In 1750, most people, if asked, would probably have said that the preindustrial configuration of the world's economy was a largely permanent state of affairs—that the world had always been like that and probably always would be. They would have had the facts on their side. Not much change had occurred by our modern standards for many centuries. To put it differently, since even low-percentage changes add up over centuries, the pace was truly glacial by our standards.

But the world was not really static. Science progressed. Florence experienced a Renaissance with a flowering of art, architecture, commerce, finance, banking and science, architecture and engineering. There are such periods when some breakthrough occurs in the minds of people and innovation occurs in a burst across a broad range of fields of human endeavor. It is still something of a mystery why this occasionally happens.

Still, viewed through an economic lens, the lives of most people did not change all that much. Growth was very low, and as a result the distribution of income and wealth approximated a zero-sum game. What one individual or group got, another gave up.

If you had suggested to a European in 1750 that in exactly 200 years, Europe would have incomes roughly twenty to forty times those of Asia, you would probably have been regarded as deranged. By the same logic, if in 1950 you suggested that in 100 years incomes in Asia and much of the rest of the developing world would be approaching the levels in Europe and Northern America, you probably would have gotten a similar reaction. But that appears to be the journey that we are about halfway through.

As humans, we first become aware of the world the way it is. We see a snapshot of the world first and the motion picture only much later. We seem to assume initially that the snapshot is a permanent state of affairs and not a moment in a journey with a constantly shifting landscape. Perhaps this is because fundamental change is, or seems, slow. And perhaps also because change is hard to anticipate or to think about in advance. Looking back is much easier.

As we get older we discover that we ourselves are on a rather longish voyage of discovery, learning, pain and joy, children, grandchildren, perhaps a little wisdom. In modern history, the external environment seems to change quite quickly too. And so, over decades, the magnitude of the changes becomes easier to see. We start to appreciate historians more, those whose job is in part to help us understand that things change, as well as how and why that change occurs. Now as before, there is always a large gap between the young, who tend to assume that the world has always been the way it was when they entered it, and the old, who can remember a world with propeller-drive planes and no Internet.

This propensity to view the snapshot of the world that we now see as "reality," as opposed to a frame in a motion picture, sometimes traps us and holds us back. Right now there are lots of developing countries, but as the term implies, that is probably not a permanent state.

The evolution of the terms describing "the other 85 percent" is interesting. At some point we stopped referring to poor countries as "backward" in favor of the term "underdeveloped." Then came "Third World," suggesting total separation. And then came "less developed," intimating that it might not be permanent. After another lag we shifted to the term "developing countries" and, more recently, "emerging economies," in a slightly delayed recognition of the fact that a fundamental and permanent change was not only hoped for but actually under way. This evolution in language signaled a growing awareness over time that these economies were not permanently lodged in a stationary state of underdevelopment but rather were in some kind of transition, albeit a long one—on the order of a century—to being high-income places.

By the time my education started to make me aware of the global landscape (the continents and the life conditions and opportunities in them), huge differences in economic circumstances across continents were part of the economic landscape. In the 1950s and sixties, most of us probably thought that this was just the way the world was configured. I know I did. I can still remember heated boyhood discussions of fairness and unfairness, and arguments about the reasons for the wide divergences. There were relatively poor countries and rich countries. The question was: Why? How could differentials of that magnitude persist?

Our natural instinct was to look for a villain, some human constraint that held in place the chains of poverty. That wasn't an entirely incorrect inclination, but nevertheless overly simple. Some felt this was permanent and others vaguely thought it might change, without really knowing how. But the snapshot view dominated. Dynamics and thinking about rapid, accelerating, and permanent change is conceptually harder and more than slightly unsettling for most of us.

3. Postwar Changes in the Global Economy

My parents, like many others born during World War I, went looking for jobs in the mid 1930s in the depths of the Great Depression. Not a great hand to be dealt. Like so many of their generation, that experience had a lasting effect on the way they saw the world and the opportunities in it. They either knew or hoped that fundamental change would occur. But they would not have bet the family fortune on it. They were basically pessimists at heart, and most of the postwar experience was a pleasant surprise.

Their hopes, focused mainly on their children and grandchildren, were for a less volatile and precarious existence. Those hopes were rewarded and exceeded, at least in the industrialized countries. The world finally pulled out of the Great Depression with the help of the extraordinary economic measures required by World War II. In the postwar period, Europe and Japan rebuilt their economies and governance structures with support from the United States and the newly created international institutions. Growth was restored. Rapid technological advancement (again accelerated by the exigencies of modern war), rising productivity, and rising incomes dominated the economic landscape in the developed countries, with the Cold War and the threat of mutual assured destruction hanging as a dark cloud over the process.

Growth rates take some getting used to. There is a rule used by statisticians and economists called the rule of 72. It says that the time it takes in years to double in size at a specific annual growth rate is that growth rate divided into the number 72. It sounds crazy, but it works. So, for example, at 1 percent growth, income (or whatever it is that is growing) doubles in 72 years. At 7 percent growth (about the highest sustained level ever achieved until recently), that figure for doubling falls to a decade. That is, at 7 percent growth, incomes and output double every 10 years. These numbers are approximate but good enough to get the general idea.

Unlike their historical predecessors, the high-growth developing countries have been growing at rates of 7 percent or more. It was the arrival of China thirty years ago and more recently India into the pattern of sustained high growth that changed the global economic landscape prospectively. The reason is that these two countries combined have almost 40 percent of the world's population of about 6.6 billion people. There had been prior high-growth cases like Korea in the postwar period. But Korea has 40 million people. Even at advanced-country incomes, the economy would be an eighth the size of the United States or the European Union. Japan was the first high-growth country and until recently by far the largest. With a population of 120 million (and shrinking) and advanced-country levels of income, its economy is less than half the size of the United States and the European Union. By contrast, a China or an India with advanced-country incomes will each have economies four times the size of both the United States and the European Union.

Many of us have never experienced an environment in which growth is that high. For reasons we will come to, the process is quite chaotic. And it is not easy to sustain.

Notwithstanding the recent sustained high growth in an increasing part of the developing world, it takes decades for countries to make the transition from poor to advanced. The poorest countries have incomes of about $300 to $500 per person. Advanced countries have incomes of $20,000 and above. To go from poor to the lower ranges of advanced, one has to double incomes five times, and then some. At 7 percent growth, the pattern looks like this:

Start	500
Decade 1	1,000
Decade 2	2,000
Decade 3	4,000
Decade 4	8,000
Decade 5	16,000
Year 53–54	20,000

Income doubles every decade, and that is very fast—the economic analogue of driving at 120 mph. Putting this all together, even at very high growth rates, it takes well over half a century to make the full transition. And of course at slower growth rates, the transitions become much longer.

Middle incomes are in the range of $5,000 to $10,000 a year. The graph below shows the transition times from poor to middle and advanced income levels for differing growth rates (1 percent through 10 percent). Clearly, most of the time is spent getting from poor to middle incomes. Once one gets to high middle income ($10,000) one more doubling will catapult the economy into the advanced category.

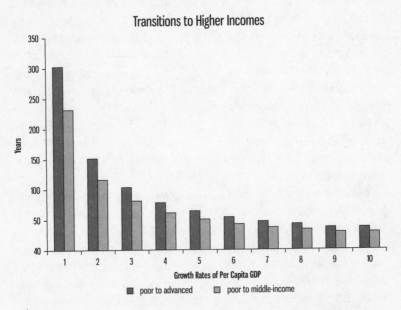

Transitions to Higher Incomes

What matters, then, is sustained growth over a long period of time. Little growth spurts followed by stagnation simply lower the average growth and prolong the process.

The last doubling from middle to high income looks easier than it is. It is called the middle income transition, or sometimes the middle income trap. It has proven for many countries to be a difficult passage, for reasons we will come to in Part II. But the time-consuming part, the transition that requires long sustained periods of growth, is the one from relatively poor to the middle-income levels.

We saw earlier that world population growth shot up starting at about the same time as the English Industrial Revolution. Thomas Malthus theorized that population growth would keep up with income growth, leaving individuals little better off and living at subsistence levels. Something close to this may have happened for much of modern history, and in a significant part of the developing world until the last fifty years. But it did not happen in the countries that broke away, starting in the second half of the eighteenth century, the current set of advanced countries. It is not completely clear why.

Growth in output and income outpaced population growth in spite of the fact that science, medicine, and public health battled with longevity and won. So people got older and lived longer. Populations rose, but even then incomes started to rise. It is that pattern, the breaking of the link between population and income growth, that is now spreading in the developing world.

A Study in Contrasts

The contrasts across the developing world are in some ways as striking as the accelerating growth in a subset of countries. In 1950, both Africa and Asia were very poor; Africa had higher incomes than Asia because of its natural resources. Asian growth accelerated slowly at first, and then more rapidly, while African growth stayed slow. Economists thought that developing-country incomes and prospects depended largely on natural resources. Before the opening of the global economy to trade in manufactured goods, that was probably true. But with the opening-up, it turned out that national wealth included human resources, whose value climbed when they became available to the global economy. Utilizing human resources has turned out to be the basis of Asian growth. And as we shall see later, natural-resource wealth by itself is not the basis of sustained growth.

By 1990, developing-country growth was well under way. The Asian Tigers (South Korea, Taiwan, Singapore, and Hong Kong) had grown to middle-income levels and were headed for advanced incomes. A number of other countries in Asia (Indonesia, Thailand) had experienced sustained high growth. China shifted gears in 1978 and went into high-growth mode. India was in the early stages of its growth acceleration.

Later on we will look in greater detail at where the high growth occurred and why. But some examples of the contrasts are interesting.

South Korea, for example, had a GDP per capita of about $350 to $400 fifty years ago (a little over a dollar a day, and about the same as the poorer countries in Africa). North and South Korea were about the same in terms of income. Today South Korea's GDP per capita is close to $20,000. North Korea has progressed almost not at all, and much of sub-Saharan Africa is experiencing growth acceleration since 2000, similar to what occurred in Korea starting in the late 1950s. For most of the postwar period Asia and Africa diverged, though that is starting to reverse now.

China began market-oriented economic reform in 1978, and GDP per capita has risen from roughly $400 then to over $3,500 now, doubling more than three times, and with hundreds of millions of people moving out of poverty. Before the 1978 reforms, China was a centrally planned economy with negligible growth and periodic disastrous episodes, like the Great Leap Forward, in which perhaps 30 million or more people starved. The Cultural Revolution, starting in 1965 and lasting ten years, was not primarily an economic policy choice, but it had significant negative economic impacts. Much talent was lost or sidelined and underutilized.

India began economic reform in the 1980s. After successfully navigating a financial crisis in the early nineties, it has grown in excess of 6 percent per annum (accelerating recently to close to 9 percent just before the financial and economic crisis of 2008–9), again with the prospect of hundreds of millions of people moving out of poverty.

In 1960, the small island state of Singapore, adjacent to Malaysia, was a fishing village with an average GDP per capita of $427. It became independent of Malaysia in 1960 and today has an average GDP per capita of $38,000, one of the highest in the world. The fishing village became one of the largest ports in the world and a major financial center. Another island state, Cuba, had a revolution, made major changes in the lives or ordinary citizens by providing education and health care, but then chose to follow the Soviet version of central planning and languished in terms of growth and poverty reduction.

The Overall Picture After World War II

The advanced countries grew at relatively high rates in the immediate postwar period thanks in large part to successful recoveries after the war, among both the victorious and the vanquished countries. Thereafter they settled into a steady pattern of growth at the rate of between 2 and 2.5 percent. In addition, there was a growth spurt at the end of the twentieth century, continuing into the twenty-first, associated with very large productivity gains resulting from the deployment of information technology—a subject we will return to later.

A few developing countries grew at high rates, and we will examine them in detail in Part II. But the vast majority did not grow much in the first few decades after mid-century, and so the gap between the advanced countries and the developing world initially widened.

Economists' Forecasts

In the wake of the unanticipated financial and economic crisis, we economists have plenty to be humble about. But that has been true for some time. It is interesting to look back at economists' projections for growth in various parts of the developing world. Of course, economic forecasting and forecasters are the butt of vast numbers of jokes ("Economists have forecasted nine out of the last five recessions"). But at the start of the 1990s it is interesting to see, for various regions, and for China and India, what those forward-looking guesses were and what actually happened.

The chart on page 24 shows expert forecasts for growth in the nineties along with the actual, and the differential between the forecast and the actual result. Generally underperformance corresponded with low (actual and forecast) growth. This was a lost decade for Africa. Things have dramatically improved since then. It was also a tough decade for the post–Cold War Eastern European countries. It probably took the best part of a decade to make the transition to market-oriented economies and policies. Their economic performance has also improved since 2000. The huge overperformer was China. Virtually no one expected sustained growth at 9 percent a year. It had never been seen before.

In fact, analysts routinely bet against China, in the past and now. I like to remind the skeptics that betting against China in the past has not been very profitable. Maybe this time is different. Probably the fact that China's governance model is quite different from what we are used to causes us to think it won't work. But to paraphrase Deng Xiaoping, different-colored cats can still catch mice.

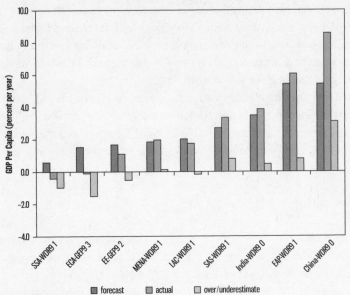

Forecasts for the 1990s—and Reality

SSA = Sub-Saharan Africa
ECA = East and Central Asia
EE = Eastern Europe
Mena = Middle East and North Africa
LAC = Latin America and the Caribbean
SAS = South Asia
EAP = East Asia Pacific

Taking a longer time horizon, in the immediate postwar period the consensus view among knowledgeable development economists and analysts was that prospects were quite bright in Africa and quite dim in Asia. Asia (East and South) was and is the most densely populated area of the world. In the 1950s it was also the poorest part of the world, and it is, relatively speaking, very low in natural resources compared to sub-Saharan Africa, Latin America, and the Middle East. It seemed a bad starting point.

The results over the next fifty years were just about the complete opposite of the prediction. Asia found a way to engage the global economy and grow at rates never before observed. African countries struggled with nation-building and governance, with lots of variation across countries. The continent's unusually high level of natural-resource wealth proved to be a curse, diverting political incentives toward capturing the wealth or the income streams they generate, and away from broader long-term growth-oriented agendas.

With the admittedly unfair benefit of hindsight, Asia invested in the only thing it had, people, and in gradual steps accelerated and sustained growth. It also benefited from the opening of the global economy to trade in a broader range of goods. Especially important for Asia was a global reduction in barriers to trade in manufactured goods. There are several lessons in this.

- First, our models and our ability to see into the future are limited, and surprises are the norm rather than the exception.
- Second, adversity is surprisingly often the birthplace of successful change.
- Third, sustainable wealth creation is ultimately built on people, human capital and knowledge, on continuous structural change in an economy, and on systems of economic and political organization that permit the productive deployment of those assets.
- Governance is crucially important. Favorable economic conditions are not enough.

4. The Origins of the Global Economy

A Brief History of the General Agreement on Tariffs and Trade (GATT) and the World Trade Organization (WTO)

Right after World War II—and little noticed at the time—a seed was planted that turned out to be one of the two main building blocks of the global economy. Leaders in the developed countries after the war set out to create a different international order, with perhaps more hope than confidence of creating a more benign and inclusive world. The opportunity was probably created by the horror of the war itself, and the devastation right after. It was a crisis. Generally, crises are opportunities for change because they weaken vested interests and resistance. The opportunity is not, however, always seized.

The United Nations was part of the new international structure, of which the General Agreement on Tariffs and Trade (GATT) was a fledgling component. The GATT started in 1947 to reduce tariffs, which are taxes on trade flows and thus partial barriers to trade.

Tariffs can be thought of in two ways. As taxes on international transactions, they are a source of revenue to the importing government, though usually not a very important one. Their main purpose is not revenue generation but rather to make goods produced outside the country more expensive than they would otherwise be, so that domestic industries are partially protected from external competition. (If revenue were the main goal, you would probably see more taxes on exports. There are such things, but they are not very common.)

A Brief Thumbnail History of the GATT and WTO

Rounds
GATT held a total of 8 rounds.

Name	Start	Duration	Countries	Subjects Covered	Achievements
				GATT and WTO Trade Rounds	
Geneva	April 1947	7 months	23	Tariffs	Signing of GATT, 45,000 tariff concessions affecting $10 billion of trade.
Annecy	April 1949	5 months	13	Tariffs	Countries exchanged some 5,000 tariff concessions.
Torquay	September 1950	8 months	38	Tariffs	Countries exchanged some 8,700 tariff concessions, cutting the 1948 tariff levels by 25 percent.
Geneva II	January 1956	5 months	26	Tariffs, admission of Japan	$2.5 billion in tariff reductions.
Dillon	September 1960	11 months	26	Tariffs	Tariff concessions worth $4.9 billion of world trade.
Kennedy	May 1964	37 months	62	Tariffs, antidumping	Tariff concessions worth $40 billion of world trade.
Tokyo	September 1973	74 months	102	Tariffs, nontariff measures, "framework" agreements	Tariff reductions worth more than $300 billion achieved.
Uruguay	September 1986	87 months	123	Tariffs, nontariff measures, rules, services, intellectual property, dispute settlement, textiles, agriculture, creation of WTO, etc.	The round led to the creation of WTO, and extended the range of trade negotiations, leading to major reductions in tariffs (about 40 percent) and agricultural subsidies, an agreement to allow full access for textiles and clothing from developing countries, and an extension of intellectual property rights.
Doha	November 2001	?	141	Tariffs, nontariff measures, agriculture, labor standards, environment, competition, investment, transparency, patents, etc.	The round is not yet concluded.

The GATT was created to reduce these barriers. Initially the main focus was postwar recovery in the industrialized economies and not in the developing nations. But the benefits rapidly spilled over to the larger group. By almost any measure it has been a huge success, though the work is incomplete and the risk of regressing nontrivial in the postcrisis environment of 2010. The GATT was supposed to become part of an entity called the International Trade Organization, which never made it through ratification in the U.S. Senate and hence never really came into existence. But the GATT survived and slowly but steadily began reducing the barriers to trade and commerce.

Eventually the GATT turned into the World Trade Organization (WTO) in the 1990s. The GATT was mainly a club run by (and initially for) the industrial countries. The WTO is a more inclusive organization, more like the United Nations than the G7. Most countries are members.

It is a change that reflects the changing size, power, and influence of some of the developing countries. It is also intended to ensure that the interests of smaller and poorer countries are represented in the process of modifying the rules that govern global trade. Widespread representation of diverse interests is, in principle, a good thing; but it makes reaching consensus harder and appears to have slowed down the process of further reductions in barriers.

The WTO has 153 members with another 30 observers, mostly with pending applications for membership. The largest country that has yet to join is Russia, and that is likely to change in the near future.

Members of the WTO

■ Original 1995
member
■ Subsequent
member
▥ Not a member

At present, the main WTO round of negotiations, called the Doha round (after the place of the first meeting), is stalled and has an uncertain future. It was supposed to be the round where the focus was on the needs and interests of developing countries, particularly the poorer ones. It has raised questions about whether the new structure can be effective in expanding global trade. We will come back to this in Part III.

With the benefit of hindsight, it is hard to overstate the importance of this postwar process of shifting the basic parameters of the global economy by engaging in cooperative behavior. The GATT was the beginning of the creation of what we now call the global economy, something that is accessible not just to the one-sixth of the world that is well off but to the other five-sixths as well. Together with cost-reducing technological advances in travel, transportation, and communication, the GATT was an essential catalyst to a second economic revolution, a much more inclusive one in which hundreds of millions of people started to experience the benefits, if also the turbulence, of growth. It is this revolution, now much easier to see than it was at the start, that is shaping the way we live.

Small Steps Toward a Global Economy

As the global economy emerged in the postwar period, the colonial system disappeared. Old colonies became new countries, some of them with very odd shapes and geographical positions. With no history of self-governance as nation states, they struggled to find their way, economically and in terms of stable governance. India created the world's largest and most complex democracy—a modern miracle. China turned to communism, adopted the centrally planned model of economic organization, and made very little measurable economic progress for twenty-nine years, but perhaps sowed the seeds of its future rise by educating the vast majority of its people. It dramatically changed direction in 1978 and became the largest (in population) and fastest-growing country in the history of the world.

What no one saw clearly was that in the postwar period, the economic party that had been running for two hundred years in a small subset of the population was about to spread to much of the rest of the world.

The implications of this new convergence are profound and extensive. The costs of things will change. Goods and services that require human time and effort will become relatively more expensive, an inevitable consequence of the eventual decline of low-cost underemployed labor in the global economy. Economic forces and incentives will try to make them less expensive by allocating more capital to labor and hence reducing the labor input required. But there are limits to substituting capital for labor, though these limits are moving as technology changes the art of the possible. The abundance of underemployed labor in the world economy has in a sense delayed the arrival of labor-saving technology. But this will end in the current century; although we still see low-cost goods at Walmart, Target, and so on, that situation won't last forever or indefinitely.

The Industrial Revolution was aptly named. It was a revolution (a long one) in multiple dimensions: standard of living, reduction of poverty, growth of knowledge, access to information, opportunity, and the application of scientific thought to the economic processes of production, communication, public health, and resource allocation. Now all of that knowledge and technology is being disseminated around the world.

The "new normal" for our younger children and grandchildren will be a world in which what used to be available only to a privileged few becomes a part of the lives of a new high-income majority. There may also still be a large minority of people who continue to live in low-growth environments. At this stage we just don't know. The hope is that their growth will accelerate too. But for a variety of reasons they may still have difficulty finding a way into the global economy, to prosper and enjoy an expanded set of opportunities. If that happens it will present a major problem, a possibility I will return to later.

5. Economic Growth

Why Are We Interested in Growth?

People don't really care about growth in any direct sense. After all, it is just a statistic that documents a certain aspect of change. Generally people universally care more about spiritual things: values, religion, their relations with the rest of humanity. In the material realm, humans care about opportunity, the chance to be productively employed and creative, about being valuable to society, about education and health—in short about those things that create the freedom and the opportunity to fulfill their potential.

Growth is interesting because these latter things are correlated with and enabled by income and wealth. More specifically, they are influenced by the *levels* of income and wealth. As an aside, wealth for the very rich is probably more valued as metric of success—beyond a certain point it is nearly impossible to actually spend the wealth. In our world, substantial wealth is a partial signal of achievement and brings with it prestige. It is pursued well beyond its capacity to add to material comfort. But for most people, wealth is much lower and is best thought of as insurance against uncertainty, instability, and interruptions in income. For most people, the main goal is a decent level of income.

Our interest is in sustained high growth over long periods of time because it is what shifts the *levels* of incomes by amounts large enough to reduce poverty and to increase the opportunity to be productive and creative. Though economic growth is talked about all the time by policy makers, investors, companies, and shareholders, it really is a means to an end.

There is one other reason why growth is important to most people. It has to do with another nearly universal value. Most of us want our children and grandchildren to have better opportunities and options than we have. This preference is especially powerful in poorer countries. From my experience working in and with developing countries, I have found the sacrifices that people will make or accept if they believe they are creating opportunity for their progeny to be quite extraordinary. In that sense, growth—sustained growth—is directly important to most of us.

There are those, and their numbers are increasing, especially in developed countries, who resist this value framework. The pursuit of growth and material wealth has gone far enough, they say. The unrestrained pursuit of higher incomes has led us to ignore the environment and the sustainability of how we live, to overestimate the value of income and material wealth in relation to happiness, and to create a value system that is more of a rat race than a chance for deep satisfaction. There is a growing body of interesting research on happiness that tends to back up this point of view.

This is an important discussion of values. Over time it may result in a formidable shift in our priorities and the economic choices that we make, pushed along by the tailwind of climate change and environmental degradation. But for the present it pertains mostly to the one billion who live in the developed economies. The rest of humanity wants to catch up. This makes perfectly good sense too. The added value of a thousand dollars of income if your annual income is $800 is likely to be a lot higher than it is if your current income is $40,000. The percentage increase is much larger for the poor person, even though the absolute amounts are the same. But, more important, for the poor person, that additional thousand dollars may make it possible to ensure that their children receive a good education.

This asymmetry is important and a potential source of misunderstanding. We should welcome the questioning of our material values in the developed world and wonder about the benefits and costs of a materialism on autopilot. But we should not assume this questioning is universal or that it is independent of one's immediate circumstances. The developing world surely cares in multiple dimensions about sustainability. But their enthusiasm for lower growth or different patterns of growth will increase as their incomes rise and come closer to creating the opportunities that are now experienced by a minority of humanity in the advanced countries.

Leadership and Politics

When I started studying and learning about growth in the developing world, I thought the subject was mainly, or even exclusively, about economics. I no longer believe that. It is not that the economic moving parts in the dynamics of growth are uninteresting or irrelevant—far from it. They are an important part of the story. But they are not the whole story. The rest of the picture has more to do with leadership, governance, institutions, and politics, and the interaction of these factors and processes with economic outcomes.

Put bluntly, growth requires investment, and that means present sacrifice for future gain. The job of leaders is in part to get everyone on board, to build a consensus behind a forward-looking vision, underpinned by a growth and development strategy that is credible. Multiple classes of participants and organized stakeholders need to be willing participants. These include labor, unions, businesses and entrepreneurs, civil society organizations, and households at various levels in the income distribution.

Many countries spend extended periods of time in no-growth or low-growth mode. It is a kind of equilibrium that must be broken and then shifted to a new sustainable pattern. Evidently that pattern breaking does not necessarily occur automatically within the economic system, narrowly defined. A shift external to the economy is required, one that changes trajectories and expectations. That external impetus usually comes from leadership, and not infrequently in a crisis or near-crisis setting. An additional nudge is sometimes provided by a favorable shift in the external economic environment. And we know demonstration effects are powerful. Seeing what is happening in other countries (easier with television and the Internet) changes leaders' and peoples' sense of what is possible.

People will make incredible sacrifices if they believe their children and grandchildren will, as a result, be better off than they are. But they do have to believe that the dynamics will work, and that the process is inclusive so that whole groups of people are not simply left out. Citizens may not impose the requirement that the government be of and by the people, but an effective government that is, and is perceived to be, *for the people* is essential.

Governance in the context of sustained growth has a lot to do with what Europeans call "cohesion." Others use the term "identity." They are not quite the same but they are closely related. Older nations have managed to build nationalism over long periods of time, a sense of belonging and of common interest. It is the shared belief that in good times and bad, the citizens are in it together. It leads to a pattern of inclusiveness, of making sure that everyone benefits and that those who experience adversity are protected, and it gives a nation a kind of resilience.

We tend to take this for granted in the context of developing countries, but we shouldn't. In Canada, where I grew up, the province of Quebec periodically considered seceding from the country for complex historical reasons but in the end mainly because many Quebec citizens do not identify with the English-speaking majority and when push comes to shove believe themselves to be second-class citizens. Scotland, similarly, has periodic secessionist impulses. The American Civil War was fought over slavery, but what underlay that division were deeply perceived differences in shared values and identity.

New young nations, particularly ones that are linguistically, religiously, ethnically, or tribally diverse, have the challenge of building this sense of identity and cohesion. Without it, and in the process of creating it, there are pitfalls. Often too much energy and talent is devoted to struggling over power and control of resources. This makes a purposeful, coordinated assault on growth and change, with its required attendant investments and sacrifices, almost impossible to accomplish.

The new postwar states of Asia and Africa have wrestled with this challenge. Great leaders like Nelson Mandela have had a significant impact in part because their moral leadership accelerates the creation of a shared sense of values and identity and national pride. Singapore, though small, is multiethnic. A key feature of the development strategy pursued by Lee Kwan Yew and his colleagues was delivering on the promise of equality and inclusiveness through employment practices and access to education and public housing.

Most Chinese identify themselves as Han, and that identity has been two thousand years in the making. It is a partially hidden but valuable asset in collective choice and governance. The miracle of India's democracy since independence in 1950 is that in the presence of extreme diversity in multiple dimensions (religion, class, caste, and language), it has created a sense of pride and national identity that attaches to their noisy, argumentative democratic structure. Creating the ability to govern itself was (and is) the foundation of their ability to make hard choices, to invest, and to grow now. There is of course a darker side to creating a national and cultural identity. Almost inevitably, the definition of an "us" creates a simultaneous suspicious definition of a "them."

As global interconnectedness increases, catching global governance up to the level of economic interdependence is important. (We will talk more about the specifics later.) Institutions will have to be developed that bring substance to the pursuit of the collective or common interest. But the authority and legitimacy of such institutions will depend in part on their ability to act evenhandedly, and on the ability of people to see their interests as common. Some modification of the notion of "us" that goes beyond national borders is probably going to be needed—a sense of a fully collective commonality of interest. Nationalism, which sometimes facilitates farsighted collective choice within the country, can get in the way when it comes to global cooperation.

I am not saying that we need to give up thinking of ourselves as Italians or Canadians. We all have multiple identifications that are part of our overall identity and which link us to others. Yet if we are going to successfully navigate a passage to more effective global governance, our evolving sense of identities is going to have to move along with it.

Where Does Growth Come From?

Let me set aside the developing countries for a moment and talk about growth in the advanced economies, the ones that have grown for the past 250 years. We are interested in growth in incomes for the reasons discussed earlier. In a market economy, incomes are determined by the productivity of labor; that is, by the output of human beings working. That productivity is in turn determined by their skills (individually and in the aggregate), by the other forms of capital that they have to work with (think of high-tech tools such as computers), and by the effectiveness of the institutions that oversee and govern the market system in which they function.

Over time, productivity can increase for people when capital is added. It can also increase when market incentives are allowed to function. One of the clearest cases is the huge jump in agricultural output in China in 1978–80 when farmers were allowed for the first time to sell any surplus they produced above the central planning target they were given. But while market incentives increase efficiency and productivity, they do not produce continuous change in productivity and incomes. Similarly, there are limits to increasing labor productivity by just adding capital. The returns eventually decline. But since the Industrial Revolution began, incomes and productivity keep rising. So the obvious question is: Where does that come from?

The short answer is: innovation.

Innovation, which is sometimes called technological progress, increases the productive potential of an economy over time. That means that with the same inputs of capital, labor, raw materials, and energy, you can produce more—or more valuable—output. You can also think of it as reducing the cost of producing a given amount of output. Some technology economizes on labor, such as eliminating manual processing of information using networked computers and modern information technology. Other technologies economize mainly on capital. The cell phone would be a good example. It requires much less capital than a landline system to set up a workable network. We shall see later that this has had a profound effect on closing the information and communications technology gap between advanced and developing countries. Some technological advances are just neutral: they economize on all the inputs proportionately.

Some readers will be familiar with the term "total factor productivity." In ordinary English, it means how much you can produce with a given set of inputs.

When total factor productivity changes in a functioning market economy, it is mainly the result of innovation and technological progress. Or (and this is important for developing countries) total factor productivity can change when technology and knowledge that already exists (say, in developed economies) are acquired, transferred, and used in a new environment. That is what happens in developing countries. The technology and knowledge, skills and know-how that exist largely in advanced countries are imported. The effects on potential output and on productivity are the same. This is the principal reason that developing countries can grow at very high speeds relative to advanced countries.

Innovation is new knowledge that is applied to add value by creating new products, by creating new production techniques, or by lowering costs. It doesn't just appear magically out of the blue. It has to be created. Modern growth theory has been devoted in large part to explaining in precise terms what the economic incentives for innovation are and how the dynamics work. It is called endogenous growth theory because the goal is to make technological progress part of the dynamic model, so that the technological underpinnings of the economy are explained as part of the functioning of the economy, rather than appearing from somewhere outside the economic system.

The insights of this theory make precise an older but powerful theory of creative destruction developed by Joseph Schumpeter. Innovation gives the innovator (or the firm that acquires the innovation) a market advantage in terms of cost or product differentiation. Exploiting that advantage generates an incremental stream of profits that is the reward for the expense or investment cost of creating the innovation. But this market advantage is transitory. In simple terms, it lasts until the next innovation overtakes and displaces it. That is the "destruction" part. This is important because it is the flip side of the coin associated with market return to innovation. Technological innovation both creates and destroys value. But when it works, the balance is positive.

The dynamics of innovation and productivity growth are fairly easy to see. New products and new firms are entering markets displacing old ones. Sometimes a firm will occupy both positions—that is, it will introduce a product that displaces one of its own products. You might ask why it would do that. The answer is potential competition. Some existing or perhaps new firm is going to do it. If the firm in question is going to experience the loss anyway, it might as well try for the benefit, even if the net increase in profit is less than it would be for the new entrant.

This process of entry and exit, of new product introductions and displacement of older ones, is the microeconomic engine that drives growth. There are complementary factors that influence outcomes. For example, a firm that successfully innovates will likely expand and may enjoy additional benefits associated with larger scale. It is common in many industries for average costs to decline with size because of the presence of fixed costs. That may make it harder for a new entrant with a new technology or product to enter. It raises the bar a bit for successful innovation. These more static complementary factors may affect productivity and growth over short periods of time, but the underlying dynamics are driven by what might be best termed "competitive innovation."

But there is more to innovation than economic incentives and transitory market advantages. The advancement of science, engineering, social science, and management science precedes and enables economic growth. The creation of our expanding scientific knowledge base has been driven in part by economic incentives. But human curiosity plays an important role. It is a very powerful, and largely noneconomic, force.

The desire to create new knowledge was, and is, augmented by the desire for recognition and respect, also a powerful human motivation. In Renaissance Florence, major artistic and architectural projects were funded by wealthy individuals. Many of these projects were related to the Catholic Church and to its churches and cathedrals. It was actually a marvelous system. Great art was created; artists worked gainfully, and some experienced expanding reputations and hence market power; wealthy families were provided with opportunities to signal both wealth and piety; and the Church had a magnificent fund-raising machine.[1]

Here we have an example of the coming together of purely economic and other types of motivation, creating a powerful engine. Perhaps the modern analogue is the funding of scientific investigation by governments. The American postwar system has been very successful and widely adopted around the world. A key feature of this system is a powerful norm that the results are to be entirely nonproprietary. The knowledge that is created is supposed to be freely available anywhere in the world. This value is inculcated in young academics in the course of their graduate training, everywhere in the world. It is a universal value. This largely precludes direct economic gain because nothing remains proprietary.

But something has to be proprietary if investors in new technology are to receive a return. So there is a handoff to entrepreneurs and the private sector. Building on the shared knowledge foundation, private interests invest to turn knowledge into technologies and products. In this downstream layer, economic incentives largely take over.

Even in the product and technology area, recognition and desire to innovate remain powerful. One can see this in open-source product development, where creativity and recognition (and possibly subsequent pecuniary opportunities) play a central role.

People like to be creative and socially useful for the recognition as much for the purely monetary rewards. In the modern era, the Western economies benefited from this powerful human impulse by providing the tools and critical inputs to allow it to function. Education at all levels, investments in basic science and engineering and biomedical sciences, access to financing, and a host of other enablers have resulted in the alignment of economic and social interests on the one hand with the most basic human motivations on the other. Now that is spreading through much of the world.[2]

Parallel Development: Prerequisites in Small Steps

Economic growth always occurs in parallel with the development of political, legal, and regulatory institutions. One can think of this as applying to national, subnational, and international levels. It's a continuous process in which increments in economic capacity and the effectiveness of government complement each other.

Much ink has been spilled debating which comes first, institutional development or market dynamics. The right answer is both and neither.

Most of us tend to think logically and linearly at least some of the time. Logic suggests we think in terms of prerequisites: the idea is that first you need this, then you can achieve that. First you need well-defined, legally enforced property rights, and then you can have investment and growth.

But in reality when it comes to growth and effective government, it doesn't work that way. Or, rather, it does, but in tiny steps and positive feedback loops. From a distance, then, it looks like things run in a smooth parallel process. But in reality there are millions of small positive interactions and feedback loops. Educational funding increases, education becomes more effective, human capital increases, private-sector investment returns rise, foreign direct investment expands, taxes and government revenues go up, infrastructure investment expands, and educational investment increases. It is impossible to keep track of all the interactions and multipliers. Small improvements and steady long-term progress move things forward a step at a time. Education becomes more affordable and over time improves the human capital, which in turn feeds into skills, management, and government capability. Greater competitiveness opens the door to the global economy, and, as a side effect, learning and knowledge transfer accelerates, adding to incomes and investment in, among other things, educational institutions.

Of course not all the feedback loops are positive. Increased demand for labor by itself might raise its price (a good thing) but lower the return on and therefore the rate of investment, which by itself might slow growth.

Thinking this way turns out to be important. India has a massive amount of infrastructure to build. India's policy makers know this. So does anyone who has visited. The country is making steady progress, especially recently, but it will take years. The infrastructure situation in India pales in comparison with that of China. And there is no doubt that China's infrastructure has helped it grow. Yet India has accelerated to high growth in the past decade. The question is: Does India have to close the infrastructure gap to grow like China? Intuitively it would seem so, but the answer is no.

India can grow provided that its educational output and infrastructure are increasing rapidly enough. To see this, note that China's infrastructure looked somewhat like India's fifteen years ago, and even then it was growing at 9.5 percent. If one thinks a gap of that size has to be closed to enable growth, it seems a goal out of reach. That can produce a kind of paralysis. And it is this paralysis, not the gap itself, that will slow down growth.

A corollary is that in a dynamic setting the search for the causes of change can be difficult. In the models that describe these processes, variables come in two kinds. One set is determined by the model and is *within* the system (in economics the term is "endogenous"), and the other set is determined *outside* the system ("exogenous") by some other set of factors. For the endogenous variables, everything is "causing" everything else—more or less. That means they are codetermined. It doesn't really make sense to talk about what causes what unless the model has an uncommon "triangular" structure.

What about the exogenous (meaning outside the system) variables? It is natural to look to the exogenous variables as causes or, in the context of growth, as necessary conditions. These economically exogenous variables describe things like government policy, public-sector investment, and external conditions in the global economy. Exogenous variables and unconstrained choices are sometimes viewed as the same. But they are not.

Models are constructs, simplifications designed to sort out the important forces and interactions. What is exogenous and endogenous is a choice. Our colleagues in the field of political economy have been busy making endogenous what were traditionally thought of as exogenous political and policy variables. The important insight is that political and policy choices are influenced and constrained by economic outcomes, and vice versa. This is enormously important work that helps us understand the interaction of politics, economics, and collective choice. It is also making variables traditionally thought to be exogenous to the model, endogenous.

Of course, that brings us back to the challenge of finding the causes and the starting points.

In fact, there is a bit of a mystery as to how these reinforcing positive growth dynamics get started and why they don't when they don't. We will revisit this later in Part II.

6. Common Questions About the Developing World and the Global Economy

The developing world is vast, varied, and confusing. Some countries are huge and some are small. Some are growing at high speed, while others have barely started to accelerate growth or are stationary. If you mention the developing world to people in advanced countries, some will think of a poor African country struggling with AIDS and other health issues. Some will think of governance issues that occasionally result in armed conflict.

Others will think of Latin America, with its higher incomes, dramatically higher levels of income inequality, slums, and drug-related governance challenges. Still others will think about dynamic high growth in East Asia and will have read stories about the Asian Tigers and the rising size and power of China and Asia. Many have wondered about the apparent conflict between, on the one hand, the accelerating growth and rising expectations in India, and, on the other, its rural poverty.

This mosaic *is* the developing world. No wonder it is hard to bring all the pieces into focus.

Foreign Aid and Growth

In the West, much of the focus of attention when it comes to developing countries has been on aid. There is the celebrated debate between Jeffrey Sachs and William Easterly on whether aid does any good at all or indeed more harm than good. Sachs argues that there is a low-income trap that can be escaped with an appropriate ongoing external investment in the poor countries. Easterly points out that the correlation between aid and outcomes in terms of economic performance is weak at best and that aid creates dependence and undercuts self-reliance and governance reform.

To be fair, both these protagonists would agree that emergency humanitarian aid (in cases of famine, conflict, and epidemics) is exempt from these debates. Its purpose is largely to protect people, with no pretense of influencing development and growth except in a very indirect way. The debate is about development aid—that is, assistance that is designed to improve economic performance and jump-start growth.

Aid, though a subject of interest in the West, is something of a red herring from a growth and development standpoint. Relatively little of the postwar growth we have seen is attributable to foreign aid. An open global trading system and relatively free flows of foreign direct investment and cross-border learning are significantly more important drivers of developing-country growth.

Until fairly recently, a large portion of the Western discussion of the developing world tended to focus not so much on the internal dynamics and challenges of growth in developing countries, but rather on how advanced countries interact with them, be it via aid, trade, the migration of jobs and people, or just investment flows. The implicit assumption appears to be that these external interactions are the principal catalysts for change.

This is an incomplete and somewhat narcissistic view. It is not that the external connections with the advanced countries and their institutions are irrelevant to growth and development. But the external catalysts interact with a complex internal dynamic whose elements are needed to complete the picture.

The questions I get asked as I travel around the world mirror the confusing nature of the mosaic.

Where Is the Income in the Global Economy?

Most of the income in the global economy is in the set of countries known as the G20, slightly adjusted to add the larger countries who are not yet members. The G20 includes the advanced countries: the European Union, Japan, the United States, Canada, Australia, and New Zealand. It also includes most of the major developing countries: South Korea (now approaching advanced-country incomes), the BRICs (Brazil, Russia, India, and China), but also Argentina, South Africa, Turkey, Indonesia, and Saudi Arabia.[1] The systemically important but missing large countries are Mexico, Egypt, and Nigeria. Over time they are likely to be included.

The G20 accounts for between 85 and 90 percent of total global income and roughly two-thirds of the world's population. The G20, formerly somewhat obscure, has come to prominence as a result of the financial and economic crisis of 2008–9. The reason is quite simple: leaders, policy makers, and observers all realized that the effective management of the global economy required the involvement of the systemically important developing countries. The shift from the G7/8, the advanced-country group (with partial participation of Russia), to the G20 occurred literally almost overnight and with next to no debate or dissent. The rest of the developing world thinks of it as a cabal and worries that its interests will not get adequate attention. But that was also true of the G7. It is remarkable what a crisis can do by way of removing roadblocks and shifting old patterns of thought and interaction.

For much of the postwar period, international economic priorities were set by the G7, and the global economy and financial systems were managed by institutions dominated by the advanced countries. We have left that world behind. But new institutions do not just spring into existence. They are created over time. Thus we are in uncharted territory in the midst of a major transition in global governance. There are very likely to be missteps and bumps along the road. The volatility and bouts of instability that we have experienced in the period since 2008 are commonly viewed as an aberration, a once-in-a-hundred-years perfect storm. To me they are more probably signals or precursors of an extended period of potential volatility and change that will be a challenge to manage and a test of the model of growth convergence that we have been experiencing for the past fifty or sixty years.

What of the rest of the developing world? There are 223 countries in the world. Roughly 200 outside the G20 have over a third of the planet's population (about 2.2 billion people, and hence an average population of 11 million each—relatively small) and less than 15 percent of the income. There are exceptions, but on average they are poor. Of these

200 countries, roughly 75 have populations of less than 2 million people. They are very small, and that increases their economic vulnerability in a number of ways.

In terms of per capita income, the G20 is at about $10,000 and rising rapidly. The remainder is at an average of around $3,300 and growing much less quickly. In both sets there is considerable variability.

The developed countries (the 15 percent from the earlier discussion), with roughly a billion people, account for 63 percent of total income. The remaining 3.2 billion people in the rest of the G20 (roughly half the world's population) have 20 to 25 percent of the income. The 200 outsiders have 15 percent or less. It is clear that the wide divergences created in the first 200 years of the Industrial Revolution are far from being closed.

Poverty in the Developing Economies?

Nations have different definitions of poverty, each designed to identify the relatively disadvantaged members of their societies. But for development and international comparisons, we need an absolute standard. That standard is normally taken to be a cap of $1 or $2 a day.

The following is a picture of the incidence of poverty globally using the dollar-a-day standard.

Incidence of Poverty

- Under 2%
- 2%–5%
- 6%–20%
- 21%–40%
- 41%–60%
- 61%–80%
- N/A

Source: UN Human Development Indices 2008

Advanced countries have very little poverty. Generally poverty declines with growth, but the pace is affected by the distribution of income. Latin America and Africa have the highest levels of measured income inequality. And so, relative to the incomes there, poverty tends to be higher. But this can get a little complicated. In very poor countries where almost everyone is poor, the measured income inequality will be low. Then, with growth, it tends to rise, as incomes rise unevenly as a result of the growth dynamics.

Clearly, in countries with very low incomes, growth is the key enabler of poverty reduction. This is evident in Asia, where growth has been high and poverty has declined rapidly. The same illustration from twenty-five years ago would have shown a lot more high-poverty dark areas in Asia.

India still has a relatively high percentage of poor people, because it accelerated later. This percentage is expected to decline dramatically with the country's high growth. But because of the sheer numbers, the highest concentration of poverty remains there. Recall that India's population is twice that of all of sub-Saharan Africa. Notwithstanding the high growth, Indian citizens, particularly those who are poor, and Indian politicians and policy makers remain concerned about inclusiveness: that is, ensuring that the benefits of growth are spread fairly evenly, particularly in the rural sector, where 70 percent of the population still resides.

Income Inequality—GINI Coefficient

■ <.25	■ .45–.49
■ .25–.29	■ .50–.54
■ .30–.34	■ .55–.59
■ .35–.39	■ >.60
■ .40–.44	■ No Data

Source: CIA—The World Factbook 2009

Of deepest concern is the poverty in poor countries that are not growing. The poor in these countries are the group that Paul Collier refers to as the "bottom billion." Not only is there poverty in these countries, but the crucial test of whether one's grandchildren will be better off is failing. The lack of growth and the absence of conditions that enable it make the persistence of poverty there the most likely outcome.

While growth is the dominant determinant of poverty reduction—and its absence the main explanation for persistent poverty—there are other important factors. Of these, the lack of access to basic services and systems is a serious de facto exclusionary device. The absence of quality education would be high on the list. So would the related issues of property rights and little or no access to credit and financial services. These latter seriously impede the ability of the poor to save and invest, to form businesses or to expand them. Underinvestment in infrastructure and in relevant technology on the public-sector side also contributes to a persistent lag in productivity growth in rural sectors in many countries where the poor are concentrated.

Global poverty is dominantly a rural phenomenon. Its reduction, in known cases, comes from growth and urbanization, leading to a decline in the rural population, a reduction of surplus labor in that sector, and eventually to an increase in rural productivity.

There are deviations from this pattern. In major parts of Latin America, urbanization outpaced growth in productive employment. As a result, poverty is not so highly concentrated in rural areas, which have been substantially depopulated, but rather in slums in urban areas.

How Big Is the Chinese Economy?

China's economy is now just under 35 percent of the size of the U.S. or E.U. economies, the two largest economies in the world. It is just at the point of displacing Japan as the second-largest economy in the world. The E.U. and the U.S. economies are similar in size, and each is just under 22 percent of the global economy as measured by output. Assuming current growth rates, the Chinese economy will become about the same size as that of the E.U. or the U.S.A. in ten to fifteen years. China has a population four times that of the United States, so its per capita income will then be about one-fourth that of the U.S.A. It will take an additional fifteen years (or perhaps more if growth starts to slow) for China's per capita income to be similar to those of the advanced countries.

One very striking aspect of this arithmetic is that China will become a major economic power (one could argue that it already is) at a time when its per capita income is quite low. This has not really happened before because no country of that size, in terms of population, has grown that fast. China has global impacts and growing global responsibilities for the maintenance and stability of the world economic system, though its income levels are still low by advanced-country standards. Most developing countries have the luxury of focusing on domestic growth and development for much longer. There will therefore be significant challenges for China in balancing its domestic growth and development with its growing international power, impact, and responsibilities. This creates a difficult internal tension within China that makes management of the global economy more difficult. I will return to these issues in Part IV.

Where Is India in Relation to China?

India's growth accelerated later than China's, and the ramp-up was somewhat more gradual. China's growth jumped up in the late 1970s, while India's growth acceleration started in the late 1980s. Assuming the continuation of recent and similar high growth rates (9 percent or above) in both countries, India is about fourteen years behind China. India's per capita income is presently about one-third that of China. The poverty reduction that has occurred in China is less far along in India. But that will change. Huge reductions in poverty are likely to occur in India in the next fifteen years. But with a lag of fourteen years or so, the pattern in India should be about the same as what we have seen in China.

There is one important qualification. The population growth rates in India and China are different. Over the past five years, India's population grew at 1.4 percent a year, while the figure for China was 0.6 percent, reflecting the one-child policy that operates mainly in the urban sector and the modern part of the economy. That 1 percent difference causes per capita income growth in India to diverge from overall growth by that same amount. China's population is older (in fact aging quite quickly) and the divergence may widen as a result. The higher rate of population growth in India will have a modest negative impact on per capita income growth there relative to China.

On the other hand, fertility tends to decline with income, with education, and with the increasing employment opportunities and empowerment of women. The fertility rates in Mexico, for example, are declining rapidly as the economy develops. It is therefore likely that as India becomes richer, its population growth rate will decline, and that will accelerate the growth of individual incomes.

China and India together account for about 8–9 percent of global GDP. That will increase over time. With populations of 1.3 billion (China) and 1.2 billion (India), together they account for close to 40 percent of the world's population.

One way to think about this is that China and India account for about 60 percent of the population of the G20 countries. In another few decades, these will be the major advanced income countries. At that point, say by the middle of the twenty-first century, output of China and India will be similar and account for almost 60 percent of the world's advanced-country income. The United States and Europe by then will each account for about 10 percent of the advanced-country total. Currently the E.U. and the U.S.A. together account for about 60 percent of G20 income. The sizes and perhaps the roles of the U.S.A. and the E.U., on the one hand, and China and India, on the other, will be reversed. How that will affect the conduct of the global economy is impossible to know in advance. But it will be a very different world in terms of the distribution of economic power.

PART TWO

Sustained High Growth in the
Developing World

7. The High-Growth Developing Countries in the Postwar Period

One way to understand high growth in the developing world is to look at the cases where sustained high growth has been achieved and to ask what they have in common.[1] Then one can ask how they differ from countries in which growth has been lower or zero. Doing this does not provide scientific proof of the drivers of growth, but it does give useful clues and leads.

There are thirteen developing countries that have managed to grow for twenty-five years or more at a average rate of 7 percent or more. Given that there are some 180 developing countries in the world, it is not a long list. But, then, it is a very high bar to clear. Otherwise the pattern of high growth would be much more widespread. In fact, until the past fifty years, it would have seemed an impossibly high standard.

The countries where sustained high growth (using the 7 percent/twenty-five-year standard) has occurred are listed the chart on page 54, along with the period of rapid growth and the starting and ending per capita incomes. At 7 percent growth, income and output double every decade. Starting at $500 per person, that income would become $2,700 after twenty-five years, still not rich by a long shot, but a huge change. At these rates, poverty reduction is dramatic.

As you can see, the list of thirteen economies includes Japan, which is a combination of postwar rebuilding and economic development. Japan and Brazil were the first high-growth cases in the postwar period. The list also includes the Asian Tigers (South Korea, Singapore, Hong Kong, and Taiwan)—no surprise there—and a number of other Asian countries:

Economy	Period of high growth[†]	Per capita income at the beginning and in 2005[‡]	
Botswana	1960–2005	210	3,800
Brazil	1950–1980	960	4,000
China	1961–2005	105	1,400
Hong Kong*	1960–1997	3,100	29,900
Indonesia	1966–1997	200	900
Japan*	1950–1983	3,500	39,600
Korea, Rep. of*	1960–2001	1,100	13,200
Malaysia	1967–1997	790	4,400
Malta*	1963–1994	1,100	9,600
Oman	1960–1999	950	9,000
Singapore*	1967–2002	2,200	25,400
Taiwan*	1965–2002	1,500	16,400
Thailand	1960–1997	330	2,400

Source: World Bank. World Development Indicators.
*Economies that have reached industrialized countries' per capita income levels.
[†]Period in which GDP growth was 7 percent per year or more.
[‡]In constant U.S. dollars of 2000.

Indonesia, Thailand, and Malaysia. One also finds Botswana, a small land-locked country in Africa, a functioning democracy that has found a way with inspired leadership and sound policy to get past the challenges of nation-building and conflict surrounding natural-resources wealth (diamonds). Botswana is thus far an outlier in Africa, though that may be about to change.

China is the largest and fastest of these cases. India and Vietnam, with their somewhat later starting points, are not on the list, but they appear to be on track to become members of this elite club with the passage of a few more years. And there may be others. Generally global growth accelerated and spread across countries in the decade starting in 2000. The economic and financial crisis in 2008 put an abrupt but probably temporary end to that pattern. We know that the major high-growth economies displayed remarkable resilience in the crisis and appear to be restoring growth to near precrisis levels (more on this in Parts III and IV). What is not known is how widespread this pattern of resilience will be across a broader set of developing countries.

The income and poverty-reduction figures in China are exceedingly dramatic and illustrative of what this kind of growth means. Per capita income, having languished from 1949 to 1978 under a centrally planned economy, immediately started to rise as a result of the introduction of market incentives and reforms. After that initial burst of productivity, mainly in the agricultural sector, continued growth was associated with a pattern of opening up the economy to the rest of the world.

As a result of these dynamics there are over 700 million people in China whose incomes have risen above $2 per day. These changes are dramatic and extraordinary in terms of the number of lives affected, but the pattern is not atypical. Growth with a reasonably inclusive pattern of the distribution of benefits is a potent weapon in reducing poverty. In fact, it is arithmetically essential because in a poor country with a low average income, even if the distribution of income is very even or equal, pretty much everyone is poor.

In trying to get inside the dynamics—the causes and the enabling factors associated with the expanding pattern of growth—it is useful to ask two related questions. First, why did this process of rapidly expanding modernization and growth start in the postwar period? And second, what do developing economies do (and not do) to sustain the high rates of growth and poverty reduction?

The answer to the first question is the global economy: the growing openness to trade in goods and services, the flows of capital, and, most important of all, the transfers of knowledge and technology.

But while the global economy is probably a necessary condition, it certainly isn't sufficient. The high variability in growth rates across developing countries is inconsistent with the view that all you need is access to global markets and knowledge. Clearly there is something else—in fact, quite a lot—that is additionally required. Which leads us to ask: What are the internal dynamics, conditions, and policies that lead to sustained high growth? Or, more bluntly: What do countries do and not do to sustain growth?

The answer to this second question is not simple. We will spend some time on that after addressing the way in which the global economy creates the possibility of sustained high growth.

8. The Opening of the Global Economy

These sustained high-growth cases were all made possible primarily by the growing openness and increasing connectedness of the global economy. The GATT removed policy barriers to trade. In parallel, technology gains in transportation and communication were driving down the costs of logistics, connectedness, and coordination. The Internet is the latest important entrant in this long-term trend. In economic terms, the costs of trade, transactions, communication, travel, and economic coordination declined, and continue to do so, driving increasing economic connectedness and integration.

Multinational businesses, armed with these reduced costs of communication, transportation, and coordination, learned over time how to manage global supply chains. The economic advantage of global supply chains is the ability to make use of high-quality, low-cost resources (especially labor) and opportunities around the world, in manufacturing, and now increasingly in services and business functions. The disadvantage is that global supply chains are inherently more complex. As a result they are subject to delays, errors, and costs associated with managing and coordinating this complex set of interconnected activity. Those disadvantages have declined steadily as a result of the combination of technology, management learning, and the removal of formal barriers and costs to trade under the GATT.

Trade that was previously theoretically possible but not cost effective shifted into the tradable category. Put another way, things that were in principle tradable but in fact were not traded for reasons of cost and capability, or because of policy-imposed barriers to trade, began to move rapidly into the traded category. Labor and knowledge-intensive services are presently in the process of shifting into the internationally tradable sector, again with the tailwind of the Internet and communications technology and applications. Markets that had local, regional, or national boundaries are shedding those boundaries. In short, technology and international policy are pushing markets toward being global. The tradable sector is an expanding subset of the world's economic activity.

This combination of factors (rapid advances in technology and international policy choices directed at expanding trade, and, more specifically, at expanding the range of traded goods between the advanced and developing countries) created a new set of opportunities. It jump-started what has come to be called catch-up growth in the developing economies.

9. Knowledge Transfer and Catch-up Growth in Developing Countries

Knowledge has to be created before it is used for economic purposes. Admittedly, the boundary between creation and use can at times be blurred. But this observation is essentially correct. Economic advancement comes from knowledge, technology, and innovation that we collectively create and then apply to create something of economic value. It is, as we have seen, the driving force in long-run advanced-country growth.

But once knowledge is created, it can be used anywhere, and over and over again. Of the many things that have economic value, knowledge stands out in this respect. If person A has it and transmits it to person B, then they both have it. This is in stark contrast to refrigerators, cars, timber, and almost everything else we think of as having economic value.

But the people on the receiving end of the transmission have to be able to receive it. Old knowledge has to be disseminated in every generation, lest the knowledge foundation of our economies and societies depreciate over time. Much of our educational investment is undertaken to that end.

In addition, of course, new knowledge is created, and then it is disseminated. The creation of new knowledge and technology is costly and consumes a lot of human resources. The dissemination would also be expensive were it not for the fact that the investment in disseminating old knowledge is already in place—or, in developing countries, in the process of being put in place. This means that the incremental cost of disseminating new knowledge is low, and much lower than the cost of creating it. In a sense, knowledge is the ultimate public good. If it is available to one, it is available to everyone with the educational background to absorb it.

In essence, this is what is happening in the developing world. There are many critical ingredients that go into high-growth recipes, but the single most important is learning—that is, acquiring new and productively relevant knowledge that already exists. Knowledge, technology, and practical know-how are imported from the global economy, and especially from the advanced countries, where the knowledge gap is largest. There are multiple channels for this transfer process: the processes surrounding foreign direct investment and engagement with the global economy through multinational supply chains are probably the most important.

This knowledge transfer and learning process has been going on for a couple of centuries. Industrialization in continental Europe and America wasn't just a accident. It came as a result of the British technological advancements. In our time, knowledge transfer causes the productive potential of a developing economy to increase extremely rapidly. It is as if innovation took a quantum step up. But in fact it is not innovation that has jumped, but rather its transfer; the dissemination of the output—knowledge.

When the other pieces of sustained high-growth dynamics are put in place, the growth rates are high compared to advanced-country growth rates and to past growth in developing economies when the barriers were higher.

Advanced countries don't grow at rates of 7 percent or above on a sustained basis. Advancing the knowledge base that underpins the economy doesn't seem to happen that fast, or fast enough to support growth at those rates. It would be going too far to say it is impossible: nothing in logic or theory precludes it. But since we know of no counterexamples, we may assume that it is very unlikely to happen in the future.

It is possible that advanced-country growth will accelerate in the future. The reason is that the size and share of the global economy with advanced-country incomes is set to rise because of developing-country growth. Size and scale matter. While the share of GDP devoted to innovation may not rise, the absolute amounts very likely will go up, increasing the pace of innovation then deployed across a large part of the global economy.

To return to the developing countries, the economic impact of knowledge transfer is a function of the size of the gap. It is hard to measure precisely because quantitative measures of knowledge have been thus far elusive. When the gap is large, as it is between an advanced country and a poor one that is just starting to grow, the transfer rate of useful technology can be rapid.

I say "can be" deliberately. Learning and knowledge transfer are not automatic. There are significant differences across countries in their learning speeds. They are due to differences in education, attitudes, and a range of factors that we need to understand better than we do now.

This accelerating growth in potential output doesn't last forever because the gap declines. Along the path, a developing country continues to import technology, but it begins to produce progressively more, too. That internally generated technology is also shared internationally. At the end of the development path, a developing country becomes an advanced country. It creates and absorbs and shares the knowledge and technology that moves economic potential and causes growth for advanced countries and for the whole global economy.

Tangible and Intangible Assets

The aspects of growth and development that we can observe most easily are the physical and measurable things: incomes, highways, ports, industrial plants, housing, patterns of consumption, exports and imports, capital flows in and out. This picture is a real and important reflection of growth and development, but it is incomplete.

There is a parallel process of accumulation of assets and capabilities that are intangible. These intangibles are much harder to measure and document. But that doesn't make them less important. We can think of these intangible assets as the accumulation of embedded knowledge: embedded not just in people, but in institutions and processes, and in how they interact. We have a lot more to learn about how these intangible assets are acquired and about the channels through which they are imported and internalized. The process of learning by doing and experimenting is surely part of it. So, too, is contact with outsiders, through education, foreign direct investment, and probably much more.

When Deng Xiaoping and a group of reformers in China decided to change direction at the end of the 1970s, they did two things. The first was to let the market mechanism work in the agricultural sector. This was a brilliant move. Most of China's population were in agriculture (82 percent). Being allowed merely to sell on the open market any increment they could produce over the planned economy quotas resulted in an immediate and very large jump in output and incomes. Prices went up, and the city residents grumbled. But they were only 18 percent of the population and were outnumbered four to one. Market incentives at the microeconomic level are powerful tools. The jump occurred even though the farmer initially could keep only the profit on the sale of the increment over the old quota. The quota part was still owed to the state in return for a basic income and access to services under the old central planning model.

The second reform was deeply insightful. Deng realized that they didn't know how to manage a market economy: they didn't have the experience or the concepts. He asked the World Bank to help. Specifically he asked the then president of the WB, Robert McNamara, to come to China to help with the transition to a socialist market economy. Prior to that, the World Bank had had no dealings with China. What Deng asked for was not primarily financial capital for investment in real assets, even though he was talking to a bank. Rather, it was for knowledge. He realized intuitively that the missing piece was know-how. And so a small group in the World Bank, acting with Chinese counterparts, set about to accelerate the importation of knowledge about market economies, bringing academics and experienced policy people from around the world to give lectures on how market economies work and how policy should be set. Some of these took place on boats in the Yangtze River and featured presentations by Janos Kornai, the late James Tobin, and others. Tobin talked about managing the demand side of the economy, a totally new and mysterious concept in a centrally planned economy.

Deng realized that the central task for development and growth was learning at all levels, in the private sector and the government. This idea has guided the approach to reform and growth and development in China for the last thirty years. It was and remains, first and foremost, a high-speed learning environment. Westerners with little contact with China don't understand this. We tend to believe that with its different political system and restricted press freedom, Chinese society is closed and cut off. Nothing could be further from the truth.

The opening of China to the global economy, of course, accelerated the learning process. Deng is reported by those who were present at the early meetings to have said that he thought that he and his Chinese colleagues and Chinese businesses could eventually figure it all out themselves, largely by trial and error. But learning from external experience and analysis would make the process a lot faster, with less chance of mistakes.

The Chinese leadership understood that the conceptual frameworks that are used in advanced market economies to predict the outcomes of taking policy actions could not be used without modification in an economy that had barely started the transition from centrally planned to market based. Armed with incomplete models and conceptual frameworks, they set out on a decades-long journey. Skeptical of theory and advanced-country policy prescriptions, they experimented and learned. They knew that the economy they were dealing with was changing its characteristics as it grew and developed. Deng famously described this as "crossing the river by feeling the stones."

This general approach also characterized the other high-growth countries, and it has become increasingly recognized as the best way to think about strategy and policy formation in developing countries. It is based on the fundamental recognition that simple one-size-fits-all formulas are unlikely to work. In some ways it is more akin to a business mind-set than it is to a policy mind-set.[1]

To summarize briefly, the high-speed growth in the postwar period in the developing world is enabled by knowledge transfer and the reduction in barriers and impediments to the flow of goods, services, and capital in the global economy. The speed is accounted for by the size of the knowledge differential and the rapid transfer of knowledge across borders.

Intellectual Property

One reads a great deal about a blasé attitude toward intellectual property rights in developing countries. Enforcement of intellectual property rights is a significant issue in recent trade negotiations, including at the stalled Doha round. An obvious question is whether or not the knowledge transfer that underpins catch-up growth is nothing less than a form of theft of intellectual property.

The answer is that it is not. The vast majority of productively useful knowledge is neither patented nor copyrighted. Some is proprietary and held within firms, and those firms transfer it voluntarily when it is in their interest to do so. General Electric has global supply chains in many of its operating divisions. When it sets up a manufacturing facility and supporting logistics in India, it is pursuing a profitable strategy of using the global economy to lower the cost of its products. It is also transferring technology to India. The transfer includes manufacturing technology, to be sure, but also management know-how. It is a voluntary arrangement on both sides. That means that there are benefits to both sides, and ultimately to workers in India and consumers in Europe. The fact that there are knowledge spillovers or transfers does not detract from the mutually beneficial nature of the trade. In a sense, India is paying for the knowledge acquisition by providing a low-wage and otherwise supportive environment. More vigorous enforcement of intellectual property rights would have no effect on this aspect of knowledge transfer and would not impede the catch-up growth process.

There is theft as well. This is a concern primarily to companies and individuals who make their income from selling intellectual property. Computer software, entertainment videos, and music, for example, are copied and sold at a discount, with none of the revenue going to the creators or the original distributors of the product. The legal and enforcement systems in many developing countries do not have the capacity, or the intention, to enforce copyright protection.

From a policy point of view, in specific countries, the issue tends to take care of itself over time, because, as countries become richer, and their economies shift in structure, the domestic producers of valuable intellectual property grow, and then they begin to demand intellectual property protection for themselves. Intellectual property protection tends to develop with growth. Probably a sensible compromise for the WTO would be to set a per capita income threshold, above which countries are required to create effective mechanisms for the protection of intellectual property.

10. Global Demand and Catch-up Growth

What is it about the global economy that makes it possible to grow at previously unknown rates for long periods of time?

The short answer is, mainly, two things: (1) a huge potential market and (2) access to knowledge. They are both important and they work together. We have talked about knowledge transfer, so now let's turn to the market.

The global market allows a developing country to specialize in producing what it is good at, relative to other countries. That specialization increases its productivity. In a relatively poor country, demand (meaning what people want and can afford to buy) is small and "uninteresting" in the sense that the range of products consumed is limited, and it may or may not (in fact, likely will not) correspond very well to what the country is comparatively good at producing. Producing only for the domestic market would dramatically limit specialization.

In the global economy, goods and services can be divided into two important categories: tradables and nontradables. Nontradable goods and services have to be provided locally either because proximity is required or because remote production and delivery are too expensive. Examples include construction, most aspects of health care, government services, hotels, restaurants, and legal services. Tradables are the opposite. They can and are produced in one country and consumed in another. Electronics, autos, industrial machinery, and certain agricultural products are examples. Exports and imports have to be in the tradable category. But not all tradables are imported for consumption. The United States produces cars for domestic consumption and export, and it imports cars too. Imports displace and exports augment domestic production.

The boundary between tradables and nontradables changes over time, usually as a result of technological innovation. Recently, for example, the Internet has allowed services that had previously required proximity and were in the nontradable category to be provided remotely and hence be internationally traded. The outsourcing of these services to India is an example of the growing trade in activities that were formerly nontradable.

In the global economy, a country produces the nontradable goods and services it needs (it has to because these goods and services are not tradable—they have to be produced locally) and then specializes in what it is comparatively good at producing for the global market in the tradable sector. The benefits are of two kinds and they are large. First, you don't produce the things you are comparatively weak at: you import them instead. The difference represents a gain in productivity. Second, by specializing, you benefit from scale economies and the dynamic analogue, sometimes called the learning curve. The more you do something, the better (more efficient) you become at it.

Economists call what a country is relatively good at "comparative advantage." It seems to be one of the more mysterious of economic concepts for intelligent experienced practitioners.

Countries produce what they are relatively good at. The "relatively" part is important. In the early stages of growth, when productivity levels are low, a country may (probably will) compare unfavorably with other countries in virtually all sectors when it comes to productivity, ranging from agriculture to manufacturing and services. But they will still trade and export the products where they have the least disadvantage and import the ones where they have the greatest disadvantage. The mechanism that makes this possible is the exchange rate for the national currency. If the country is unable to export anything and is busy importing, it will be borrowing money abroad, and that has its limits. Eventually the domestic currency will decline in value relative to other currencies, making exports cheaper for foreigners and imports more expensive for citizens. As this happens, some sectors will become competitive enough to export.

Incomes and wealth are determined by absolute (not relative) productivity levels. Trade, on the other hand, is determined by relative productivity levels across sectors. The goal of a poor country is, through investment and knowledge absorption, to increase absolute productivity, and hence incomes. One way to get started at this is to quickly shift to sectors where one is relatively more productive. This is what trade—and the large global marketplace—allows. That starts the knowledge transfer process, and then the growth engine is up and running.

In a poor country that is isolated from international markets, both the size and composition of the domestic market (more exactly, market demand—what people want and can afford to buy) constrain the producing side of the economy. The global market essentially removes those constraints. Any single developing country is small with respect to the global market. Once it finds an area in which it can compete, it can expand without limit. As it does, it specializes, learns, achieves greater scale, and becomes more efficient. Productivity rises and incomes reflect that and start to rise.

This highlights another "advantage" developing countries have, particularly those countries in the early stages of growth. They are small in relation to the global economy. Take a sector, say labor-intensive apparel, and assume that a country has a 10 percent market share globally. Now suppose the apparel part of the export sector is growing at 15 percent a year while the global economy is growing at 5 percent. Then, after a year, the market share of the clothing manufacturing export sector for that country will be 11 percent, not a large change in absolute numbers, but the growth rate is very high.

The hard part about comparative advantage is that it is not a static condition. It shifts continuously over time, in parallel with investment, human capital acquisition, and, ultimately, with prices and wages. Consider an example. At some point in the 1970s the Asian Tigers (Hong Kong, Singapore, Taiwan, and South Korea) were major exporters of apparel and shoes. These are labor-intensive industries, and these countries with their educated workers and low wages had a comparative advantage in these goods. If you look today, there is almost no apparel or shoe manufacturing for the mass market in any of these countries. It disappeared in the 1980s. More accurately, it didn't disappear, but rather moved to other locations, namely Indonesia, Vietnam, Bangladesh, and China. It moved because wages rose and these countries ceased to be the logical place for high-quality, low-cost, labor-intensive manufacturing. When people say that economic activity is constantly moving around in the global economy, this is what they mean.

Comparative advantage shifts continuously as incomes rise, human capital deepens, education and work experience grow, and learning occurs. Economic activity shifts around the global economy, driving structural shifts in both developing and advanced economies. The structural change combined with innovation drives the sustained growth. Without it, productivity and growth will stagnate. Growth strategy and policy have everything to do with accommodating and supporting the structural shifts and the learning that goes with it by avoiding barriers and structural impediments and by investing in supportive human capital, knowledge transfer, institutions, and infrastructure.

I recall a trip I made to Korea in the mid-1980s to give a lecture. At that time, the local media had discovered that the labor-intensive exports that had driven so much growth for two decades were becoming uncompetitive. Wages were too high, and people were going to be thrown out of work. Some suggested that it might be desirable or necessary to hold wages down to prevent this calamitous outcome. I was a little taken aback. I reminded them (without noticeable effect) that the point of growth and development was to have higher incomes. What they were describing as a problem was actually a signal of success.

The static view of the world always has great attraction. One of the more significant mistakes in growth-oriented policy is to find a formula that works and then to stay with it for too long.

Sustained growth and structural change go hand in hand. The structural change driven by shifting prices and market forces is the crucial input to productivity and income growth. There is a very powerful tendency to resist the change, especially when it comes to the job- and company-destruction part of creative destruction. The pressure to resist comes from policy makers who want to stick with a known formula for success. It comes also from the people who bear the brunt of the job transitions and the anxiety that goes with it. And it comes from vested interests, namely the export sectors, who may have considerable political and policy influence. The main job of government is to facilitate structural change by investing in human capital, protecting people in the transitions through income support and access to basic services, and then to let the market forces and investment incentives work. All too often governments protect the sector (through excessive downward management of the exchange rate or with subsidies), the companies, and the specific jobs. This is the functional equivalent of throwing sand in the gears of an otherwise well-oiled machine. It will negatively impact productivity and incomes—and, eventually, growth.

11. The Internal Dynamics of Sustained High Growth

At the start of Part II, after describing the known cases of sustained high growth, I suggested that this kind of growth was enabled by the expanding openness of the global economy, driven by both technological forces and international agreements and policy changes. I hope the preceding chapters have been persuasive in outlining the reasons why the global economy is the critical enabling environmental condition.

I also suggested that access to the global economy, though necessary for catch-up growth, was not the whole explanation. If it was, there would be more examples. Clearly there is something else—in fact, quite a lot—in addition that is required. Now, the second question, the reader will recall, has to do with the internal dynamics, conditions, and policies that lead to sustained high growth in the context of an open international economic system. More bluntly: What do countries do and not do to sustain growth?

We know the answer to this in the most general sense. It is the private sector that is the proximate driver of growth. Governments by and large do not create new products, enterprises, or jobs. They aren't very good at it. When they do try to organize the productive sector directly, as in various forms of central planning, they fail. All the twentieth-century experiments in planning an economy collapsed under their own inefficiency and from the lack of incentives.

There is an alternative view. Governments should do as little as possible. This has the virtue of recognizing the critical role of private-sector dynamics. But it has the major defect of missing the important complementary role of the public sector: in investment and in policies that overcome transitory market deficiencies in the context of developing economies where market, legal, and regulatory institutions are in transition and where informational shortfalls impede performance.

What governments do in successful cases of high growth is to create an environment in which private-sector investment is profitable. That turns loose the competitive dynamics that we talked about before. So the question really comes down to what policies and investments on the public sector or government side at various stages of growth and development are needed to create strong investment incentives and unleash the private-sector dynamics.

To get at this we can ask: In what countries has growth occurred, and what did they do that seems to have enabled the sustained growth acceleration? Do they have common characteristics that help us understand this extraordinary shift? We can also ask about the low-growth countries, with a view to determining what pieces or ingredients are missing there. A combination of the two should give us a sense of what is needed to sustain growth.

12. Key Internal Ingredients of Sustained High-Growth Recipes

Reliance on Markets and Incentives

Growth requires the use of markets to provide price signals, create incentives, and guide the allocation of resources. Markets are a way of decentralizing decision making. Competitive markets also create powerful dynamic incentives to lower costs or improve quality.[1] There have been numerous attempts to replace markets with planning systems and command-and-control approaches. All of these experiments in centralized economic management have failed because of very poor economic performance, and they have been largely abandoned.

These failures result in part from an inability to calculate all the resource allocation requirements accurately. But the more fundamental reason is that centrally planned systems lack incentives for people and organizations to do what the plan says. They find ways to do something else: work less, free ride, and so on. When incentives are reinserted into the system to solve this problem, it starts to look like a market system.

Keep in mind that this is not market fundamentalism, a belief that largely unregulated markets are optimal and self-regulating and that regulation largely produces second-best results. Lots of markets have problems—such as externalities and informational gaps and asymmetries—that require regulation to improve performance.

Growth Is Driven by Continual Structural Change

Taking advantage of the static-efficiency benefits of market allocation and the more important dynamic gains in productivity coming from competition, and the previously discussed forces of Schumpeter's creative destruction, entry and exit is easier to say than to do. It is a quite chaotic process, especially at high-growth rates. Jobs, companies, and sectors are created and eliminated by the forces of innovation and competition. If you take a snapshot of a rapidly growing developing economy at ten-year intervals, the changes from picture to picture will be dramatic. The composition of the economy shifts. The jobs people do change. Education levels rise. Industries that were once competitive and a source of rising productive employment eventually decline and are replaced by others. These are the dynamics of Schumpeter's creative destruction.

In some respects it is not unlike biological evolution. Markets and investors conduct experiments. Many fail, but the ones that succeed get replicated and change the economy, along with employment opportunities and incomes. The experiments, of course, are not random, as in the alteration of genes in biological evolution, but rather they are driven by the purposeful searching for new investment opportunity in a competitive economic environment, and by the shifting incentives caused by changes in prices, most especially the price of labor.

You can see this in the differing rates of growth of the manufacturing, agriculture, and service sectors in the high-growth economies. Generally manufacturing and eventually services grow much faster. The economy undergoes a process of urbanization as the new manufacturing and service jobs are created mostly in urban environments, where modern economic activity occurs.

Protecting People and Not Jobs

As the structure evolves, and as firms come and go, people need protection in the form of income and access to basic services during these transitions. Too often the legitimate need for protecting people and families has taken the form of policies designed to protect companies, jobs, and whole industries from competition. Sometimes the competition that is blocked out is domestic and sometimes it is foreign. But the effect is simi-

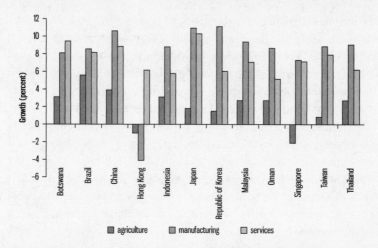

agriculture   manufacturing   services

Sources: World Bank, World Development Indicators 2007; for Brazil: World Bank calculation using data from World Tables 1976, World Bank, and Institute of Applied Economic Research (IAER), Brazil (http://www.ipeadata.gov.br); for Japan: World Bank calculation using data from World Tables 1976, World Bank, and Maddison, Angus 2001: *The World Economy: A Millennial Perspective.* Pairs: OECD.

Note: The calculation apply for different periods indicated in parentheses because of different degrees of consistent data availability: Botswana (1965–2006); Brazil (1955–73); China (1965–2006); Hong Kong (2000–06); Indonesia (1960–2005); Japan (1955–73); Republic of Korea (1970–2006); Malaysia (1970–2006); Oman (1988–2004); Singapore (1975–2006); Taiwan (1965–2006); and Thailand (1960–2006).

lar. It slows down the process by which productivity increases and growth occurs. Blocking the foreign direct investors has the additional disadvantage of slowing down the knowledge transfer process. India's earlier slow growth was partly attributable to a distrust of foreign investors and a relatively low level of foreign direct investment by multinational firms. If you look at the data for India and China, for example, the differences are dramatic. Of course this is changing now with India's growing openness.

It is a strategy mistake, albeit an understandable one, to protect people by protecting their jobs. The short version of a better approach is: protect people, not jobs. It is easy to say but harder to do. Protecting companies and jobs is politically easier and tends to have the support of the incumbents (business and labor) and interests vested in the status quo. These interests are usually antithetical to new competition and growth. Sometimes they are politically quite powerful.

Protecting people means providing income support during periods of unemployment, effective retraining, and subsidized access to health, education, and other basic services. Note that these steps do not protect people from change. This safety net will always be viewed as an imperfect substitute for job protection and employment security. But the best long-run protection for people is an economy with robust and growing labor demand and a high rate of new productive employment creation. There is obviously a chicken-or-egg issue to be seen here in the interaction of economic dynamism and the protection of people through new employment creation.

There is a special problem with older workers in an economy that is rapidly changing structurally. Older workers are less mobile and hence much more vulnerable. The returns on retraining are lower because of the shorter time horizon in terms of their future working life. For these people, transitional-support mechanisms may not be sufficient. The answer has to be a social commitment to longer-term income support—that is, a comprehensive and protective social security system.

Investment and Savings

Knowledge transfer and learning drives the growth in productive potential. Investment turns it into a reality. By looking at sustained-high-growth cases, one can find some evidence about the levels of investment and saving required to support high growth. With the thirteen sustained-high-growth economies as a benchmark, it appears that investment needs to be in excess of 25 percent of total output or GDP. That is a big number. There are no counterexamples to this observation that I am aware of. This standard is based on observation, combined with a certain amount of common sense, and does not derive from theoretical considerations alone. It is also consistent with simple growth arithmetic. Typically for a developing country in early stages of growth, the capital-to-output ratio is in the neighborhood of 2.5, and labor is often in a surplus condition. If we accept that configuration (and ignore frictions), an investment rate of 25 percent would be consistent with growth approaching 10 percent, a bit high, but in the right range.

Investment is expenditure whose purpose is to increase the tangible and intangible asset base of the economy. Those expanded assets increase the output of the economy and the productivity of labor. Incomes rise with increases in productivity, and people benefit broadly over time. At the most basic level, investment is the deferral of consumption and the satisfaction of current needs, and the use of those (invested) resources to increase the incomes, consumption, and opportunity in the future. Later, when we discuss savings, we will talk about whose consumption is being deferred.

Tangible assets include: plant and equipment of firms; buildings of all types; and infrastructure (roads, ports, airports, electricity distribution grids, and telecommunications networks). Intangible assets include: knowledge; education; and human capital (which can be thought of as embodied learning).

Investment also divides into private- and public-sector components. Private investment is undertaken by companies and entrepreneurs (with the support of external investors), the prime motive being profit or a good return on investment, given the risks involved. These activities in conjunction with the knowledge-transfer process are the source of the new productive job creation. They are the proximate drivers of growth.

Private investment is high when there is opportunity in the form of high risk-adjusted returns and when entrepreneurs and companies have access to capital that is appropriately matched to the risk characteristics of the investment. In the developing world, the banking sector is usually more developed than venture-capital sector. As a result, there is a tendency to use debt financing even when the risks would make equity investment more suitable. This leads to inefficiency in the funding process and can reduce overall investment.

While private investment is the proximate driver of growth and job creation, government nevertheless has a crucial role to play. Certain kinds of investments do not lend themselves to private-sector incentives. The reason is that the benefits are so diffuse and spread out that there is no practical way for the private investor to charge for all the benefits. The social return (meaning the benefits to all those who receive them all added up) exceeds the private return to the investor, and that gap may cause underinvestment if left to the private sector and households alone.

The principal public-sector investments that are needed to support growth are education and infrastructure. Both of them positively impact growth by raising the returns to private-sector investment (both domestic and foreign). The analysis of the cases of sustained high growth suggests that public-sector investment in the range of 5 to 7 percent of GDP is required to sustain growth in the 7 percent range. Again, this guideline is inductively based on data from both high- and lower-growth economies. The importance of public-sector investment lies in its capacity to raise the return to private-sector investment. Its impact on growth is therefore indirect but important.

Consider an example. A global producer of brand-name apparel is looking for places to manufacture its product. The global economy is highly competitive. The multinational firm looks at a number of countries as potential sources of labor supply. It will want to achieve a certain quality standard and keep the costs as low as possible for competitive reasons. Developing countries are essentially competing for this business.

What do they bring to that competition? An educated (and thus fairly literate) population that is relatively easily trained in new skills is a major asset. In return the developing country can reasonably ask for and expect the training of workers and managers, skills that will benefit the broader economy over time. Infrastructure that lowers the costs and time associated with the movement of product in and out of the facilities and through ports or airports is also a key component of the multinational calculation. Reliable electric power and telecommunication services are another requirement. Not all of it requires direct public-sector investment.

There are other ingredients. Licensing and permits can be more or less easy to accomplish. Labor-market regulations and structures can provide more or less flexibility. If there are high tariffs, tariff relief on the needed imported inputs to the manufacturing process will help increase the return on investment for the multinational. Note, however, that the reduction of tariffs must be selective. A more sweeping reduction of tariffs may not be wise and can be inconsistent with the aforementioned challenge of moderating the pace of opening up. It may also cause a drop in government revenue that is too steep in the short run. Eventually the opening-up process will reduce tariffs more broadly and the special tariff-relief provisions will not be necessary.

Not infrequently, multinational companies ask for tax relief for a period of time. As a way of sharing the risk associated with entry into a new economic environment, some tax relief can be justified. But it should be temporary and decline over time as the risk is resolved. However, this type of subsidy (and there are other forms) tends to become permanent, and when that happens it becomes costly. A good general principle is that if a subsidy is required on a long-term basis to sustain the activity (meaning, to make it profitable), then the original investment should be viewed as a mistake and the activity allowed to go away.

These decisions can be tough. In 2008, the government of St. Kitts in the eastern Caribbean decided to withdraw the subsidy to the sugarcane industry on the island. It was costing the government $30 million a year to keep it in business with no evidence that the level of the subsidy would decline over time. But the sugarcane industry was the major source of employment on the island. It was a difficult and courageous decision. The government knew there would be short-term pain but also knew that the longer-term growth and prosperity depended on shifting the structural characteristics of the island's economy.

Savings Matter

Saving is the deferral of present consumption into the future. At the country level, there are three components of savings. The one that normally comes to mind and is most discussed is the savings accrued by individuals or households. Generally these savings are channeled through private intermediaries and end up as investment, which can be either domestic or foreign. A portion of private saving goes directly to investment via the purchases of houses and consumer durables that have an extended usable life. Another bit may be lent to the government.

The other two components of saving are government and the corporate sector. We have already seen that government makes important investments. If it fully finances these out of its revenues, then it does not run an overall deficit and its savings are by definition equal to its investment. Otherwise it may run a deficit and borrow that amount from citizens or foreigners. If the borrowing is from citizens, the government's negative saving is matched by household savings, so overall savings are unaffected.

The corporate sector also invests. Normally it finances that investment out of its own income, the part that is not distributed to its shareholders, which is called retained earnings. In that case, corporate saving is equal to its investment. It may also borrow or issue shares—in either case, the financing is from others' savings (domestic or foreign). If the corporation's retained earnings exceed its investment, the remainder is lent out to someone else.

If one adds up all three categories of saving, the total may equal investment, or it may exceed or fall short of it. An excess of savings over domestic investment goes to foreigners to finance their investment. Conversely, if savings are below investment, foreigners are financing some of the domestic investment. The difference between savings and investment is equal to the trade (or, more precisely, the current account) surplus.[2] If savings fall short of investment, the difference is a trade deficit and is equal to the net foreign capital inflows that are used to make up the difference between investment and saving. In common-sense terms, if we sell more to other countries than we buy from them, we send back the difference as savings, and that partially finances their investment or their consumption.

Evidence and experience suggest that developing countries are best served by financing most of their investment from domestic savings. That means not running persistent large trade deficits. This may be a little counterintuitive. In principle, it should be possible for rich countries to finance some of the investment in developing countries when the investment returns are attractive. The problem is that if you rely on foreign saving to finance investment, you become vulnerable in a number of ways. If there is a negative shock or a period of adversity (internal or external, as in the crisis of 2008), the capital withdraws. More precisely, the portion that is liquid and mobile withdraws. Interest rates rise and investment slows down. If the accumulated debt to foreigners becomes high, the government may choose to default. The anticipation of that limits the availability of foreign financing.[3]

If a country borrows externally and the obligations are specified in a foreign currency, then there is additional currency risk. If the domestic currency loses value, the size of the external obligations increases by the same percentage. Because of this risk, borrowing in another currency has come to be called the financial equivalent of original sin. But it's not that uncommon. Asian countries suffered in this manner in the Asian financial crisis of the late 1990s; more recently, Eastern European countries and citizens were borrowing in euros and Swiss francs before the crisis of 2008. When their currencies declined during the crisis, it put these countries, and the external financing banks, in distress.

The world does not run as smoothly as we would like. Countries are subject to internally and externally generated shocks that are not, and probably cannot be, fully anticipated. From the point of view of developing countries, the crisis of 2008–9 is an external shock. Credit and financing contracted precipitously owing to extreme distress in the advanced countries' financial systems. This left countries reliant on external financing highly vulnerable. The countries that weathered this storm best generally have low current account deficits and are able to sustain high levels of investment financed by domestic saving.

Saving domestically to finance most of domestic investment does not solve all of these potential problems, but it does mitigate the risk and the impact and significantly improves resilience.

Public-Sector Investment: Education and Infrastructure as Public Goods

We noted earlier, in discussing the sustained-high-growth countries, that high levels of savings and investment are required. We also noted that the government component of investment needed to be in the range of 5 to 7 percent of GDP to sustain high growth. It is clear that public-sector investment is a crucial ingredient. The principal categories of government investment are education and infrastructure.

Education is an investment that creates public benefits as well as private returns. Normally in most countries it is either subsidized or paid for by government and is an important part of public-sector investment. Education is the crucial foundation of the learning process that underlies catch-up growth. That is not to say that all learning occurs in schools. Far from it. But formal education provides the tools that enable the other, more disparate, learning processes: training on the job, experimenting, and learning by doing. Literacy and numeracy would be the essential core, along with a problem-solving orientation and certain noncognitive attributes like curiosity.

Educated people turn into productive employees, entrepreneurs, political and policy leaders, artists, performers, writers, and more. To be sure, some of the benefit is captured by them in their incomes. But certainly not all. Take, for example, the entrepreneur who founds a successful company that creates incremental productive employment for a growing number of people. The social benefits of that investment include the enhanced salaries of all the people who come to work there. That is not part of the narrow economic private return but is a huge part of the broader social return. This does not mean that the entrepreneur needs to be subsidized. The private return (not to mention pride of accomplishment and recognition and respect) may very well be an adequate incentive. But note that the return depends in part on the availability of employable people, which in turn depends on the effectiveness of their prior education. In effect, the subsidy is indirect.

In many poorer developing countries, underinvestment in education is common, and understandable. But there is another problem. Given the level of investment, the output as measured by literacy and the acquisition of measurable cognitive skills is disappointingly low. The efficiency of the investment that does occur is low. There are a number of causes of this inefficiency, including inadequate teacher supply and training, and poorly constructed incentives for teachers and administrators. The effect is to lower potential productivity and growth.

More generally, governments invest in things whose benefits are not easily captured by the private investor. These investments are crucial and complementary to private-sector investment. They increase the range of possible profitable private-sector investments and the returns to them.

China's investment and savings levels after the reforms in 1978 have been at or above 35 percent of GDP, clearly exceeding the minimal standards. This is at the very top end of the range of experience for developing countries. It is hard to know exactly how much of the total investment is public-sector investment because the state-owned enterprise sector is large and its investments hard to categorize. Notwithstanding the challenge of being precise, there is no question that government investment in China is high and at the upper end of the range even for high-growth countries.

These levels are quite startling. Remember that domestically funded investment is that part of output that is not consumed today but instead turned into assets that yield increased output later. In a poor country with per capita income of, say, $600 (well under $2 a day), not spending one-third of that income for day-to-day needs like food and shelter is certainly a major sacrifice. It means, in effect, that the part of income available for immediate consumption is $400. The remainder goes to creating assets that enhance future income.

Investment rates at these levels in relatively poor countries (enabled by domestic saving) demonstrate a startling willingness to sacrifice present for future benefits. That intertemporal choice (that is, the choice to invest now and consume later) is made by people, and to some extent by governments (because the government is also an important investor). The future orientation turns out to be crucial, because without it, sustaining the investment that underpins the growth becomes impossible.

India is a slightly different case from China. While India's overall investment and savings have been high, the government component of it has been an ongoing challenge. It is not much of a secret that public-sector investment in growth-enhancing assets like infrastructure has been lagging in India. This challenge is not the result of a shortage of overall savings nor an unwillingness to invest. India's investment and savings rates run in excess of 25 percent of GDP, which means that India invests at a high rate and finances almost all of it from domestic savings. Rather, the issue is with the government budget (revenues and expenditures) and the political economy and incentives that surround it. Noninvestment expenditures and income transfers use up much of the government revenue. That makes it difficult to sustain a public-sector investment program in the 5 to 7 percent of GDP range.

India is closer to the more normal case. The pattern of underinvestment on the public-sector side is very widespread in developing countries. This is not the whole explanation of subpar economic performance, but it makes a significant contribution. The problem is that in relatively poor countries, immediate needs of citizens for income support, health care, and basic services are high relative to government revenue. Political pressure urges the allocation of scarce government revenue for meeting these basic needs. The public-sector investment part therefore tends to be crowded out. And that reduces the returns to private-sector investment and growth.

You might ask how India can be in high-growth mode if it has a historical pattern of underinvestment in infrastructure, one of the key requirements for sustained high growth. In fact, India's growth has accelerated in part because its investment in infrastructure has notched up. Remember the earlier discussion of prerequisites? It is steady progress that is required to sustain the growth. In India's case, a difficult fiscal situation with a persistent deficit means that not all infrastructure can be financed by government investment and savings. Part of the solution that India is implementing is a set of partnerships with private investors (some domestic and some foreign) to finance and construct needed infrastructure. This is a more complex model to implement than the Chinese one, where infrastructure is entirely publicly funded. But it appears to be working.

In India, the job is not yet done. There are frequent brownouts in much of India. The electrical distribution system is still somewhat fragile. Water supply is unreliable in many cities. Companies, including those in the important services export sector (IT and business process outsourcing), rely on continuous supplies of electric power and therefore must maintain backup power systems, which are expensive and not the most efficient solution to the problem in the long run.

Malnutrition Among Children

The Commission on Growth and Development held fifteen workshops on a wide range of subjects related to growth and development. One of those workshops, held in 2007, was devoted to the linkage between public health and economic growth. We asked experts about the linkage. The answer that came back was that it depends on what aspects of health one is talking about. But one pattern in particular stood out. Children who are undernourished over extended periods experience a nearly permanent diminution in their ability to acquire both cognitive and noncognitive skills. It is a very long-lived effect. It adversely impacts educational outputs, damages productivity and income potential, and, at a more macroeconomic level, hinders growth. Most important, it is deeply unfair, because it is largely irreversible and it harms the most vulnerable. This impact on economic performance is not the main reason that so many religious and charitable organizations focus on nutrition and famine relief, but it is a good thing that they do.

In 2007 and '08, before the financial and economic crisis, commodity prices went rocketing up, with oil and food grains experiencing among the highest relative price increases. The resulting inflation was huge. Rice, the staple of many diets around the world, more than doubled in price over an eighteen-month period. The reasons for these price spikes are somewhat complex and perhaps still not completely understood. But that is not the point. Price increases of this magnitude had rather mild effects in advanced countries, but among the world's poor they constituted a crisis. Poor people in developing countries devote as much as 50 percent or more of their income to food. If the price of staple grains doubles, that is tantamount to a reduction in already meager incomes ($6 a day or less) of 25 percent.

The financial and economic crisis could be said, somewhat ironically, to have "solved" this problem, at least in the short run. But while it lasted, there was a growing problem of malnutrition and even famine among the poor, including children. The World Bank, to its credit, stepped in aggressively. Nations lacked redistributive institutions and mechanisms and had to resort to economically dysfunctional measures like export and price controls. Both of these efforts damage the supply-side response that is the longer-term solution to the problem. India and Thailand are the two largest rice exporters in the world and both had to resort to export restrictions to protect their own people.

The commodity price spike produced what amounts to the equivalent of a global famine for the poor. It made clear that we need much more effective countermeasures and "circuit breakers" (domestic and international) than we have now to prevent long-term damage to people, and especially to children.

The Productive Deployment of Underutilized Resources

Developing countries in the early stages of growth have another somewhat perverse advantage. Prior to achieving growth mode, a relatively poor developing economy usually has a lot of underemployed labor, a reflection of the fact that there has not been much incremental productive employment creation. This underemployed labor resides in traditional sectors, such as agriculture. Labor markets don't really form in the normal sense because the marginal product of labor is so low that income gets determined and distributed through family and village structures, and not really by the normal market and pricing mechanism.

The reason this configuration creates an advantage when growth starts is as follows: when incremental productive employment opportunities are created and labor is drawn into new sectors (including those for exported goods), the economic impact on the traditional sectors is negligible because much of the labor being drawn away is essentially redundant. The opportunity cost of drawing away the labor is very low. You get the benefit from the new output and incomes with little or no loss of output in the older part of the economy.

The identification of this aspect of the high-speed dynamic is the work of Nobel laureate Sir Arthur Lewis.[4] Lewis understood this dynamic. He also worried that the large supply of underemployed labor would hold down the wages and delay the raising of incomes of the newly employed. This is a legitimate concern. Counterbalancing it is the fact that wages and incomes rise immediately as rural labor moves to the high-growth and more productive part of the economy. So there is an immediate benefit for workers and their families.

An interesting recent example of the underlying market forces comes from India. In June 2010, *The Financial Express* in India reported that "BPOs (Business Process Outsourcers) eye rural frontiers to expand their territories. For this they are tempting the women folk to join the BPO centers running there. The BPOs are offering hefty payments, often 10–15 percent more than mandatory minimum, along with other attractive perks, reports Goutam Das of *The Financial Express*." The business-process outsourcing firms, a major growth sector in the Indian economy, are running short of talent to support their rapid growth. This has led them to develop an employment model that enables them to tap the large potential labor pool of women in rural areas. This has all kinds of beneficial effects, ranging from growth to equity to opportunities for younger women to gender equality.

Of course, this process does not go on forever. As labor is drawn away, eventually there is a potential impact on traditional sectors. But then a surprising thing happens. With much less essentially free labor, these sectors start to substitute capital.[5] As they do, labor productivity rises. In addition, in agriculture, at a certain point along the path, depopulation of the rural sector advances to the point where land consolidation becomes feasible, and that further facilitates the move to capital intensity.

In the normal course of events in a rapidly growing developing country, labor in traditional sectors falls while output stays constant and then eventually rises.

Urbanization

Urbanization is at the heart of the growth-and-development process. People change their employment as new industries are created. They also move physically. Experience and research tell us that modern economic activity occurs in urban settings. It appears to require person-to-person contact—proximity. Sometimes the need for proximity is obvious. It is hard to imagine assembling a car without having workers present in the factory. But that is not the whole story. Proximity also seems to be important in facilitating information and knowledge transfer and sharing; also in enabling complex transactions. I discussed earlier the importance of knowledge transfer in catch-up growth. Modernization and structural transformation is accompanied by—and requires—urbanization.

We saw earlier that in the high-growth countries manufacturing and services grow much faster than agriculture, and that the composition of the economy shifts dramatically. Both are urban activities, for the most part.

One might object at this point that modern information and communications technology, including the Internet, have perhaps modified these proximity requirements to some extent. They have, but not completely. To be sure, productive participation in certain kinds of processes or supply chains is consistent with remoteness. Indeed, the increasing accessibility of valuable but physically remote human resources and talent is one of the most important trends in the global economy. But modern economic activity still requires a degree of proximity. It is an odd mix. We still don't have a good taxonomy to describe which activities require proximity and which ones lend themselves to a geographically diverse set of inputs.

In the chart on page 86, the rural population as a percentage of the total is shown for two large high-growth countries, India and China. Though the rates are different, this pattern is characteristic of all cases of industrialization, including that which occurred prior to World War II in the countries that are now advanced. It goes on until the rural population drops below 20 percent of the population. China and India are currently in the midst of this process. China's rural population is still just over 50 percent of the total and India's is still in the neighborhood of 70 percent. There are many millions of people left who will eventually move to urban environments.

In the early stages, the productivity differentials between the rural and urban sectors are very large. Urban productivity levels normally exceed the rural ones by factors of between three and six times. This is to some extent reflected in income differentials. The flow of people across this boundary therefore tends to produce rising average incomes and rising income inequality.

One might reasonably ask why everyone doesn't move to the cities and to higher-income employment once this process gets started. Part of the answer is, they can't. It takes many years for private investment to

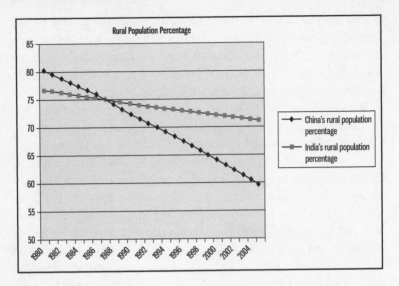

create the incremental productive employment opportunities and for public investment to build the urban infrastructure. The other part of the answer is that they do move, hoping to capture a place in the new economy. Not all succeed. This normally causes the urban inflow to outrun both the capacity of the employment-generating engine to create employment and the government's capacity to create urban infrastructure. The result is urban poverty and slums, which can be found in many cities in the developing world. Managing this so as to maintain a balance is a large challenge.

There is no known complete solution to this problem. The best way to mitigate this imbalance is to invest simultaneously in the agricultural sector, in education, in productivity-enhancing technology and its dissemination, and in infrastructure that enables connectivity to the rest of the economy. This component of growth strategy is too often neglected. The focus is frequently narrowly focused on the higher-productivity export sectors. Investing in the rural sector contributes to growth (though not as much as in the growing urban sectors) and, equally importantly, to equity by diminishing somewhat the tendency toward rising income inequality. And it moves the system in the direction of having rural-to-urban migration driven more by opportunity in the urban areas than by its absence in the rural sector.

It is not a perfect solution. Urbanization is a generally chaotic process in which inbound migration almost always outpaces urban infrastructure, capacity, and job creation. Charles Dickens documented this side of the British Industrial Revolution—not its prettiest. But it can be managed to some extent by a balanced program of investment and development in both urban *and* rural sectors.

Inclusiveness and Equity

Inclusiveness turns out to be an essential part of sustaining growth. "Inclusiveness" in economics is a term that came from India initially but is now used widely. It refers to the distributional aspects of growth. The main ideas are (1) that people should not be left out or excluded from the opportunities created by growth, and (2) there should be limits to the amount of inequality in income and access to basic services that are tolerable. There are two reasons why paying attention to inclusiveness is crucial. One has to do with sustaining support for the policies that generate growth. The second has more to do with the growth dynamics themselves.

Central planning failed not just because you cannot efficiently and centrally manage static resource allocation in a complex environment, but also because the dynamics require entrepreneurship, diversity, and decentralization—in short, a bottom-up process. You want as many entrepreneurs, rich or poor, as you can get. That is one dimension of inclusiveness.

Governments are not entrepreneurs. Centralized economic decision making smothers new business development. If you take that away, the dynamics are simply missing and growth is about dynamics. In this sense, sustained growth has to be an inclusive phenomenon. We have no counterexamples.

There are of course naturally centralized functions that are critical inputs. Examples would include effective macroeconomic, fiscal, and central-bank management of inflation and government finances. These are complements to but not substitutes for the entrepreneurial dynamics.

But can you have too many entrepreneurs and too many new entrants and small firms? In the course of a long experimental learning process, countries have sometimes restricted competition on the following argument. In small economies (and most tend to be small in the early stages, when people are relatively poor on average; even countries with large populations are economically small), having lots of competitors in an industry may sound like a good idea. But there is the chance that they will fragment the industry and leave no one big enough to be efficient. Why? Because we know that there are economies of size and scale in many industries. The policy choice that seems to follow is that it might be best to restrict entry, so that the number of competitors remains small enough so that each of them, or at least some of them, can become big enough to capitalize on the economies of scale and hence be efficient and internationally competitive.

There is nothing particularly wrong with this logic in a static framework. But it is incomplete and ultimately wrong in practice. It turns out that the gains in productivity from allowing relatively free entry of new rivals with new ideas, products, and technologies simply dominate in size the potential static efficiency gains of restricting entry. So the preferred choice from experience is to let the entry and exit process run and not to worry too much about scale and static efficiency.

The second part of inclusiveness has to do with fairness. People care a lot about fairness. They will make sacrifices if their children and grandchildren will be better off; however, they will not do this if the sacrifices are shared broadly but the opportunities created are not. Thus the most important dimension of inclusiveness is equality of opportunity—not leaving people or whole groups (however defined) out. Experience over a broad array of countries, some successful and others less so, suggests that a failure in this dimension is toxic and frequently fatal for growth and development. The political support for the policies and investments that sustain growth will be eroded and the policies will be abandoned. Worse, in some cases, major asymmetries in the area of inclusiveness lead to conflict—usually fatal to growth as well as to the participants.

There is one further dimension of inclusiveness. People understand in general terms that markets and the growth dynamics cannot be expected to produce equality of outcomes. It is inherent in the dynamics that not everyone can move to cities and to higher-wage employment opportunities at once. There is a tendency for income inequality to rise during part of the process. Experience indicates that people will accept this up to a point. But extreme inequality of outcomes, in terms of income or access to important services like education, is a problem, to the point that it will cause resistance and increase the likelihood of derailing the growth process through political channels.

13. Opening Up: An Issue of Speed and Sequencing

We know that economies that sustain high growth are ones that are open to, and take advantage of, the global economy. There is, however, another level of subtlety that intrudes. It has to do with the speed of opening up a developing economy to the global economy, and hence to potential competition.

There is general agreement that what underlies high sustained growth in the early stages is a process of creating huge numbers of new productive jobs in the tradable/export sector, drawing people by these new opportunities from traditional sectors such as agriculture, where there is usually surplus labor and, as a result, low productivity. But if opening up to competition causes job destruction that is faster than job creation, the net effect is negative and the growth strategy will lose support and become politically problematic.

Thus, while an effective growth strategy does involve opening up to the global economy and needs to avoid permanent protections for domestic companies and sectors, the opening-up has to be modulated so that the job destruction and job creation engines are roughly in balance. This is an important practical dimension of policy.

Structural change is not an issue confined to developing countries. It arises with increasing frequency and urgency in advanced countries too. As developing countries become larger and achieve higher incomes, their impact on advanced countries and the global economy is greater. With openness on the one hand and declining costs of transportation, communication, and coordination on the other, economic activity is moving around the world at an accelerating pace. Just as in developing countries, job loss and frictions related to mobility can run ahead of job creation.

Policy makers and politicians have to deal with these realities. There is always domestic political resistance to trade liberalization more or less in direct proportion to the speed and scope of the structural shifts being imposed. The challenge is to find the right balance between accommodating structural change, maintaining a reasonable balance between new job creation and job loss, and protecting and supporting people and families in transitions. Pragmatically this balance probably needs continuous adjustment while both internal and external conditions evolve.

In the advanced countries, we really haven't faced up to this yet, though perhaps the evolution of thinking is in the right direction. Yes, openness in the global economy needs defenders. But openness must go hand in hand with economic and social protection mechanisms for those adversely affected by structural shifts, and adjustments must be made as the external environment changes. And these adjustments have to be balanced against the collective interest in a relatively open global system.

America has prided itself on having an innovative and flexible economy. That has historically meant less comprehensive social and economic safety nets than one finds in much of continental Europe. The argument is that the best form of protection for workers is a flexible, adaptive economy that creates new jobs rapidly and facilitates rather than impedes employment transitions for people. There is a lot of merit in this approach. But we don't have to be rigid about it. If structural change in the global economy has accelerated and has as one of its effects more frequent and widespread adverse impacts on people in terms of loss of employment and depressed incomes, then we can and should shift the balance toward greater investment in the transitional support mechanisms. The balancing act requires that we do this while retaining as much of the flexibility as we can in order not to impair the new company-, job-, and sector-creating engine.

The issue of facilitating structural change has become more urgent as a result of the economic and financial crisis. The financial sector grew beyond what is needed to allocate capital and distribute risk efficiently. At some point the financial sector in the United States accounted for 40 percent of total profits of private corporations. The "new postcrisis normal" will quite likely have a restructured and slimmed-down financial sector. The obvious question is: Where will the excess highly educated people be employed, and with what incomes?

The more general point is that for the most part policies are not right for all time but are constantly in need of adjustment, particularly in times of rapid change. In the developing world, because the growth rates and the speed of structural adjustment are so high, the lesson is driven home rather quickly. But it is a good principle to adopt on a broader front in advanced countries as well.

14. The Washington Consensus and the Role of Government

In the late 1980s, a group in Washington lead by the gifted economist John Williamson developed what came to be known as the Washington Consensus (WC). It was a set of ten general points that were felt at the time to be the critical ingredients of successful growth and development. The focus was on economic policy and was mainly macroeconomic in character—though not entirely so. Much controversy has surrounded this approach to growth and development, particularly in Latin America.

The original version looks like this:

Washington Consensus: Original Ten Guidelines

1. Fiscal policy discipline
2. Redirection of public spending from subsidies ("especially indiscriminate subsidies") toward broad-based provision of key pro-growth, pro-poor services like primary education, primary health care, and infrastructure investment
3. Tax reform—broadening the tax base and adopting moderate marginal tax rates
4. Interest rates that are market determined and positive (but moderate) in real terms
5. Competitive exchange rates
6. Trade liberalization—liberalization of imports, with particular emphasis on elimination of quantitative restrictions (licensing,

etc.); any trade protection to be provided by low and relatively uniform tariffs

7. Liberalization of inward foreign direct investment
8. Privatization of state enterprises
9. Deregulation—abolition of regulations that impede market entry or restrict competition, except for those justified on safety, environmental, and consumer-protection grounds and prudent oversight of financial institutions
10. Legal security for property rights

The first thing that needs to be said is that at face value, these are sensible guidelines largely supported by development experience and by economic analysis. It is hard to quibble with fiscal stability as a supportive condition. And there have been many cases of the opposite behavior in a range of countries, leading inevitably to poor economic performance, or worse.

Subsequent experience has led to modifications and additions. Freely floating exchange rates determined by global capital markets are still seen as appropriate for advanced countries but, since the Asian financial crisis in the late 1990s, not for developing ones. The WC guidelines refer to public (meaning government) spending. "Public spending" lumps together government consumption and public investment, masking to some extent the importance of the government as investor in assets that support the private-sector growth dynamics.

Various items were subsequently added to the list or emphasized more: things like investment in human capital and issues of equity and the distribution of benefits. These additions have come to seem quite central in the intervening years. Interestingly, they involve components of the overall growth recipe in which government has a key role to play and which go beyond macroeconomic stability.

And yet, reasonable as they seem to be, the Washington Consensus prescriptions have become quite controversial. Why is this? I think the answer lies not so much in their content as in the way they were variously interpreted and used in different parts of the developing world.

Proponents and defenders of the WC say that failures on the ground result from incomplete or ineffective implementation, not from a flaw in the formula. Critics came to view it as a statement of market fundamentalism, or neoliberalism, later captured by the shorter, more memorable and less helpful formula: "Stabilize, privatize, and liberalize." It came to be seen as an assault on the state, on expansive government, and as a prescription for limiting government's role as much as possible. To the best of my knowledge, this was not Williamson's intention. The problem with the Washington Consensus lay not with the ideas, but rather with their interpretation and implementation. The WC was inappropriately taken as a fairly simple formula that, properly implemented, would ensure success in any country at any stage of development. Understood as a one-size-fits-all formula, it has major problems.

Roughly speaking, the Asian countries took what was sensible from the Washington Consensus, added to it, and provided an overlay of skepticism and pragmatism that worked rather well. Latin American countries, on the other hand, tended to take the slimmed-down, limited-government version and experienced limited and lower growth.

The most basic pitfall when interpreting the Washington Consensus is to confuse the means and the ends. The end goal, we presume, is supposed to be growth and development. The means are policies, broadly defined. Our models and conceptual and empirical understandings of growth and development, while improving, are far too incomplete to permit confidence that a single formula (that focuses mainly on policy and government activity) can successfully apply to all countries and across time within countries as the structure changes. The chance that it is incomplete or misses an important economic or political element of the dynamics, like proper sequencing of policies, is very high. By and large, successful high-growth countries set growth and development objectives as high-priority goals and then essentially experiment their way toward improved performance, using theory, common sense, and sensible guidelines as aids.

Part of the problem with the application of the WC is that the policies came to be viewed as the objectives, as ends in themselves. The results in terms of growth, in that view, should be whatever they turn out to be. It is a mistake of the first order to confuse means and ends. The only exception is a world or context in which there is a known perfect match between policies and outcomes—that is, a world in which the models are accurate and complete. Then it doesn't matter whether the means are taken as the ends, because the results are the same.

But that is certainly not the case in the complex world of growth and development. By and large, successful countries have maintained focus on sustained growth, recognized that the means are not all that clear, and adopted a pragmatic, experimental, and navigational approach to stimulating and adapting to change. Those who assumed that guidelines for policy and strategy were a formula for success were often stunned when it didn't actually work. In fact, the successful high-growth countries made no such assumptions and adapted and augmented what were sensible principles to create their own recipes. Those who took the WC guidelines to be a formula for success made the policies the objectives, afterwards frequently arguing that incomplete or imperfect implementation explained the absence of results.

There is now a strong and justified feeling among experts and practitioners, based on experience, that growth strategy has to be country- and context-specific. But John Williamson never intended, as far as I know, that the Washington Consensus become an ideology whose central tenant was that governments always screw things up and that the proper approach was to limit government activity to a bare minimum.

The correct insight that markets and market dynamics are of critical importance morphed into the simplistic view that the problem is government. It has taken more than a decade to correct this mistake. As the report of the Commission on Growth and Development (May 2008) said, quoting W. Arthur Lewis, "governments may fail either because they do too little, or because they do too much." Effective governments and markets are both essential ingredients. They are not in competition with each other but rather complementary parts of the process. To be sure, governments *can* be too big and intrusive. But they can also be too small and ineffective.

There is another pitfall in writing the government out of the script, one that applies to developed as well as developing countries. There is a widespread view that growth dynamics reside entirely in the private sector. In this view, when you are thinking about policy, for the most part you are thinking either about enabling structure, such as the legal and regulatory framework, which tends to be static or slow moving except after a crisis, or about shorter-term macroeconomic and monetary policies that are cyclic in character. In order to carry out these functions, you don't have to know much about the dynamics and incentives in the private sector that generate growth, long-term employment increases, and structural change. That's convenient for policy makers, because these latter things are much harder to think about. Much easier not to, and to be backed up by a framework that implies you don't have to.

But the reality we find in the history of developed countries, as well as in the current developing ones, is that growth comes from a complex interaction of the public and private sectors, with effective governments investing, building institutions, and actively filling in gaps.

The successful developing countries have come to understand and exploit the interaction of public and private sectors in sustaining growth. Public-sector investment in infrastructure, in human capital, in institutions that facilitate information transfer and diffusion, and, in many cases, in housing and real estate, has played a crucial role in growth because it increases the returns to private-sector investment. It may also help achieve equity and inclusiveness, which in turn create continued political support for the growth-oriented policies. The same approach can be seen in the history of the advanced countries, but somewhere along the way we seem to have lost the framework, especially in the United States. In the postcrisis environment, where structural change is crucially needed to restore growth, there is practically no talk of public-sector contribution to growth and long-term employment.

And so, these days if you ask such questions as "Where will employment come from?" or "What will be exported?" or "What does the government need to do to enable the private sector to get there?" you will probably find a vigorous debate about this in most developing countries, but in developed countries you will also probably find that the implicit assumption is that the answers will be determined in the private sector. In June 2010, *The New York Times* published an article the gist of which is that markets (that is, market participants) are starting to worry that politicians and policy makers in the United States appear to be assuming that if they sort out the fiscal situation and exit the stimulus at the right speed, the private sector will take care of structural change, accelerated employment, and growth.[1] They are right to worry. It just isn't so. The fiscal and monetary balancing act, with deflation on one side and sovereign debt risk on the other, is surely important. But it isn't the whole story. The rest has to do with fundamental structural change.

15. Managing One's Currency in the Course of Growth

Exchange rates are prices. In an open economy, they are very important prices, as they determine the relative price of tradable and nontradable goods and services. If the value of a country's currency goes up, its exports become more expensive to others, while its imports become cheaper than they were, and cheaper relative to domestic goods and services, which now cannot be easily traded. In simple terms, exchange rates determine the competitiveness of the export sector and the tradable portion of the domestic economy.

For many years leading up to the currency crisis of the late nineties in Asia, the conventional wisdom was that exchange rates should be set by market forces without government (which usually means: central-bank) intervention. These are called floating exchange rates and they move in response to global capital and trade flows. After the postwar system of fixed exchange rates broke down, this was the approach of the advanced countries for the most part, and it was the recommended approach to developing countries.

Most of the developing countries, however, managed their exchange rate by buying and selling their own currency, using foreign exchange. Thus the actual global system was a kind of hybrid, with floating rates in advanced countries (except Japan), and developing countries managing their currencies in various ways. But for most of the postwar period, the developing countries were not big enough for this hybrid system to cause problems or tensions. That is no longer the case. Emerging economies have become big enough to have larger systemic impacts on the global economy. China's yuan is closely managed to the U.S. dollar, and much of Asia does not deviate much from either the yuan or the dollar. This behavior has potentially large systemic effects in the global economy and is the subject of much current controversy.

Developing countries had good reasons to manage their currencies. Absent intervention, the exchange rate and net capital inflows and outflows tended to be volatile. Most countries used capital controls as well as direct interventions in their currency markets to limit this volatility. After the Asian crisis of the late 1990s, developing countries accumulated foreign reserves for the purpose of having ammunition to stabilize their currencies in the event of an unexpected rapid outflow. This form of self-insurance is now widespread and proved useful in the crisis of 2008, when high-speed capital outflows occurred because of balance-sheet damage in the advanced countries.

Developing countries, too, manage their exchange rates to ensure that their export sector remains competitive. As we have seen, exports are a key driver of growth. The idea is that you don't want enthusiasm in the global capital markets to price your country out of the product markets your export sector participates in. Since the crisis of the late 1990s, the advice to developing countries is no longer to let their exchange rate float, but rather to plan to do that in the long run while managing it in the meantime in parallel with the development of the financial sector and the real economy.

Managing the currency is not risk free. Holding the exchange rate down too much for too long by accumulating reserves causes structural change to stall, and with it productivity gains and growth. It is widely accepted that managing the exchange rate is not a good way to make up for poor productivity.

Until recently in emerging economies the balancing act associated with management of the exchange rate was considered largely a domestic-growth and development issue, albeit a rather complex one in which the best practices and associated benchmarks are not fully worked out. The impacts on the global economy were not sufficiently material to make the subject one of great interest to the advanced countries or to the global economy as a whole. This has changed in the past ten years. With the growing size and impact of the developing countries, and of China in particular, exchange-rate management has become an issue and an element of global balance as well as of domestic growth and development. This renders the issue much more complex.

Currencies of major countries have been known, since the time of the Bretton Woods Agreement, to be an area that requires international coordination. But with the abandonment of that system, we lost the international structures to carry this process out. And we need new ones, anyway, to incorporate the needs, interests, and challenges of developing countries. At best we are just at the beginning of building these new international capabilities. In the meantime, we can expect more conflict, disagreement, misunderstanding, and, probably, imbalance.

In June 2010, China announced a resumption of the managed appreciation of the yuan that began in mid-2005 and was suspended in mid-2008 in response to the crisis. Subsequently, the appreciation has thus far been modest. Directionally, this is surely the right policy for China and the global economy. Some view it as a major step forward in dealing with rebalancing global demand. I don't think so, but let's leave that argument to Part III.

16. The Middle-Income Transition

Most countries that grow to middle-income levels slow down, and some even stop growing. The exceptions are relatively few: Japan, Korea, Taiwan, Hong Kong, and Singapore. Here we explore some of the challenges associated with making this transition. It is important. China is entering the middle-income transition now. Brazil is successfully restarting its growth as a middle-income country. India is about ten to fifteen years from entering the same process. Russia is a middle-income country in which it is at present unclear whether the structural dynamics of sustained growth have been initiated. Much in the global economy will depend on the success of these upcoming navigations.

Middle-income transition refers to that part of the growth process that occurs when a country's per capita income gets into the range of $5,000 to $10,000. At this point, the industries that drove the growth in the early period start to become globally uncompetitive due to rising wages. These labor-intensive sectors move to lower-wage countries and are replaced by a new set of industries that are more capital-, human capital–, and knowledge-intensive in the way they create value.

This transition turns out to be very problematic. There is a very strong tendency to try to hold on to the known successes. And it is hard for policy makers to sit idly by while competition shrinks known sources of employment. The techniques for resisting the structural evolution are many: subsidies, increasing protection in the form of tariffs, management of the exchange rate so as to keep the cost of exports down, and

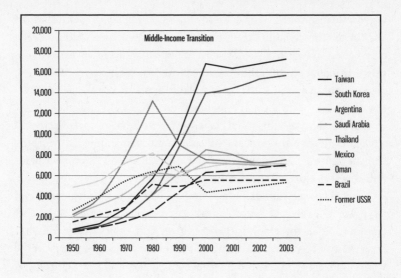

the like. There are potentially powerful domestic interests that create pressure in this direction.

As a result, there is a tendency for growth to stall at this point. The graph above illustrates this effect, and also two of the exceptions—Korea and Taiwan. In both these cases, policies were adapted to promote rather than impede the microeconomic structural transformation. Similar exceptions are the city-states Singapore and Hong Kong (before its formal reconnection with the PRC). Though not shown on the graph, Japan also maintained high growth through the middle-income transition.

In talking about structural change earlier, I spoke about my trip to Korea as it was entering the middle-income transition. There was universal concern about the loss of growth momentum. High-quality, labor-intensive manufacturing was migrating to lower-cost countries like China. Jobs and industries were threatened. The press framed the issue in terms of what was needed to protect the competitiveness of the declining industries and their employment. This was perfectly natural.

What was more unusual is that the government saw that the structural transformation was inevitable if incomes were going to continue to rise. It therefore dramatically shifted the focus of policy and public-sector investment away from targeting labor-intensive export sectors and toward education, applied research, and attracting talent back from abroad. It withdrew from much of its earlier industry-level planning and support and turned the dynamics over much more to the private sector. Korean companies, stalwarts of the low-cost manufacturing era, invested in developing global brands. They became powerhouses in research.

Samsung, a manufacturer of household appliances, astonished Western observers by announcing its intention to develop and make semiconductor memory chips. This was viewed as lunacy in the West. But ten years after the announcement, Samsung produced the first working 256-megabit memory device, a major milestone in the semiconductor industry. The external skeptics have quieted down.

As you can see from the graph on page 101, South Korea continued to grow and is now very close to advanced-country income levels. What is not visible in the graph is that it is a very different economy than it was twenty-five years ago. It may be the most advanced country in the world in terms of broadband Internet connectivity and use, for example.

What happens in the middle-income transition is a combination of positive and negative forces. As incomes rise, labor-intensive processing industries with relatively low value added become internationally uncompetitive relative to other countries in a less advanced state. They are replaced by higher-value-added industries and functions within industries, both upstream in the value-added chain in product development and more capital-intensive parts of manufacturing, and in the downstream part with marketing, global reach, and brand building. Service industries grow in size and employment to serve a growing and shifting pattern of domestic demand as the middle class grows in size and consumption. The new emerging economy is more capital-, human capital-, and knowledge-intensive. The pattern of importing knowledge and technology starts to shift from importing technology to developing and exporting it, part of the journey to advanced-country status.

The key inputs to this process are education, investment in research, and urbanization. The government stops targeting specific labor-intensive and export-oriented sectors for development. It stands back to let the market forces take over. It becomes less hands-on at the microeconomic level. This transition is more than a little scary and requires a leap of faith. What is disappearing is highly visible, while what is hoped will appear is much less so.

There is also a structural change on the demand side in the middle-income transition. At about this point, a middle class appears and grows.

With higher incomes, they buy more, and they buy different things, more closely matched to the production side of the economy. Therefore, an important part of the supply side of the economy grows and shifts its focus to domestic demand. Exports also shift to high-value-added activity and continue to be a driver of growth. But the domestic market, with its rising incomes, starts to assume a more prominent role in determining the structural evolution and patterns of growth of the economy. In short, more growth is traceable to the domestic-economy demand than is true at earlier stages.

The more advanced parts of the complex Chinese economy are now at the middle-income transition stage, particularly in the wealthier coastal areas. The critical question for the future of the country and the global economy is whether the mandatory economic restructuring that has characterized the past thirty years of sustained high growth will continue and shift in a way that supports the microeconomic evolution of the economy. Without it, growth will begin to slow.

Thus far, China's economy and its policy makers have been flexible and have accommodated the structural change. Indeed, policy makers in China appear to understand very well that continued growth requires more rapid structural transformation. But there is some dissent. As profit margins shrink in the labor-intensive manufacturing sector, pressure builds to protect the known source of employment growth, the pattern that worked so well in the past.

I will come back to China's structural challenges in Part IV, when I discuss the prospects for sustaining growth in the postcrisis environment that we are now living in.

17. The Political, Leadership, and Governance Underpinnings of Growth

Economic Freedom

In this chapter, I want to talk about what we do and do not know about the relationship between governance and economic growth—or, more generally, performance. It is a subject about which there are many strong opinions, some only vaguely related to the facts and evidence that we have.

One way to begin is to ask if the economic dynamics that we have already reviewed suggest anything about governance. Clearly they do. The microeconomic dynamic is associated with investment for profit, entrepreneurial activity, entry, and exit. It is a decentralized, bottom-up process. To function, it requires a certain kind of economic freedom. In the modern era, that freedom includes access to markets and to financing, as well as a system of government and governance that allows people to exercise this freedom by making investments and forming businesses without excessively burdensome approval processes or outright restrictions. It also depends on some system of property rights. For the process of investment to operate, people must be able to own assets and buy and sell them. And it relies on a reasonable degree of stability, without which investment risk is elevated and investment suffers.

Some would say that for innovation and entrepreneurial activity to thrive, one also needs some degree of freedom from extreme poverty, where all energy is devoted to survival. Though most of us would be intuitively inclined to accept this, recent research suggests that the vigor of entrepreneurship among the world's poor, when other enabling conditions (such as property rights and access to finance) are present, is plentiful and impressive. This should at least give us pause before we quickly assume that entrepreneurial vigor is a product, as opposed to a cause, of rising incomes.

Economic freedom and inclusiveness are very closely related. Innovation of the type that drives productivity growth is largely a bottom-up process. It requires lots of people with different backgrounds, perspectives, interests, and proclivities. Diversity is a good thing in this context because it multiplies experiments. I think it is fair to say that there are no examples of sustained growth where this type of freedom is missing.

Growth and the Form of Government

Economic freedom is not the same thing as democracy in the sense we ordinarily mean the term, although they overlap. Democracy is a more comprehensive idea. In a healthy, well-functioning democracy, economic freedom is part of a larger package of individual freedoms. But another important feature of democracy is voice: that is, involvement of the individual in making social choices.

A significant number of the high-growth countries are not democracies in this latter sense, at least for part of the growth process. In many of these cases, a second feature of democracy beyond the sphere of individual freedom of action, namely the right to have a voice in making collective social choices, tends to come later.

This is not an argument for democracy; though, clearly, democracy embodies a set of values that most people care about deeply. Nor is this an argument against democracy; I am certainly not suggesting that democracy is an impediment to growth. This is simply a caution against assuming that the governance underpinnings of sustained high growth are coterminous with democracy. That is not supported by the evidence.

There is, however, more to be said about forms of governance and economic performance over time. By giving people not only economic and other kinds of individual freedom, but also "political voice," democracies are safer in two senses. First, in a democracy, if government adopts policies that are selfish, misguided, or at variance with the interests of the majority of citizens, it can be stopped, at least in principle. Autocratic regimes can proceed along destructive paths with far fewer built-in features to stop and reverse the process. Second, democracies pay attention to distributional issues, and these are important. Nobel laureate Professor Amartya Sen has said that famines do not occur (or are much less likely) in democracies. That is in part because in functioning democracies distributional issues are politically salient, and when dealing with a negative shock, the "pain" is spread around through redistribution mechanisms of various kinds.

If one constructs an overly simple 2x2 matrix in which the horizontal options refer to governance, democratic or autocratic, and the vertical dimension has two options, excellent economic performance and very poor performance, that gives us four boxes. There will be lots of countries in every box. In other words, there are both high-performance and low-performance democracies. There are also high-performance autocratic systems and many others where the economic performance is disastrous.

What should we make of this? The growing field of political economy and development is providing some answers, and more will follow in the future. In the meantime, it seems fair to say that the form of governance is not in itself determinative. If it were, not all the boxes would have numerous entries.

Where does that leave us? I have come to believe that success in economic performance is highly correlated with the combination of the following four attributes:

1. The government takes economic performance and growth seriously.
2. The governing group has values that cause it to try to act in the interest of the vast majority of the people (as opposed to themselves or some subgroup, however defined).
3. The government is competent and effective, and selects a viable sustained-growth strategy that includes openness to the global economy, high levels of investment, and a strong future orientation.
4. Economic freedom is present and is supported by the legal system and regulatory policy.

Autocratic systems often fail to meet one or several of these criteria. The result is widespread slow growth and a failure to reduce poverty—not terribly surprising, given that growth and poverty reduction are often not even objectives. But there are exceptions.

China is an interesting case because since 1949 it has been in both economic performance categories: poor for about thirty years after the revolution, and then excellent for the three decades since 1978. Is this pattern consistent with the criteria above? The Communist revolution swept away residual elements of class and caste dating back to the days of the empire and the transitional republic. The state took ownership of all the assets, eliminating concentrated ownership of land and other assets by individuals, families, and subgroups. That made it unlikely that policy would be dominated by formerly wealthy special interests. They set out to educate everyone and even prior to the reforms of 1978 achieved very high literacy rates by developing-country standards (on the order of 85 to 90 percent for both men and women). But prior to 1978, economic freedom did not exist, markets didn't function, and central planning failed, as it did everywhere else. The intent was there, and some of the pieces too, but the growth strategy, if one could call it that, was flawed. The poor performance reflected a poor choice of strategy, which itself was based on the prevailing ideology. Per capita income growth was negligible: incomes were about $500 or less by 1978.

From 1949 to 1978, China was missing items 3 and 4 above. But the reforms of Deng Xiaoping and his colleagues instituted markets and incentives, allowed a growing amount of economic freedom, and began opening up the economy to allow interaction with the global economic environment. That, in combination with the focus on growth—namely, the intent to have the growth be inclusive, very rapid learning, effective pragmatic management of the economy, and skill in navigating in the face of great complexity with incomplete models—led to thirty years of growth, and growth of the highest known average rate to date, about 9.5 percent.

Most autocratic systems have performed much worse, and in many cases that is because the governing group is interested in power, or their own wealth or that of a subgroup, or something other than the future well-being of the whole population. The improvement of the conditions of the general population over time—that is, growth—is simply not often a priority. But even for those with "better" intentions, strategies are often flawed. When power is relatively concentrated, the governing group can proceed without the sea anchors of opposition or public debate to slow them down. This means that they can act quickly. That is fine if they are going in the right direction, but much less fine if they are not.

A number of the high-growth Asian economies (Japan, Korea, Taiwan, Singapore) are interesting hybrids. While democratic in form, they had extended periods with a dominant single party. These structures allowed for relatively rapid implementation of growth-oriented policies. But the dominant structure had to be maintained by garnering popular support and by setting up the details of the political structure so as to make it easier for the dominant party to remain in power. That ensured at least some degree of inclusiveness. But it also distorted the policies, and to some extent the economies. The Liberal Democratic Party in Japan stayed in power for a long period of time by maintaining support in the agricultural sector and in the small-business sector (principally owners of retail businesses). That has had lasting effects on the structure of parts of the economy.

Most of these systems evolved over time into more conventional multiparty democracies, in part because the growth process produced educated middle and upper-middle classes that demanded more "political voice" in collective decision making and social choice.[1]

What of democracies? Well, as with autocratic systems, there are clear successes: India, the world's largest and probably most complex democracy; Botswana, one of the smallest; Chile in the post-Pinochet era; and Brazil since the mid 1990s under Presidents Cardoso and Lula da Silva. All are democracies that have seen high economic performance. But there are many democratic countries where success has been illusive. Building consensus around growth-oriented strategies and policies is more complex in a democratic setting, though perhaps a little more surefooted. But the effect is to slow things down. However, even that is not the major failing.

In governments that have a democratic structure, there are multiple possible reasons for poor economic performance, just as there are in the more autocratic or hybrid cases. At the risk of oversimplification, they seem to me to divide into two broad classes. In one set, the intentions of those in power are good but their strategy choices are flawed, much as in the China (though not democratic) of the first thirty years after the Communist revolution. Another example of this would be Tanzania under President Julius Nyerere. He is widely and rightly admired for his leadership and postindependence nation-building gifts. But by his own account, he and his government chose a form of socialism that did not unleash the nation's growth dynamics, and economic performance was modest.

There is a second (and distressingly large) group of formally democratic countries in which the form of governance is democratic but the system isn't working. In many of these, the governing group uses its mandate and its control over resources (including the police and military) to stay in power, to enrich itself (or a subgroup of which it is a part), and to suppress opposition or buy support. These pathologies are particularly widespread in countries with natural-resource wealth, where being in power means control over the resources and enrichment of the governing party.

These dynamics are highly destructive in many dimensions, of which only one is growth and economic performance. They are the object of intense scrutiny in the field of political economy and development. Understanding them, however, and knowing how to change them are two different things. For many of the poorer countries in the world, breaking the cycle and the destructive political dynamics and embarking on a different path is undoubtedly the main challenge.

Generally, the solutions need to come from within. Externally imposed solutions or improvements lack legitimacy, for understandable reasons. External intervention is not welcome, even in states with governance problems. Citizens of countries that are poorly governed will not generally be enthusiastic about external intervention except in extreme cases where the social order has broken down completely. In those cases the intervention is justified on broad humanitarian grounds, rather than for reasons having to do specifically with fixing up the governance structure or improving economic performance.

During the work of the Commission on Growth and Development (2006–10) I was frequently asked what could be done about failing states. While external influences can conceivably help under certain circumstances, effective change can come only from within the country itself. Sometimes that means there isn't that much outsiders can do. The opportunities for external assistance usually arise only after positive internal change gets under way. They can take the form of investments and concessionary lending with the goal of increasing the rate of acceleration of growth, thereby adding to the support of the incumbent leadership.

What are the catalysts for change when it actually occurs? One prominent one is a crisis, or a series of them, or just chronic poor economic performance. In such situations, political gridlock can break down and create an opportunity for change. The mere opportunity for change does not, of course, guarantee a positive outcome.

An awareness of just how poor the performance is can also act as a catalyst. Communications technology has dramatically changed the ability of almost everyone in the world to learn about how others live. In places where growth is low and poverty is high, that awareness can translate into heightened dissatisfaction and can increase the pressure for a change of direction and for better results over time. Demonstration effects can be quite powerful. I don't have any doubt that the increasingly visible growth of China and India will change the ordinary citizen's sense of what is possible and hence the demand for change in many other parts of the world. It is reported that Deng Xiaoping's thinking was materially influenced by visits in the 1970s to Singapore and then to New York (to the UN), neither of which he had seen before. It also seems fairly clear that the growth of China has had a galvanizing effect on India.

That being said, the persistence of malfunctioning governance and poor economic performance in many countries strongly suggests there aren't any universally known, broadly applicable, and reasonably sure-fire solutions.

In cases of successful sustained growth, leadership at the top appears crucial. Leadership that is generous and inclusive, uncorrupted, and able to build consensus around a reasonably compelling vision of what the future might look like and what it will take to get there (including sacrifices), is very powerful, especially at the start and in the early stages, when there are as yet no results to point to. Later on, success creates momentum and support for growth-oriented strategies, so that sustaining them, while never easy, at least enjoys the performance of the recent past as a tailwind.

I have asked friends in India (including those from political parties outside the government) whether a change of government would produce a major change in direction with impacts on growth and strategy. The uniform answer has been no, that the basic approach to growth and development is now firmly embedded in the politics and in the minds of citizens. Turning back or away from the present course would not be a viable political option.

One of the reasons leadership is even more critical early on is that institutional depth in policy making is limited in the early stages of development. The analytical capacity we in the United States associate with the Congressional Budget Office, the National Academies, and numerous think tanks both guides and constrains the policy-making process. Building that kind of institutional infrastructure is in fact just as much a part of the development process as the economy. Part of the challenge is to build increasingly effective government and surrounding institutions over time. Before that is well under way, a heavier burden for making crucial choices therefore falls on the leadership group. It is easy to make mistakes—indeed, it is inevitable. Effective leadership lies in part in recognizing them, acknowledging them, and correcting them promptly.

Leaders also need to change the political structures in response to the evolving economic reality in a growing economy. Among the high-growth cases, including Korea and Taiwan, the dominant political party structures came under stress as the middle and professional classes expanded. The political rules and procedures—and sometimes even the constitutional underpinnings—needed to change to accommodate the desire for expanded participation in policy-priority setting. The result has been a relatively peaceful set of transitions to multiparty democracies. But this evolution required active choices by political elites under the threat of a much more disorderly breakdown in governance.

18. Low-Growth Economies in the Developing World

The majority of developing countries in the world have not yet achieved a pattern of sustained growth. These countries used to account for a very large majority of the world's population. That is no longer the case. By moving India and China and their 40 percent of the world's population into the sustained-high-growth category, the balance has tipped. Nevertheless, there remain about 2 billion people in countries where growth has been low or where there are periodic growth spurts that are not sustained.

What explains this divergence in economic performance, and will it persist or disappear over time? These are questions of interest not only to those who live in low-growth developing countries but also to the rest of the global community. Sustained lack of progress in a world where the majority is experiencing expanding opportunity has problematic consequences in many dimensions.

Those in the poor and low-growth economies are much more vulnerable to shocks, including climate change. Adaptation to major climate change is expensive and will not be affordable in these countries. Many of them are in parts of the globe believed to be most vulnerable to potentially damaging shifts in climate—mainly in tropical climates or on low-lying islands. One of the cruel ironies of climate change is that those countries likely to be affected most adversely by the climate change are those least likely to have had a major role in the buildup of CO_2 in the atmosphere.

An international response on a quite massive scale may be required, as outlined by the United Nations and the World Bank.[1] It may or may not be forthcoming if and when the time comes. Thomas Schelling and others have pointed out that, long term, the best defense is growth and increased income and wealth in these countries.

There is also a security challenge associated with persistent lack of growth. Experts disagree about the causes of conflict. While most experts do not believe that terrorism and other forms of destructive activity directed toward people, countries, and assets are caused in a simple straightforward way by relative economic deprivation, they do agree that recruiting people to these activities is a lot easier in environments characterized by low economic growth that lack social and political opportunity.

In many low-growth countries, the demographics are such that large numbers of young people are entering the job market with little real prospect of productive employment. There is a massive, and growing, youth unemployment problem. Addressing it requires higher growth in the relevant countries. But even that is not enough in the short to medium term. These efforts needs to be combined with expanded migration for work options. But the point is that the problem has external impacts: it creates a fertile recruiting ground for terrorist and antiestablishment organizations, both within these countries and internationally.

On the economic side of the equation, the most common causes of poor economic performance are lack of openness to the global economy and underinvestment by government in crucial assets, principally infrastructure and education.

I won't comment further on the global-economy issue. We know that sustained high growth in isolation is not possible. There is a growing awareness of this, and the number of cases of isolation is very small now.

Public-sector investment well below the levels required to sustain high growth is widespread. In both infrastructure and education, there are quantity and quality dimensions with variations across countries. That is, the levels are often too low, and the effectiveness or efficiency of the investment in producing outputs for a given commitment of resources is also low.

Why is this so? There are a number of reasons.

In poor countries, the immediate demands of day-to-day life get translated into political pressures and end up crowding out investments with longer-term returns. This has led some to hypothesize that there is a "poverty trap." I don't think this is the right way to think about it. Forgoing present consumption for future growth is a choice—a tough choice, but still a choice. In the high-growth countries this choice was made in favor of the future, admittedly at some considerable cost in terms of near-term consumption. If poverty traps or low-level equilibria were unbreakable binding constraints, China in 1975 should have been in one of them. This makes me somewhat skeptical of the purely economic version of the poverty trap argument.

Dysfunctional governance is a different story. In many countries, governance fails and the investments that are required to improve the conditions for the citizens in general and to support growth are not high-priority items. We have encountered this before in the section on governance. It is a prescription for low growth, and for divisive, and at times violent, politics. The reinforcing incentives and behaviors surrounding the maintenance and misuse of political power are very difficult to alter. To me, these look more like traps than the purely economic ones. But, surely, the debate will go on.

Probably the most challenging aspect of the underinvestment problem lies in the quality, as opposed to the quantity, dimension. In many countries, there is a significant commitment of resources to education, for example, but the results are at best disappointing and highly variable across countries (and across regions within large countries). Something goes wrong between the inputs and the outputs as measured by real skills acquisition.

This problem is ubiquitous and not confined to a specific subset of developing countries. It does occur in poorly performing developing countries. But it also occurs in high-growth cases like India, where many of that country's northern states have documented educational "quality" problems. If left unattended, those problems will retard the growth in those areas. It is also a problem in some developed countries, such as the United States.

The "quality" problem—that is, the low level of outputs per dollar of investment—has multiple causes. Sometimes it is just a shortage of competent teachers. In other cases, public finances are such that it is hard or impossible to attract talent by paying competitive wages. In still other cases it can be traced to political patronage systems: teaching jobs are sometimes awarded as compensation for political support, and the incentives are disconnected from the educational output measures. Educational output is simply not an embedded incentive in the system.

The labor-market structure can intervene in a negative way if unions defend teachers and administrators in the face of evidence of poor performance as a way of maintaining economic power. Seniority systems have adverse incentive properties but are defended by unions as part of the political economy of maintaining support. Measurement is also part of the problem. If educational investment is measured by years of schooling and graduation rates at various levels, that will tend to be the focus. It has been observed (correctly, I think) that you tend to get what you measure for. But more certain is the proposition that what you don't measure for will largely be ignored. The point is that it is hard but important to measure real outputs such as the acquisition of cognitive skills, and then to try to achieve measurable targets in spite of institutional, political, and incentive structure obstacles.

In a world in which knowledge and connectivity are increasingly the basis of value creation, failures in the educational system are the surest form of exclusion there is.

19. Natural Resource Wealth and Growth

Some advanced and developing countries have a lot of oil, natural gas, and/or minerals. Others are potentially very productive in agriculture. These are different forms of natural resource wealth. In principle it should make these countries better off in some way. Indeed, some advanced countries, like Canada and Australia, have natural resource wealth and appear to have benefited from it. In developing countries, resource wealth should make it easier to make the investments that underpin steady growth, and with less short-term sacrifice than is normally the case. However, that is not how it usually plays out.

Most of the high-growth developing countries we looked at earlier are not particularly resource wealthy. On the other hand, a significant portion of the historically poorer and lower-growth developing countries *are* resource wealthy. Africa, for example, has an unusual amount of natural resource wealth. Paul Collier counts fully a third of the countries in sub-Saharan Africa as wealthy in natural resources. The question is, why does the ownership of valuable national assets correlate negatively with national income and growth? The answer, in the broadest sense, seems to rest on governance distortions and mismanagement.

There are three problems that are created by natural resource wealth. The most troublesome is the distortion of political incentives away from the normal functions of government and toward capturing the wealth, or the income that flows from the wealth. Since the payoffs can be pretty high, this leads to a whole variety of deviations from well-functioning democratic processes. Sometimes autocracy displaces democracy, backed up by police and military force. Then the autocratic power is used to appropriate the natural resource wealth rather than invest it in assets that are supportive of growth. In other cases, the outward form of democracy is retained but the incumbents controlling the wealth use a portion to stay in power by "buying" support. A variant of this approach is to pay off those with tribal or ethnic connections. Outbreaks of violence and conflict are not uncommon when certain groups are favored over others. In all dimensions these various divergences from the normal idealized functioning of government are fatal to economic performance. The investment climate is damaged by conflict, by the risk produced by political instability, and by the absence of investment in complementary public-sector assets.

In a sense, the distributional issues when there is natural resource wealth sometimes simply overwhelm and displace all future-oriented collective interests in growth. The costs of decades of lost growth are staggeringly high.

It doesn't have to be this way. Botswana is a case in point. Botswana is a high-growth country whose growth began shortly after independence in 1966. Diamonds were discovered later. Growth has been maintained and accelerated, and dependence on foreign aid has declined to almost nothing. Botswana is small and land-locked and should be a troubled country, but it is not. A key element of its success dates to when President Seretse Khama, who came from the Bamangwato tribe, on whose traditional lands the diamonds were found, took the position that the diamonds belonged to the country as a whole. This position was supported by the tribe. Tribal procedures for making collective choices consultatively are well developed. So instead of having a fight over the ownership of the natural resource wealth, it became the property of the central government and an asset belonging to all the citizens. The government owns a substantial portion of the mining operations and deploys the revenues to maintain investments in people and institutions that support growth and development. The political, financial, and legal underpinnings are impressively developed. The Botswana case illustrates that the natural resource "curse," though pervasive, is not inevitable, and that leadership matters at crucial points. This all could have taken a very different course.

The second set of problems associated with natural resource wealth and income are more technical. Managing resource wealth to accelerate and sustain growth is actually quite complicated. For a full treatment of the steps in the chain, from extraction of the resources to capturing an appropriate fraction of the revenues, and then to investing them in ways that support and do not hinder growth, some readers may be interested in reading the newly developed Natural Resource Charter.[1] It is an attempt to lay out the priorities and steps needed to turn natural resource wealth into a sustainable pattern of growth.

For our purposes, it is sufficient to note that even well-intentioned governments do not necessarily know how to carry out these steps. Capturing the revenues in a transparent way through a combination of auctions, royalties, and taxes, while avoiding corruption, investing effectively in infrastructure and education to jump-start the economic diversification that supports growth, and investing an appropriate fraction of the income abroad so as to maintain a competitive exchange rate and an appropriate intergenerational distribution of wealth are also complex management challenges.

My own view is that the Natural Resource Charter will help, but that expecting this kind of expertise to be developed on a timely basis in multiple countries, many of them small and still quite poor, is unrealistic. A better short-to-medium-term approach would be to try to develop a trusted international institution to which oversight of some of these steps could be partially outsourced. What is needed is a trusted international technical advisory group that comes free of biases and its own agenda. For Africa, a natural place to develop this institutional capacity would be the African Development Bank.

The third challenge is really an aspect of the second. Suppose that the government collects its share of the revenues and invests a portion of them in public assets up to the capacity of the economy to make these investments efficiently. Suppose further that these investments do not exhaust the revenues. What do you do with the remainder? There are two issues here. You need to invest some of it abroad, else the exchange rate will rise to a point where the only viable exports are the natural resources. That will choke off export diversification and even cause competitive problems for domestic industries serving the domestic economy when those products can be imported. Failing to counteract these forces is referred to as the "Dutch disease," a term coined by *The Economist* in 1977 with reference to the impact in Holland of the discovery of a huge natural gas field in 1959. To prevent this effect, you have to invest some of the proceeds abroad, much as do the sovereign wealth funds in the Gulf States.

The other choice is between investing or consuming the resource income now. In a poor country, especially if it is growing, it is appropriate to consume more of the income now rather than spread it out evenly over future generations, which, by virtue of the growth, will be richer. Intertemporal income redistribution, the movement of income to present from future generations or the reverse, should favor the relatively poor people, and in a growth environment, that group is the current population. The main constraint is avoidance of the Dutch disease problem.

20. The Challenge for Small States

Many of the poorer and lower-growth countries are small, a significant number being island states. They face challenges on two fronts. First, because of their small size they are almost by definition undiversified, and hence vulnerable to shocks in the industries that they do have. Second, the cost of governance declines with the size of the population. There are fixed costs. As a result, in a small state, effective governance costs a lot more per person. Therefore it tends to be underprovided.

From an economic standpoint, many of these smaller countries should not be countries at all but parts of larger, more diversified, national units. Indeed, that has been the direction of movement in the eastern Caribbean, with beneficial effects—a kind of partial economic integration combined with the sharing of governance functions and overhead costs (like the court system and the central bank).

There remains the nontrivial political challenge of forging these larger units. The European Union has relevant experience in this. It has mechanisms and pathways for expanding membership and areas of cooperation built into its structure. An intriguing idea is to use the E.U. infrastructure model for expansion and extend it to a broader array of countries. Or, if that puts too much of a burden on Europe, a variant would be to take the European experience and create a new entity that could become the union for a wide range of small states.

There are many variants of this kind of proposal and thinking. It is worth pursuing. My view, for what it is worth, is that the problems faced by the numerous small poor states are too hard to solve on a stand-alone basis, and that to rely on that approach is very unlikely to produce the hoped-for results. There are seventy-eight countries with populations of less than 2 million, and sixty-eight of those have populations of less than a million. While partial political and economic mergers are difficult, they may be the only realistic alternative for countries of this size.

Smaller, poorer states should not be left to wrestle with their vulnerabilities and challenges on their own, either individually or in combination. They need periodic help. Providing that help is the international analogue of delivering on the idea of inclusiveness in a domestic national setting. We know that the latter is an important part of growth at the national level. Internationally, it is both morally and strategically important. And it is one of the primary functions of the International Monetary Fund and the World Bank to provide support when needed.

21. The Adding-Up Problem

Thus far we have focused largely on growth strategies and dynamics at the developing-country level. The global economy is the main enabling external factor. Any single developing country is small in relation to the global economy. It therefore has a very small impact on global prices, asset prices, and a range of other variables. But being individually small does not imply that small developing countries are collectively small.

You might object that if a significant number of countries pursue similar strategies at the same time, the individually small become the collectively large, and thus the arithmetic won't work. Something may go wrong that isn't detectable in the country-by-country view. This is an important point.

This example is an instance of a general class of issues called "adding-up problems." Are numerous individual rational choices made at the level of nations collectively infeasible or suboptimal? Or, more bluntly, when everyone does the same thing, can it work? In this case, the issue is whether the developing countries will flood the markets with the goods that they tend to be good at producing—labor-intensive goods and services. If this was to happen, two adverse consequences might occur. One is that the relative prices of these kinds of goods would be driven down, making these sectors less profitable and less growth generating. The other is that the flood of goods would provoke protectionist responses in the form of tariffs, quotas, or other barriers in the consuming markets, including the advanced countries.

Thus far the growth of the emerging economies has not fundamentally altered the openness of the international economy or shifted prices so dramatically as to slow developing-country growth. The record, however, is not completely clean. There have been instances in which quotas were imposed. Japanese automobiles were subject to American-imposed quotas in various categories of cars in the 1980s. In that case, Japanese auto companies responded by expanding their U.S. manufacturing capacity and continued to expand their market share. They also cleverly moved up the price/quality spectrum, shifting toward luxury cars for the imports. The quotas imposed were on units, not total sales in dollars. The result was that the unit imports were the same while the total dollar value of those imports rose.[1]

The main reason that the potential problem has not become a major impediment to developing-country growth is that countries have started at different times. Furthermore, the early starters exit and move on. The Asian Tigers are of advanced- or upper-middle income levels, approaching advanced-country income levels, and so the labor-intensive manufacturing is long gone. China is large enough to have actually lowered the relative price of manufactured goods in the past fifteen years. One might guess that the addition of India might overload the global market. This could happen, but India is behind China by about fourteen years, and much of the Chinese economy is at the point of transition out of the labor-intensive "processing" industries, or segments, in the global value-added chains. So while the jury is still out, there is a reasonable chance that the sequencing and timing will be such that the global economy has the requisite absorptive capacity.

As we have seen, the natural sectoral positioning of economies (the mix of things they do, or what economists call comparative advantage) evolves over time as incomes rise, so that labor-intensive industries that drive growth in early stages shrink and disappear and are replaced by industries that are more capital (both physical and human capital) and knowledge intensive.

This evolving landscape does not guarantee that the adding-up problem will not bite. It just creates the possibility that it will not. But in truth, there is a reasonably good chance that the dynamics will work out. The late starters are currently really quite small in relation to the global economy (less than 15 percent of the global GDP). The global economy seems to have accommodated the growth of China and India (following behind) without hitting a wall in terms of absorptive capacity or provoking a massive protectionist response from the consuming nations. Crisis-induced slow growth in the developed economies may cause this dynamic to shift in the protectionist direction, but we will come to that later.

By the time the current set of relatively poor countries that may be beginning to enter the high-growth phase are collectively big enough to have an impact (we are talking about at least two decades of high growth), China and then India will be well into the middle-income transitions, making large amount of economic "space" for the new arrivals. Remember that once you get outside the G20, there is only between 10 and 15 percent of global GDP left at present. With high growth in the large emerging economies, it will be decades before that number is much larger. Even if the entire non-G20 group starts to move to advanced-country status in unison, it will still account for less than one-third of global GDP and therefore will be unlikely to encounter the adding-up challenge.

There is, however, a view among poorer countries that it is difficult to compete with China as long as China is in the labor-intensive export sector. Paul Collier and others have argued for time-limited preferential treatment of African exports by advanced countries to overcome this advantage and to help jump-start the export diversification and growth process. In fact the United States has such a program, called AGOA (African Growth and Opportunity Act), passed by Congress in 2000. It is viewed by development policy experts as quite successful. Europe has some similar programs but these are hampered by rules concerning origin restrictions on the value-added chain. Silk garments made in Africa with silk imported from China do not qualify, for example, because the local content requirement is not met. Too much of the value added is contributed by imported silk.

Technically this argument about competitiveness is largely incorrect. Late starters can compete, but public-sector investment is required to make them competitive. That investment is lagging in many places. But as a practical matter, these preferences will not damage China or India, and if they don't work, they won't have cost anything either. It is worth a try.

One factor that relates to size is important. Large countries, even in the early stages, have a potential advantage in that if they are serious about growth, their domestic economies are prospectively large and of great interest to multinational corporations. This will attract the multinationals' attention, and cause them to make the up-front investment in learning to operate in a new environment with a view to both the expandability of exports and, in the longer term, supplying the large domestic market. Small countries do not offer these inducements. That makes it more difficult to get the attention of the multinationals and hence harder to open this important channel for knowledge transfer.

PART THREE

The Crisis and Its Aftermath

We have looked at the rapidly changing structure of the global economy and seen that if the trends of the past few postwar decades continue, the structure will continue to evolve quite quickly. We have also spent some time on the high-growth dynamics in the developing world. The conditions that cause, support, or impede this growth are important not only for growth and development strategy, but also because they provide a basis for trying to assess the opportunities and challenges that lie ahead.

The questions that are both interesting and potentially important for all of us are the following:

Will the high-speed growth in the developing world continue? On what does that continuation depend? Are there economic and environmental headwinds that will slow the growth and reduce the opportunities? Will the countries that have thus far not grown much—or, when they have, only fitfully—achieve a pattern of steadier and higher growth, or will the world divide into a majority that is relatively rich and a minority that remains relatively poor?

Will all this growth be sustainable in terms of energy availability and cost, and in terms of the environment (air quality, climate change, water availability)? If the answer is maybe, then what actions, including ones undertaken at the international level, are required to move the answer in the direction of yes?

Is an interconnected global economy governable and manageable? Or will the tension created by the mismatch between governance structures and interdependence and interconnectedness increase and eventually snap, causing something to happen to restore the balance, either by creating new governance structures or by reducing the connectedness?

In a partially governed, partially globalized world, is extreme volatility of the type we experienced in the recent financial and economic crisis likely to be the periodic norm, with adverse consequences for the global economy as a whole, and especially for the more vulnerable people and economies in it?

In Part III we explore the impact of the crisis and its aftermath on the developing countries, the lessons they have taken away, and their prospects for growth in the future.

Then, in Part IV, we will turn to some positive trends and to some major challenges to growth in the coming decades, including a set of adding-up problems that are new and require a kind of cooperative, collective action on a scale that is new.

I think of the challenges and major hurdles to be overcome for the advancement of the global economy, and especially for the interests of the developing world, as falling into three categories:

1. Periodic instability and volatility and the responses to it
2. Rebalancing the global economy and restoring demand in a sustainable pattern
3. Adding-up problems (in other words: Are the strategies and policies of individual parts of the global economy consistent with the evolution of the whole system in areas such as energy, the environment, food, and industrial composition?)

22. Emerging Markets During and After the Global Crisis

Before the currency crisis of 1997–98, the advice from advanced countries and the international financial institutions (principally the International Monetary Fund and the World Bank) to developing countries, with respect to their financial systems, was, in essence, "You should look like us," meaning they should adopt the same open financial and economic policies as we do. After the '97–'98 experience of instability resulting from a toxic combination of open financial systems, weak internal regulation, lack of transparency, and, in some cases, external debt denominated in dollars or euros, the advice changed. It became, "You should eventually look like us, but proceed at a measured pace as your financial systems deepen and mature." It was translated into action more or less as prescribed, but with the addition of a widespread accumulation of reserves to provide a buffer against volatility in capital flows and exchange rates.

Now, in the aftermath of a crisis that began with extreme distress in the advanced countries' financial markets, the structure and regulation of the advanced-country systems are in the process of significant and permanent change in terms of regulatory structure and investor behavior.[1] The lightly regulated model, with its strong presumption that self-regulation will be a stabilizing influence, has been rejected along with the assumption that sophisticated participants in sufficient numbers accurately perceive and manage shifting systemic risk. As a result, the "like us" part of the modified prescription to emerging markets is no longer well-defined and won't be until a new system, currently under construction, is in place and has operated for long enough to have been tested. The destination and the partial anchor it provided for the evolution of financial-sector policy in developing countries are no longer clear.

In fact, for the thirty-five years leading up to the crisis, the international financial system was a hybrid. The developed countries maintained floating, market-determined exchange rates, had open capital accounts, and generally did not intervene in their own currency markets. Japan was something of an exception, with some management of the exchange rate and, over time, a considerable buildup of foreign assets, called reserves. The U.K. tried to support the value of the pound sterling in 1992 to keep it above the agreed limits in the run-up to the introduction of the euro and was overcome by the markets, particularly by George Soros, who took short positions against the pound. Eventually the reserves were exhausted and the pound was devalued.

The developing countries, despite persistent advice to follow the developed-country model, did not take it. For the most part, they managed the currency, maintained inbound and outbound capital controls, and, after '97–'98, acquired a growing set of foreign currency assets as reserves. This hybrid system worked for an extended period because it met the diverse needs of the developed and developing countries—and, importantly, because the developing countries in the aggregate were not large enough to have significant negative external effects on global balance and stability. In the past ten years, because of growth, this situation has changed and the hybrid system is breaking down.

The crisis, with its origins in the advanced-country financial systems, has raised questions about our grasp of the evolving structure of the system and our ability to keep up with its shifting risk characteristics, a prerequisite for effective self-regulatory defenses. Evidently, this gap in our knowledge became too large in the current crisis, a combination of difficult-to-access information and incomplete models for processing the information.[2]

What will policy makers in developing countries make of all this, and how will their responses affect investment opportunities and returns in emerging markets?

First, they will watch with great interest the advanced-country process of reconstructing the financial regulatory systems as the possible new objective. They will assess whether the new structures meet their own needs or require supplementary steps, and they will review the pace and sequencing of the opening of the capital account. Given the heightened level of uncertainty about the sources of systemic risk and instability, a slowing of the pace seems rational and very likely to be the outcome.

Second, they will study the international transmission mechanisms that were at work in the deepest part of the crisis (the first eight months) and the range and robustness of circuit breakers. There were two primary transmission channels, one financial and one in the real economy. The financial channel consisted of the rapid exodus of capital from emerging markets to advanced countries to deal with badly damaged balance sheets, problems of capital adequacy and potential solvency, and margin and collateral calls. The result was an immediate and sharp credit tightening in developing countries and rapid exchange-rate movements that saw emerging-market currencies depreciating, the only exception being China.[3]

The use of reserves to stabilize the net capital flows has been the most important domestically controlled circuit breaker. Basically, when capital flows out rapidly, a country with reserves can sell its foreign assets and bring the money home, thus creating a reverse, countervailing capital inflow. Those countries with reserves used them for this purpose and took additional steps to mediate the flows to ease credit in various sectors of the economy. Countries without reserves had few options and remain highly vulnerable and dependent on a recovery of the international system or on balance-of-payments assistance from an initially underfunded IMF.

Two conclusions will likely be drawn from this experience. First, the perception of the importance of reserves as a defensive weapon will be elevated. Management of the current and capital account will be carried out in such a way as to include or expand this element of self-insurance. Second, the IMF (on the decline as the crisis broke) is now perceived as quite important in stabilizing volatile global capital flows. Or at least the importance of the function is better understood and the IMF will now be challenged to reform its governance structure in order to meet the challenge.

The IMF's starting resources at the onset of the crisis were $250 billion—not nearly enough to deal with the impact of the capital exodus from emerging markets in the fall of 2008. Its resources were expanded by the G20 to $750 billion, though that was not until several months into the crisis. Important potential sources of these expanded resources, including the countries with large reserve holdings, will insist on reform of the governance structure.[4]

The developing countries have taken note of the fact that in the developed countries, the role of governments (including central banks) expanded during the crisis from that of referee and regulator to major player, as purchaser of a wide range of assets and supplier of liquidity and credit. When government supplies capital, it acquires a considerable say in what the private-sector institutions do. The government's focus is quite understandably on the domestic economy and financial system and on preventing excessive damage to the real economy.

The emerging markets see this clearly and understand it. Their conclusion is quite certain to be that it is of high importance in their own financial systems to have a significant fraction of the financial sector, especially the banking sector, domestically owned and controlled. In a crisis, foreign-based institutions are required to focus elsewhere. It is imperative to have a functioning set of stable domestic institutions that are able to work with government to respond to the crisis and restore credit availability, and that are big enough to safeguard the economy's needs for safe savings channels and credit intermediation. Domestic ownership in this context does not necessarily mean state ownership. That will depend on the country.

One would therefore expect that domestic ownership of a substantial part of the financial system would become or remain a priority, a relatively long-term one, and that foreign entry will perhaps be more tightly controlled.[5] Additionally, the emerging-market balance sheets were largely free of toxic assets. This is perceived as a good thing as it removed a significant element of instability present in the advanced countries. Regulatory controls on the products that domestic entities and investors can sell and hold will be the expected response.

This is not to say that emerging markets will conclude that straightforward securitization, properly regulated, is a bad idea. Spreading risk and lowering capital costs are clearly beneficial. The trend in emerging markets toward expansion of the nonbank, marketable securities mechanism for providing credit as the capital markets and institutions mature will therefore continue, though at a measured pace. But the products are likely to be kept simple by regulation. And the pace may slow for a while as the advanced-country regulatory structures are thought through and revamped—and these, over time, will serve as better models for emerging markets.[6]

The crisis exposed fault lines and vulnerabilities that are less visible in calmer waters. One of those fault lines is the extreme difficulty in responding to global issues that require cooperative behavior to achieve anything like a first best outcome. In a crisis, one is fortunate just to get rapid and effective emergency responses at the national level; the collective multinational interests tend simply to be shunted aside. In view of these difficulties, the international cooperation in the 2008 crisis response was actually quite impressive.

But there is a more basic point. It is increasingly clear that there are limits to globalization in the context of a governance structure that is largely nation-centric. Under pressure, national policy choices will be driven by what is in the best interests of the country, and the outcome will be a noncooperative one, whether we choose to call it an equilibrium or not. For a single nation to act otherwise is to expose itself to risk, as the financial-ownership case illustrates. Anticipating periodic bouts of instability, nations will take actions to limit their exposure. It will take many forms: reserve currency holdings, fiscal dry powder, limiting the openness and exposure of the financial system, probably increasing stores of food and fuel. All of them can be thought of as different forms of self-insurance. They are individually rational and collectively produce only a second-best outcome.

A more fundamental set of questions concerns growth and engagement with the global economy. Growth has accelerated in the developing world over the past twenty years. Sustained high growth now characterizes the economies of about 60 percent of the people who live in developing countries. We know that this kind of growth has been enabled by the leveraging of the global economy for productivity-enhancing knowledge and by using the huge global demand and marketplace to expand rapidly in areas of comparative advantage. Several issues are raised by the crisis, issues that are being discussed and debated now.

Will or should developing countries abandon the high-growth, open-economy strategy, or will they adjust and continue? Does the slower global growth associated with the "new normal" imply that the developing-country growth strategies and policies won't work anymore? Is the crisis perceived as a failure of the advanced-country financial model, or perhaps of the whole market-based capitalist system in the real economy? Has the perceived balance of benefit and risk in exposure to the global economy tipped toward the risk side?

The openness of the global economy should not be taken for granted. Protectionist measures increased as part of the crisis response. While not ideal, this was pretty much inevitable. One can think of it as the political price for aggressive commitment of public resources to shore up the financial sector and to create a fiscal stimulus. Will this pattern be reversed or continue in the current negative direction? Will the deficit in global aggregate demand created by the elevated saving of the U.S. consumer responding to his damaged balance sheet persist, or will it be eliminated by higher consumption elsewhere in the world? If the deficit persists, will it be harder to remove elements of protectionism and resist additions to them in an environment where there is a strong incentive to use policy to capture market share?

Much of this will be revealed over time. But I think it is possible to make some educated guesses and to identify some of the major policy challenges, domestically and globally. A lot will depend on the way in which the global economy and various countries emerge from the crisis.

There are voices in every country that claim the system failure extends well beyond the financial sector—indeed, that the failure extends to the whole market-based (capitalist) system. That type of view can be found in some developing countries. In a country where that view prevailed in policy and strategy setting, the government would expand the scope of its involvement in the economy, and openness to the global economy might be reduced. Much of the competitive dynamics associated with high growth would be lost or diminished.

I don't think the dirigiste view will prevail. The benefits of market and capitalist incentives are well understood, and the track record of growth with an open global-economy strategy is now long and impressive. The alternative view of the crisis, the one that seems to be winning out, is that the advanced-country financial systems failed badly, but not the whole market-based edifice in the real economy. The evidence favors this more balanced assessment, and I believe it is winning out—if not everywhere, at least in most developing countries, and certainly in the large systemically important ones.

As a result, growth and development strategies are likely to be retained, although with some perhaps important modifications and shifts in emphasis and priorities. The basic open-economy, high investment and savings growth strategies will continue to work. But the returns measured in growth may be lower in the postcrisis period because of lower growth and structural challenges in the advanced economies. There is a difference between strategies and outcomes. The strategies will be modified but not abandoned. The outcomes will be less spectacular for a period of time as a result of the lower global growth, particularly in the advanced countries.

Much of the future of the developing world will depend on the restoration of openness in the global economy. With the G20 in the lead, removing the protectionist measures as the perceived need declines and restoring the openness of the global economy will likely be accomplished. It may take some time. It will be much harder in an environment of slow developed-country growth and high unemployment, and in light of a shortfall in global aggregate demand. It is clear that the entire global economy has a shared interest in an expeditious adoption of a coordinated set of policies to address the growth and structural issues on both supply and demand sides. We will come back to this set of global challenges in Part IV.

On the openness of the trading system, completing the Doha round, which is currently stalled, would be a major step forward. It is important to developing countries. Completing Doha and moving on would send a substantive message about the G20's commitment to maintaining an open global economy.

This rather important multinational agenda will be easier to accomplish if global aggregate demand can be restored quickly, for the incentive reasons discussed earlier.

The large U.S. deficits and rising debt, unaccompanied as yet by a credible plan to exit and restore fiscal balance, are causing some concern. It has started to be reflected in the bond markets and in the statements of those developing countries holding large reserves in dollar-denominated assets.

China has floated several times now the idea of a super-sovereign currency via special drawing rights at the IMF. The idea is to avoid relying on the U.S. dollar as a reserve currency. This is unlikely to be a realistic possibility in the short run for the global economy, though it might provide a risk-mitigation mechanism for central bank reserves. The bottom line is that the global economy is dependent on U.S. resolve to control domestic inflation, government deficits, and debt levels. There really isn't any good alternative as of yet.

What can we expect, then, from the emerging countries in terms of shifts in priorities and focus? The resilience of the large developing economies during and after the crisis will tend to confirm the wisdom of the their initial conditions: low external debt (and low debt in general), low household debt, clean and well-capitalized financial balance sheets, domestic ownership, reserves, current accounts in balance or surplus. The main change in emphasis will be a continued and elevated focus on resilience. Instability originating in the developed countries was a surprise. "Fool me once, shame on you; fool me twice, shame on me" captures the overall mind-set.

They will become broadly more conservative for a while. They will push for the continuing and restored openness of the global economy. Their financial markets will be structured and regulated with greater attention to partial insulation from external instability with a focus on effective circuit breakers. That probably means domestic ownership of a substantial part of the financial system (particularly banking), restrictions on the holding and trading of more complex assets, and a controlled pattern of foreign entry.

Knowledge transfer, the key driver of catch-up growth, will continue to be important. While the pace of opening up may slow somewhat, the pattern won't. Multinational corporations will continue to seek supply-chain and market opportunities across the globe. Many of those opportunities will be in high-growth emerging markets. Reserves will continue to be viewed as expensive but important insurance against the adverse impact of volatility in global financial flows, as well as a consequence of managing exchange-rate appreciation in an environment in which low interest rates in developed countries are causing a flood of inbound capital flows into emerging markets, threatening inflation and asset bubbles. A greater emphasis on funding domestic investment (public and private) from domestic savings so as to reduce aggregate dependence on foreign financing seems likely, and probably advisable, though it may slow growth.

The fiscal and sovereign-debt stress in the developed countries as a result of the crisis and the response has focused attention on initial conditions and on the importance of countercyclicality in fiscal policy so that there is some dry powder in the event of a large external shock. This lesson has not been missed in the developing economies. Note has been taken that the advanced economies are running without much capacity to respond to future shocks.

The crisis and the immediately preceding shock in commodity prices exposed another fault line. Crises and periods of economic instability have large distributional effects, as well as aggregate ones. Some people or businesses are hurt more than others. And some countries are more adversely affected than others. The food and energy price shock, and then the financial crisis, have caused developing countries to start to pay more attention to building transfer mechanisms that will allow them to redistribute quickly. In the food-price spike during 2007 and the first half of '08, poor families who spend as much as 50 percent or more of their income on food (mostly grains and oils) were threatened with malnutrition and starvation. Many countries did not have any effective mechanism for redistributing food or income to them. Some countries, including major food exporters, were forced to resort to price and export controls, neither of which is an ideal response from a global perspective, because you want the high prices to create incentives for a supply-side increase in output.

The food-price spike was complicated by the fact that subsidies for biofuels, designed to reduce dependence on petroleum, were believed by many to have contributed to rising demand and higher prices and shortages. Empirical estimates of the magnitude of this effect varied widely, tending to correlate highly with the economic interest or political viewpoint of the analyst.

Here we have an example of two things. One is that policies can have unintended consequences. The second is that the response driven by national priorities differed from a cooperative global response. The latter would have required abstention from price and export controls and rapid redistributive activity, including across national borders.

More generally, for a full global system to continue to develop, it will need enhanced coordinated oversight with objectives that are not purely national, and it will require an ability to deal with adverse distributional issues across countries. The unevenness of the impact of both the financial crisis and the prior food-price spike across countries is clearly visible, though the precise details differ. Being able to handle these distributional issues effectively is an important part of the long-term buy-in to the global economy. It is the international version of the inclusiveness that we encountered before in a domestic setting. The international system is a very long way from having this ability now.

23. Instability in the Global Economy and Lessons from the Crisis

The global economy and financial systems are going through a major crisis that could have turned into a worldwide depression. We knew before the crisis that the global economy and financial system had, with the passage of time, become more and more deeply interconnected. We also knew that the management, regulation, and oversight of the global economy had fallen well behind the growing connectedness.

Furthermore, leading up to the crisis, there were unusual (and counterintuitive) patterns, such as the low savings and high deficits in the United States, and the reverse in a number of developing countries. The ratio of housing prices to rental rates were abnormally high, suggesting a bubble in housing prices.

There were lots of signs of potential trouble. But I think it is fair to say that there wasn't that much concern about it. There was a widespread view that the system was largely self-regulating, with an important proviso that its various parts (domestic economies within nations) were properly managed.

The crisis has important lessons. It has called into question the theory that the financial system is largely self-regulating.

There are at least two major issues embedded in a blizzard of complexity that need to be acknowledged and then addressed. Or, failing that, the consequences of *not* addressing them effectively need to be analyzed carefully by policy makers, investors, and businesses. One consequence is periodic instability in the global financial system. The second is structural imbalances that come from noncooperative equilibria or disequilibria in the policy-setting process by nations. In this chapter, I will talk about periodic systemic risk and instability and address imbalances; I will discuss the challenge of rebalancing in the next.

Periodic Instability

The financial system appears to be capable of becoming periodically unstable. Why that is and what the sources of this instability are are the subjects of intense debate and important ongoing research. During periods of instability, systemic risk rises, assets become highly correlated, debt rises as a contributing factor, normal risk-mitigation strategies such as diversification and insurance (various hedging models) either don't work or work much less well than usual. Drastic intervention is required to prevent indiscriminate destruction of businesses as credit channels close and credit dries up completely.

Absent that kind of dramatic intervention, large-scale crises of the type that we have just experienced can easily turn into extended depressions. When the financial system fails, it brings down the rest of the economy, often referred to as the real economy (or Main Street), by which we mean the nonfinancial portion. In this respect, the financial sector is similar to a small number of others: transportation, telecommunications (including the Internet), and energy. In all cases, a major failure has extensive negative impacts on the rest of the economy.

Because of the external effects of failure, these sectors need to be managed, overseen, and regulated more conservatively. Even if within the sector the risks are perfectly understood and internalized by the participants, the external risks to the economy and the public purse, domestically and globally, are not internalized or factored into the decision making. Conservative regulation is needed to limit the potential for external damage to the economy.

Notwithstanding these "externalities," the prevailing (though not unanimous) view was that the financial sector was largely self-regulating. This statement needs to be qualified. It is recognized that there are informational asymmetries that, left unattended, would negatively impact the performance of financial markets. Companies inevitably know more about their future prospects than the average investor. Occasionally very perceptive analysts can get out ahead of them. If allowed to persist, this built-in asymmetry would create a signaling problem for the high-quality companies. It is not clear that there are enough effective signals embedded in the market, though there are some, such as dividend policy. Absent effective signals, investors have difficulty distinguishing among companies in terms of return and risk, and then they get averaged together in the market. The better-quality lower risks may look elsewhere for capital, perhaps to the private markets, where the informational gaps can be closed. That causes a decline in the risk-return frontier in the public markets. In the extreme case, the market in securities can unravel. In any case, the cost of capital is higher.

This class of problems is sufficiently severe in terms of its impact that it has not been left unattended. It is also well understood. All mature capital markets have disclosure regulations designed to reduce the asymmetry in the information available to companies and investors. Also, there are insider-trading rules that disallow the use of better information by company insiders in trading for profit in a given stock.

There is also some consumer-protection regulation. The theory is that a class of relatively naïve consumers can end up in situations where they do not fully understand the products they are buying or the contracts they are entering into. Regulatory intervention takes two different forms in this case. Some kinds of investments are restricted to investors who are presumed to understand the characteristics of the security or contract. They are off limits to others. Not everyone can buy into a private equity fund. There are balance-sheet requirements. Other kinds of contracts (such as abusive mortgages) are disallowed, or, more recently, should have been disallowed, on the grounds that the risk is too high and that a subset of investors will enter into them without a clear understanding of the contract terms and their implications.

Banks are also regulated, but for a different reasons. They are highly leveraged, and have balance sheets in which the term structure of the liabilities is much shorter than the term structure of the assets. They take deposits (i.e., they borrow money from us) that can be withdrawn at any time and then lend the funds to companies or households in the form of mortgages, college loans, etc. In other words, banks borrow short and lend long. This works as long as depositors have confidence that they can get their money out. When they have that confidence, most of them leave their money in, and the liability side of the bank, which is very short maturity, is stable. However, if the bank gets into trouble or is perceived to be at risk of insolvency, then a few depositors lose confidence and take their money out. In short, a bank's solvency is entirely dependent on confidence.

In a sense, this is the simplest form of contagion. Deposit insurance is designed to slow this contagion down, as well as protect the depositors. But that means that in all banking systems, risk is transferred to the government. While the owners of a bank can lose their money (the equity in the bank), their losses are often a small fraction of the total losses. The remaining losses fall on the depositors, or, if the latter are insured, on the government, and hence the taxpayers. To prevent that from distorting bank behavior in the direction of excessive risk taking, banks are regulated in terms of capital requirements and credit quality. That means they have to have a cushion to fall back on, and there are regulatory limits on them in terms of the kinds of risks they can take in making loans.

Banks are one of the two principal channels for intermediating credit in advanced economies. The other system, now called the "shadow banking system"—a term coined by Paul McCulley of Pimco—circumvents the banks. Loans such as mortgages are originated by banks or other entities, and then packages of these loans are put together and ownership shares in the packages are sold to investors. Generally, ownership shares in these packages are traded on markets. On the way through, a rating agency is supposed to opine on the quality of the loans or other assets in the package. This wise multistep process is called securitization. Because the loans are packaged, the risk of default on any one of them is spread around. Risk is diversified, and in principle the cost of the capital may be lowered.

There is actually nothing wrong with this model of intermediating credit, provided the steps are undertaken competently and investors receive accurate information about the risk characteristics of the products they are buying.

The problem in the period leading up to the crisis was that this portion of the financial system was only lightly or ineffectively regulated. Packages of loans were rated improperly, in part because of incentive problems: the originators and securitizers paid the rating agencies. Another aspect was complexity. The rating agencies didn't understand the products and their risk characteristics. The combination of complexity and adverse incentives turned out to be toxic in the extreme.

Where did the complexity come from? Simple securitized packages of loans were used as the basis to create new derivative securities that divided the original packages up into tranches based on a hierarchy of risk. Tranches vary by exposure to default risk. The top tranche has the least exposure and the bottom the most. Interest rates reflected the risk exposure for each tranche. These tranches were then risk-rated and frequently misrated by the agencies. Then the apparently safer tranches were packaged (in theory, reducing risk further) and then purchased with relatively high levels of leverage, the equity portion then being sold to investors. We ended up with an inverted pyramid of assets and debt.

Buyers of these assets included major global financial institutions and institutional investors like pension funds, endowments, and sovereign wealth funds. They clearly did not understand the risk characteristics of these securities and were attracted by the returns. They also relied on the rating agencies in lieu of doing in-depth research on the securities themselves, and thus that system failed. The result was extensive balance-sheet damage in the crisis among major financial entities, including banks. That caused the sudden tightening of credit and the danger of a credit lockup leading to a depression.

In the course of this evolution, debt in the financial sector and the household sector rose dramatically, and the real underlying risk characteristics of the securities were hidden from view or lost. It is now reasonably well documented that many senior executives and boards had no real idea about the nature of the securities. Complexity reigned, and in-depth risk assessment was replaced by the more general notion that financial innovation had reduced the risks. Rather, it hid them.[1]

The securitization industry was highly profitable. It is surely true that the excesses that one can see with hindsight were caused in part by a process of looking for additional opportunities for securitization. Mortgage and other loan originators were created to generate new loans for the securitization machine. This was undoubtedly much of the motivation behind subprime lending, and it was allowed to occur because of lax or nonexistent regulation.

The effect of this evolution was a rise in leverage and systemic risk in the financial system. And it went largely unnoticed. In parallel, the interconnectedness of the financial sector increased in a way that was very difficult to track, because of the sheer complexity and the lack of data.

The shadow banking system probably moved into what physicists call a critical state. Systems in critical states have distributions or possible outcomes that obey a power law.[2] For our purposes, that simply means that the tails of the distribution are fat, and that extreme events become more likely, especially large negative movements in asset prices.

In short, the shadow banking system was set up for a major disruption. The freezing of credit sent the financial system and the economy into a double downward spiral: with asset prices falling (housing had already started to level off in 2006), household balance sheets were damaged, leading to a sharp decline in consumption and an increase in savings, followed by drops in investment and employment, which further reduced the profit expectations of corporations and fed back into more downward pressure on asset prices. One can think of this as the interaction of the balance sheets and income statements of the economy in a reinforcing downward spiral. In a normal economic downturn, these dynamics are present but the asset declines and the balance sheet damage is comparatively minimal, so that the downward plunge is much less violent. Furthermore, as we are now seeing, the balance-sheet damage will take years to repair (the process is often called deleveraging) and the recovery will be much slower and more difficult.

Self-Regulation

Asset bubbles are often attributed to irrational exuberance, a state of mind among investors in which the prevailing view is that asset prices will only go up. But there was more to this crisis than simple irrational exuberance. The risks embedded in the system shifted dramatically with the complexity of the securities and the rising interconnectedness of balance sheets. Those risks were misread and underestimated. That misinterpretation of risk led to rising debt levels that would have been reasonable had the risks been accurately perceived. The rising debt levels increased the systemic risk and caused the correlations among asset classes to rise. It was a perfect storm.

The prevailing view now is that this was largely a failure of regulation. Regulatory failures surely contributed, but it was more than that. While lax, incomplete, or nonexistent regulation played a part, the failure of investors to take defensive action and, more fundamentally, to see the rising risk stripped the system of its self-regulatory characteristics.

Alan Greenspan and others believed, prior to the crisis, that sophisticated participants in the financial markets normally correctly perceive and monitor risk, even as it moves dynamically, and then take actions to mitigate the risk. The aggregate effect of those actions is to limit the growth of leverage, the rise in asset prices—and, hence, the systemic risk. Clearly this did not happen.

It is highly doubtful that financial stability can be achieved with only external regulation, unless it is so heavy-handed as to impair the main financial functions of allocating capital and spreading risk. A complementary and important component has to be the self-regulatory properties of the system. It is this component that failed most prominently in the buildup to the crisis. Further, the regulatory and self-regulatory components are related. The models, data, and frameworks that investors and regulators use to assess the state of the system are, if not identical, at least substantially related and overlapping. And at present they are incomplete.

Where does that leave us? Postcrisis, much effort and brain power is quite properly going into understanding the dynamics of the evolution of structure and risk. A complementary effort is going into improving regulation of structure and disclosure to enhance the likelihood that risk can be tracked more effectively. One thing that has become clear is that connectedness means that risk cannot be addressed only with an institution-by-institution approach. Risk resides at least in part in the balance-sheet connections; that is, in the system's structure. There is a growing body of evidence that these connections have evolved over time as a result of financial innovation and new risk-spreading products. A major challenge before us is to assess the impact of shifting and growing patterns of interconnectedness on systemic risk and stability.

All of this is a work in progress. In the meantime, the regulatory strategy is going in the direction of increasing regulatory coverage to the shadow banking system, rating agencies, and derivatives markets, and to increase the capital, reserve, and margin requirements so as to limit the buildup of leverage. The idea is that with more effective limits on leverage, even if risk is misestimated, the damage can be somewhat limited.

There is work to do on the academic side, too. It is increasingly clear that the dynamics of the network structure of the financial system and risk are imperfectly understood and not effectively captured in the models we have available. The data are also incomplete. Regulators in the midst of the crisis privately admit that the incompleteness of the information, both domestically and internationally, meant that they were flying at least partially blind.

It is hard to know in advance what the outcome of a renewed research effort in this dimension will look like in a few years. It is possible that complexity will impose itself and we will find that while the forces at work can be understood, the system's complexity defies precise measurement or forecasting. There are physical systems like this: earthquakes and avalanches occur because of known forces, though they are not forecast well and have fat-tailed power law–like distributions. In the case of avalanches, we intervene with explosives to trigger the fat-tailed events in a more predictable way so as to limit the damages. With earthquakes we take defensive action in the form of building codes and emergency-response capability, and then just wait. We adapt to the unpredictability.

Many seem to assume that if we correct the most obvious regulatory failures, we will remove the potential for instability in the financial system. Perhaps this is true. But it does not seem a wise bet to me. For an extended period during which a new system is in operation and is tested, it seems wiser to conclude that the global system will be periodically and somewhat randomly systemically unstable. This will affect the extent of globalization in various dimensions, and it will also affect the behavior of investors, businesses, and policy makers in advanced and developing countries. We will look into some of the dimensions of that shortly. But first I want to look at a second major challenge to growth in the medium term, and perhaps longer.

24. Stimulus in the Crisis and the Need for Cooperative Behavior

In the midst of the crisis, it was fairly clear to knowledgeable leaders, policy makers, and analysts that a major multinational effort at stimulating the various national real economies to prevent a downward overshoot in the economic contraction was needed. Such an effort was correctly viewed as a complement to the interventions by central banks to restore credit and to the interventions by central banks, reserve holders, and the IMF (with initially very limited resources) to stabilize the international capital flows caused by the crisis.

The problem with an international stimulus program is that, in an open global economy, there are leakages. A commitment of resources in one country spills over to others in the form of an increment in demand due to trade. Complicating matters further, countries have varying degrees of capacity for stimulus without jeopardizing their domestic fiscal stability, owing to different initial conditions. Citizens and taxpayers naturally did not like the idea of their resources being spent on reducing the impact of the crisis in other countries. The way to limit these spillovers is to introduce, in parallel, protectionist measures that channel domestic demand toward domestic production.

This is a clear example where the cooperative and noncooperative outcomes differ. The cooperative outcome would have been a coordinated set of stimulus packages sized by capacity combined with a commitment to abstain from protectionist measures. That is clearly not the outcome we got. But it was not a complete failure either. What we got were stimulus packages of varying sizes with particularly large ones in the United States and China, two systemically important countries, combined with some protectionism. In Europe the stimulus packages were more muted, in part because the social security and insurance systems embodied more automatic stimulus, and in part because within Europe the leakages are very large and hence the collective-action challenge is quite difficult. Some countries—particularly small, open economies—are better off with free riding than with stimulus packages with protectionist measures. Many did that and hoped for the best.

The result was neither a fully noncooperative outcome (we did get some significant stimulus) nor a fully cooperative outcome. During a crisis, it is unrealistic to expect a fully cooperative outcome. But the point of this short story is that in the international economy, there are circumstances in which the noncooperative version of the game yields quite distinctly suboptimal outcomes, and sometimes destabilizing disequilibria as well.

25. Rebalancing the Global Economy and Its Consequences for Growth

Let's turn now to the need for rebalancing the global economy, especially on the demand side. Prior to the crisis, people pointed with some frequency to what were then referred to as "global imbalances." U.S. household savings had declined to zero as a result of the run-up in asset prices (including housing). This is an understandable and rational response to increased wealth—spend a small part of the windfall each year. Of course, like everyone else, U.S. consumers mistakenly thought the gains in asset values were permanent. We now know that in some sense they weren't real. But behavior is driven (in real time) by beliefs and not by whether they turn out to have been accurate.

With household savings close to zero, the overall savings in the United States amounted to less than investment. Rising federal deficits (after 2000) as a result of a variety of policies including reduced taxes and the Iraq War contributed to the savings deficit. The government was spending more than it took in, and households were spending all their disposable income. When savings fall short of investment, the difference is made up by foreign capital inflows—think of these inflows as other peoples' savings outside their own country. This showed up as a U.S. trade deficit of growing size.[1] If you consume and invest more than you produce, you have to buy the difference from other countries, which results in a trade deficit: because your output is your income, if you are spending more than your income, you have to "borrow" the difference (also from outside) to finance it. So the trade deficit equals the net capital inflows (which means borrowing from other countries), and, conversely, a trade surplus equals the net capital outflows (or the lending to other countries).[2]

So where did these U.S. net capital inflows (external borrowing) come from? They came from countries running trade surpluses, the Gulf states, oil producers, China, Japan, and much of Asia, and a few other countries like Germany—though much of Germany's surplus was absorbed by deficits in other E.U. countries. The E.U. trade surpluses and deficits are never all that large.

When people looked at this situation, they thought it was peculiar and wondered if it was sustainable. Opinion was divided on the latter question. With hindsight, we know that we should have seen that the U.S. side was not sustainable because it was based on an asset bubble whose existence was largely the result of financial-sector disequilibrium. But that didn't happen, because financial innovation was believed to have reduced risk in the system. The rising asset prices were not, for the most part, seen as a bubble.

The persistence of high consumption and low saving and high asset prices was made possible by the complementary excess savings outside the country in the surplus countries. After all, if a country, disconnected from the global economy, tries in vain to consume more than it produces, it experiences inflationary pressures in the real economy, as people try to bid for the product that is there. And normally the central bank responds to inflationary pressure by raising interest rates, which in turn increases savings, reduces consumption, and reduces investment, and brings things back toward balance. That sequence, meaning the inflation and the central bank's response, did not happen in this case because the posture of the rest of the world was accidentally accommodative.

Analysts now debate the imbalances' contribution to the crisis. Some take the view that the imbalances were the main cause; others argue that the growing instability in the financial system due to various causes (regulatory and other) were the main culprits and the root cause. I tend to agree with the second view, though the imbalances played an enabling part. Since both conditions appear to have contributed to the crisis, I am not sure this is a productive debate. It tends to devolve into debating which of the two evils you would rather have if you had to choose: a major financial disequilibrium or the global savings and investment imbalances.

One version of the imbalances-as-main-cause argument is that the excess savings outside the United States caused interest rates to be low and borrowing to be excessive. This is not right. Europe had higher interest rates by its central bank policy. The Federal Reserve played a major role in leaving interest rates low after the Internet bubble collapse and 9/11, presumably because there was no sign of inflation. The persistent low-interest-rate policy of the Fed was a mistake and did contribute to the excess leverage component of the crisis.

To deal with the imbalances prior to the crisis, starting in 2006, the IMF initiated a quiet process among a group of major countries (a subset of what we now think of as the G20) to address the global imbalances. It produced no tangible results, for understandable reasons. While most thought the global configuration was at least odd and counterintuitive (a conundrum), the participants were happy and prosperous enough not to take overly seriously the argument that there might be an abstract risk. The problem seemed perhaps a little too theoretical. There certainly was no unanimity on the need to take urgent action.

This last is a persistent problem for contrarians, whether they be policy makers, analysts, or investors. Even if one believes, correctly, that the dynamics are unstable, it is hard to prove and next to impossible to be specific about the break points in systems that are in critical states. Geologists have the same problem with earthquakes. But without a certain level of specificity it is hard to know whether or not to heed the cautionary warnings, or, indeed, when to take action. Normally we end up doing what we were doing, waiting until something actually happens.

The Forward-Looking Version of Global Imbalances

Whatever the merits of the precrisis view of imbalances, the forward-looking version of global imbalances is a matter of first-order importance for growth and the performance of the global economy. The crisis caused, among other things, extensive balance sheet damage to U.S. households. As a result, U.S. household savings is rising rapidly as people who thought their assets were sufficient for retirement and their jobs secure find otherwise and adopt a much more conservative posture. This is not a short-run cyclical phenomenon. It will take several years for households to deleverage and restore their net asset positions. Even in the longer run, a return to very low savings rates seems unlikely.

The effect of the altered behavior of the U.S. consumer is a reduction of global aggregate demand of something like $1 trillion. In addition, the likelihood of slower growth in the advanced countries going forward—of, say, 1 percent—introduces an additional ongoing shortfall relative to precrisis growth of about $350 billion.

In a low-growth environment, the rising tide that lifts all boats stops rising. Growth (and employment) becomes closer to a zero-sum game. A country's market share in the global economy is very important in sustaining growth, and the incentive to use protectionist measures to capture share is elevated. Of course the collective result is notably inferior. Second, the growth aspirations in the developing countries cannot all be achieved. That doesn't mean every country will fall short. It seems likely that, in the market-share battle, the stronger, larger countries will prevail and others may experience diminished prospects and growth. Thus far, the postcrisis evidence we have points in that direction. However, the rebound in growth in the major emerging markets is having a surprisingly large spillover benefit within the group, as well as for the poorer developing countries.

The rebalancing issue, then, concerns whether the aggregate demand can be replaced and protectionism largely avoided (or at least not increased above the legacy levels of the crisis) in an orderly way. In principle, the answer is clearly yes. If the surplus countries can reduce their surpluses in ways that sustain their growth, most of the aggregate-demand shortfall can be recouped over time. To accomplish this will require structural change in a number of countries in both the surplus and deficit category, the United States being by far the largest of the latter.

It will also require cooperative behavior. That is to say, there are significant risks in acting unilaterally or getting out ahead. The noncooperative outcome is likely to be a continuing shortfall in aggregate demand, with slower growth globally. The threat of expanded protectionism is higher, too. Growing fiscal imbalances in the U.S. and Europe, with attendant risks to longer-term interest rates and to the orderly adjustment of the dollar and the euro, are present risks.

On page 154 is a picture of the global imbalances looking backward and forward. It comes from the April 2010 *World Economic Outlook* of the IMF.

It is quite clear that China (and Asia more broadly) represents a large and growing part of the surplus side of the imbalances historically and is projected to be an even larger part in the future, absent coordinated

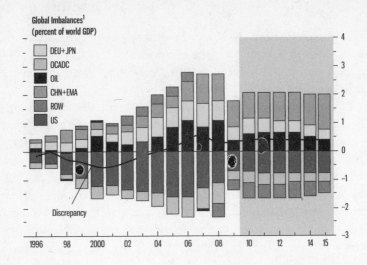

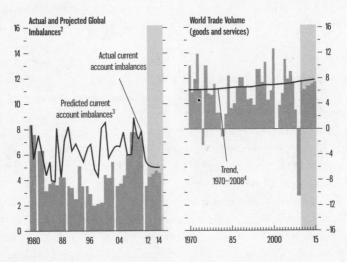

Source: IMF staff estimates, International Monetary Fund, *World Economic Outlook*, April 2010, Figure 1.6.

[1]CHN+EMA: China, Hong Kong SAR, Indonesia, Korea, Malaysia, Philippines, Singapore, Taiwan Province of China, and Thailand; DEU+JPN: Germany and Japan; OCADC: Bulgaria, Croatia, Czech Republic, Estonia, Greece, Hungary, Ireland, Latvia, Lithuania, Poland, Portugal, Romania, Slovak Republic, Slovenia, Spain, Turkey, and United Kingdom; OIL: Oil exporters; ROW: rest of the world; US: United States.

[2]Measured as standard deviation of country-specific current accounts in G20 economies.

[3]Based on a ten-year rolling regression of global current account imbalance on world GDP growth and oil prices.

[4]Average growth rates for individual countries, aggregated using purchasing-power-parity weights; the aggregates shift over time in favor of faster-growing economies, giving the line an upward trend.

corrective action under the G20. On the deficit side (the lower part of the top chart), the United States was a large fraction of the historical total. Its deficits declined in the crisis but continue to be projected to be half the total deficit side in the future. Oil (meaning oil-rich countries) remains substantial surplus countries going forward. Clearly, much will depend on the evolution of energy prices. These surpluses are much less easy to eliminate. In fact, the oil-rich countries should run surpluses and the countervailing deficits should be spread evenly across the remainder of the global economy.

But there is some reason for cautious optimism. Reducing excess savings in the high-surplus countries like China should not adversely affect growth. In fact, done properly, it should accomplish the reverse— that is, help sustain the growth while shifting the drivers of growth toward the domestic economy. Earlier I argued that high levels of savings and investment are a key component of sustained high growth in developing countries. But there is a big difference between high savings to support a program of high investment, on the one hand, and excess savings that go well beyond the investment levels in the economy, on the other. High investment is crucial to growth, and matching high domestic savings is the safest way to finance it. But sometimes savings exceed investment, even when investment is high as a percentage of GDP. Excess savings serve no useful purpose in sustaining growth and development. China is a recent example of this, and is now large enough to be systemically important.

Surpluses and Reserve Accumulation in Developing Countries

Why would a low- or middle-income country end up saving more than it invests? Well, in fact many don't: generally they do the opposite. So it is not inevitable. The deficit countries save below the investment level, run trade deficits, and import capital to make up the difference, a risky strategy in a potentially volatile global financial environment. So excess savings definitely do not occur automatically.

There are a number of factors that combine to produce surpluses in the high-growth developing economies. In many developing countries, social insurance and retirement programs are underdeveloped and people self-insure against illness and other adverse shocks. They tend to save more as a result. It can be thought of as a failure of insurance and risk-spreading mechanisms. In growing economies, investment returns are high, and that attracts savings by the corporate and household sectors.

But there are deeper reasons for the tendency to run surpluses that have to do with growth strategies. The case of China is instructive. China is a high-growth economy and has been since it abandoned central planning and other unfortunate experiments in economic management in 1978, and replaced them with markets and incentives, and then a process of opening up the economy to the rest of the world.

The results have been spectacular: average real growth rates in excess of 9 percent per year for over thirty years; incomes and total output increased by thirteen times. And China appears thus far to be bouncing back from the 2008–09 crisis faster than any other economy, pulling much of Asia along with it.

Because of the favorable dynamics, investment opportunities are numerous and returns are substantial. This investment climate has been supported by a strong underpinning of public-sector investment. A favorable investment environment causes households to save and businesses to invest. Foreigners want to invest, too. China allows and encourages foreign direct investment by companies because of the accompanying knowledge-transfer effect and until recently gave this kind of investment favorable treatment in terms of taxes. Favorable treatment included special export zones with supportive infrastructure and tariff relief on imports of intermediate products that would go back out embodied in exports. Most of these special incentives are being phased out now, as they are now not needed and have begun to produce distortions.

For the most part, China has had controls on other kinds of inbound investment, particular financial investment. And there have been controls on outbound investment and financial flows, too. Purely financial investment has generally been discouraged on the grounds that it is highly mobile and can leave as fast as it arrives, creating potentially destructive volatility in the capital markets. These controls are being relaxed slowly, as the economy (particularly the financial sector) matures and becomes less prone to shocks. The institutional and informational depth of these markets will increase over time, making the system more resilient. But there is a long way to go. This pattern of controls is common in developing countries.

Notwithstanding the capital controls, some inbound financial and real estate investment manages to find its way in.

The combination of high-investment returns, the pattern of controls and leakages, and limits on outbound capital flows causes the net inbound capital flow to be large. Here "net" means the sum of inbound and outbound flows. Those large net inflows combined with the trade surplus puts upward pressure on the exchange rates. That is, outsiders want to buy the yuan (the domestic currency) using dollars, euros, and pounds. The policy makers fear that if allowed to proceed freely, the appreciation of the currency would cause an excessively rapid deterioration in the competitive position of China's export sector in the global economy, with the result that its growth, which has been in part dependent on exports, would slow down.

China therefore moves to prevent the appreciation of the yuan, or at least to limit it. It does this through the central bank, the People's Bank of China (PBC). Authorized investors buy yuan from banks using dollars in order to build plants or buy property. The banks trade those dollars for yuan with the PBC, which then takes the dollars and buys dollar-denominated assets, for the most part U.S. government bonds. The PBC also sells domestic bonds to sop up the money that was added to the system by the foreign inflows—in order to keep inflation under control. Buying dollar-denominated assets like U.S. government bonds has the effect of holding down the value of the yuan relative to the dollar.

The alternative would be to sell the dollars for yuan in the international currency markets. That would cause the dollar to depreciate against the yuan, or, equivalently, the yuan to appreciate. So in buying dollar assets they are neutralizing the upward pressure on their own currency. If the PBC slows down on buying foreign assets, as it started to do in mid-2005, the currency would appreciate, albeit at a measured pace.

The holdings of dollar (and other major-currency) assets are referred to as reserves. By being willing to accumulate reserves, China's central bank can control the pace of appreciation of the currency. And it goes the other way, too. If there were a sudden shift in market sentiment causing people to want to sell the yuan (as in the recent crisis), the PBC could also sell dollar assets and buy yuan, thereby reducing the downward pressure on the yuan. In short, using reserves, they can exercise some control over potential market volatility. One can think of this as a kind of self-insurance against market risk. And by being willing to accumulate reserves, they control the rate of appreciation of their currency and hence one of the key parameters that determine their relative competitive position in the global economy.

Not all countries have this degree of control. You need reserves, and to accumulate them, the sum of the trade surplus and net positive inbound capital flows has to be positive. But generally the high-growth economies (ones that have succeeded in bringing the critical components together in a viable growth strategy) are attractive investment environments and meet these conditions.

Most successful developing countries are broadly similar in that they intervene in the currency markets, hold reserves of varying magnitudes, and have controls on the flows of various different kinds of capital, with the general policy approach being the reduction of those controls as their economies grow and the financial sectors deepen and mature.

This kind of intervention in markets is not popular among economists and policy makers in advanced countries. The practice is referred to as currency manipulation. The shrillness of the criticism ebbs and flows over time, as experience with volatility and crises has suggested that in the early stages of growth, completely open capital accounts are not ideal and somewhat dangerous in terms of destructive volatility.

In the summer of 2008, as the crisis hit, China stopped the appreciation that had begun in 2005. The yuan remained pegged against the dollar until June 2010, when the managed appreciation was resumed. During that period, China was subject to increasing pressure to let the yuan appreciate more freely, on the grounds that it was causing distortions in the global economy and damaging the growth prospects of a wide range of countries—in short, it was engaging in excessively noncooperative behavior.

Management of the exchange rate is often portrayed as a simple zero-sum game in the press. In fact, it is more complex than that. Managing the level of the exchange rate against major advanced-country currencies requires judgment. It has benefits and risks, and it provides lots of opportunities to make mistakes. The benefit is control of both the competitive position of the export sector and of the volatility associated with excessive (and at times short-sighted) exuberance coming from foreign investors with respect to the economy's prospects. As this exuberance waxes and wanes, the exchange rate swings from possible overvaluation to the opposite. It is not an environment conducive to sustained long-term investment in the export sectors, or in the economy generally.

The objectives of investors and of the government representing the interests of the people are often not coincident. Investors focus on return on investment. In a developing economy with a large traditional agricultural sector that is changing structurally and sending people into the modern part of the economy, inclusive growth should be the focus. Governments count new productive employment and rising incomes as benefits. These benefits are not directly part of the private return to investors.

The risks lie in overdoing it; that is, in trying to substitute a low-valued currency for real productivity growth. The appreciation of the currency is an important part of the pressure on the economy to increase productivity and to change structurally. Holding the exchange rate down too much and for too long will cause the structural transformation that drives growth to slow, locking the economy into labor-intensive manufacturing and services. This will ultimately result in holding down wages and incomes and cause growth to stall.

To sustain high growth with rising incomes, the developing economy has to exit from the early-stage labor-intensive industries and replace them with new sectors that are more capital, human-capital, and knowledge intensive. That transition is "forced" by the rising incomes. But if the exchange rate is used to undermine that pressure, the export sectors will not change, and the domestic market will not grow at an appropriate rate.[3]

The best (though imprecise) test of whether or not an economy is on the growth track is to determine if productivity is continuing to rise and whether the structure is changing relatively rapidly or not. Productivity in a developing economy does not grow indefinitely by doing the same things but by deepening the capital and knowledge underpinnings and using them to move to different kinds of economic activity. We have seen this before. Sustained growth requires structural change.

The Excess-Savings Issue

Do the growth strategies just described imply that a set of high-growth developing countries will save more than they invest, thereby running trade surpluses? An undervalued currency certainly pushes it in that direction by making exports cheaper and imports more expensive than they would be at a higher exchange rate.

Despite all the attention focused on it, however, the exchange rate is just one factor. There are a host of others that determine the level of savings in relation to investment. So the answer is no, excess savings are not a mandatory side effect of the other parts of a high-growth strategy.

Reserves can be accumulated when domestic savings and investment are in balance and the trade surplus is small. The reason is that net private capital inflows are often positive in growing developing economies. Reversing those flows, in whole or in part, will result in reserve accumulation, even without a trade surplus.

26. The Excess-Savings Challenge in China

Through most of the long period of growth starting in 1978, China's balance between savings and investment was relatively even. Sometimes there were modest surpluses or deficits, on the order of 3 percent or less of GDP. But around the year 2005, the pattern shifted. Investment remained high, and even accelerated upward, but savings followed and surpassed it. By 2007, the last full year prior to the crisis, China was investing at 45 percent of GDP and saving at about 55 percent, the difference being a current account surplus of 10 percent of GDP, with an equivalent amount of investment, roughly $420 billion, outside the country. Reserve growth was even higher because high net private capital inflows continued even as the trade surplus expanded.

The rapid increase in the trade surplus came as an unwelcome surprise to Chinese leaders and policy makers. It was not anticipated. Nor

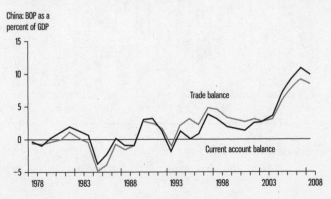

was it a good thing. Western countries and policy gurus described this as mercantilism in its post–British Empire second incarnation.[1] China received routine lectures on the importance of accelerating the appreciation of its currency.

The surpluses were not strategically important. Reserves were already substantial as a result of prior net large inbound private-capital flows. They did nothing for growth, which was already high and due for a transition to greater reliance on the domestic market. This transition was made more urgent by the crisis, the temporary collapse of trade, and the prospect of slower growth in their major advanced-country export markets. The threat of protectionism added to the urgency.

The more advanced parts of China's economy are well into the middle-income transition. The structure of the supply side of the economy is shifting away from the labor-intensive sectors, which are being replaced by higher-valued-added industries and by services. The human-capital and knowledge intensity of the economy is rising. But the demand side of this transition is extremely important, and this is where the economy needs an additional structural shift. The graph below shows the pattern of rising savings.

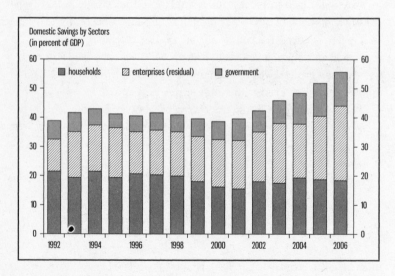

The rapid increase in saving as a percentage of GDP, since roughly the year 2000, is the result of a dramatic increase in savings in the corporate sector, combined with a contribution from rising public-sector invest-ment. Enterprises in the corporate sector capture about 25 percent or more of total income and they invest pretty much all of it. A substantial part of the corporate sector is owned in whole or in part by the government. In virtually all of the formerly state-owned-enterprise sector, govern-ment ownership has declined as stock is allocated to employees or sold in public offerings. But in no case that I am aware of has the government-ownership share fallen below the 50 percent threshold. The income gen-erated in the state-owned subsector never passes through the household sector or the government sector in the form of dividends. It is reinvested on autopilot. Corporate investment of retained earnings turns automat-ically into savings by the corporate sector.

Underlying this trend is something even more important. As na-tional income has risen, the fraction of total income and output going to households in the form of disposable income is low (by comparison with virtually any other country, advanced or developing) and is falling. Since the mid-nineties, disposable income has fallen from around 70 per-cent of GDP to under 60 percent. In most countries, household income is higher and household savings lower.

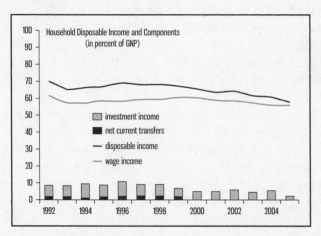

The household savings rate is high, about 30 percent of disposable income, which translates into 18 percent of GDP, or about one-third of total savings. This puts consumption at around 42 percent of national income, well below the norm in advanced and developing countries. It is not large enough to drive growth and guide the structural shift of the economy away from an export- and investment-led model to one more focused on the rising consumer sector.

Much of the discussion of reducing excess savings focuses on social insurance and pensions and reducing the precautionary motives for savings—that is, reducing the 30 percent figure. This is not misguided, but it is only part of the story. The principal complementary change has to be to expand the fraction of national income going to the household sector.

The low fraction of GDP going to disposable household income in China would be less of a concern if taxes were high and the revenues were deployed to provide a vast array of services—basic pensions, health care, education, and continuing education. But that is not the case. The old social-insurance and safety nets that were provided by the state-owned enterprises (SOEs) before the reforms have been dismantled and largely not replaced.

This strongly suggests that there are two things that need to be done in combination. One is to get more income into the hands of the households for consumption, to expand the power of the domestic market to drive growth. The second is to use the income from the SOEs to expand the services provided to households. This will lower the household savings rate, although by how much we do not know. But it will certainly reduce the incentives for self-insurance in the household sector, and if done properly will also help alleviate the problem of growing income inequality and unrest related to it.

The immediate objective should be to reduce savings by about 10 percent of GDP to get it back into line with investment. That will reduce the trade surplus. To accomplish this it is necessary to redirect income from the corporate sector to households by dividing out corporate income to the major owner (the government) and then using that income to reduce taxes and increases social services and insurance. These are major changes and entail a diminished role of government in the economy over time. There will be resistance.

These are the essential structural changes on the demand side of the economy to drive growth from the household sector of the domestic economy and to have the structure of the economy be guided by a larger and richer domestic consumption sector. Over time, this shifting pattern will have the effect of lowering the surplus and crucially maintaining the growth momentum. If China tries to eliminate the surplus with the exchange rate alone, it probably won't work, because with the current structure, excess savings is deeply embedded. The main effect of driving down the surplus with the single policy instrument of the exchange rate would be to slow growth—something not in the interests of the country or the global economy.

By and large, Chinese policy makers understand these parallel structural changes that are needed to shift the growth model and sustain growth, though there is internal debate about timing. Externally, the level of understanding of the structural shifts needed to sustain growth while reducing the trade surplus is much lower. China is regularly labeled a currency manipulator and urged to appreciate its currency. If this is done by itself, without the complementary structural changes, the main effect would be lower growth, an outcome that is, again, in no one's interest.

The Doha round of negotiations began in 2001 as the first major round of trade agreements under the WTO, the successor to the GATT. The agenda was very ambitious, as we saw in Part I in talking about the origins of the global economy. This round was also supposed to be focused on liberalization, for the benefit of developing countries. It has yet to be completed and there is some question about its future. Some policy makers and commentators have recommended dropping it and starting over. Developing countries, for the most part, want to see it successfully concluded. The G20 has highlighted its commitment to global openness, but that has not yet turned into an effective process to get things going again. It remains to be seen whether it will.

The Doha round and the current system face a couple of key issues. First, this unfinished round was ambitious and complex in scope. That may have increased the difficulty of reaching a final agreement. Some knowledgeable analysts have suggested that the Doha round be narrowed down so that it can be passed and we can move on. Narrowing the focus, however, is controversial. Such a step could very well be viewed as a failure of the WTO system and of the original intent at the start of the round.

Second, the WTO has many members. In principle they are all supposed to agree in order to conclude an agreement. By contrast, the GATT was less democratic. Agreements were largely worked out among OECD countries, with developing countries going along because they had little alternative. By and large, the direction of movement over successive rounds was beneficial to developing countries. Undoubtedly there were issues of importance to them that were left unaddressed. But this problem remains with the new structure. With so many countries with diverse conditions and interests having a voice, this system may be too cumbersome to successfully finalize results.

The United States has expressed an inclination to reopen the round to revisit issues that were settled earlier. The developing-country view is that this is risky and unwise. The American president does not now have fast-track authority. The round could easily get bogged down in renegotiating the old issues rather than on focusing on the few remaining ones. The concern, especially in the developing world, is not just that the Doha round will go into limbo, but that the effectiveness and authority of the WTO will be damaged to the point that it loses its effectiveness as the guardian of global openness.

The GATT and the WTO are built on the principle that the global trading system needs to be a rules-based system. The rules are meant to be clear and applicable to all. The dispute-resolution mechanisms are elaborate and designed to deliver on this principle.

In general this is the right framework. It does, however, create tensions in two dimensions. One has to do with volatility and shocks. There is a legitimate desire on the part of developing countries to introduce some flexibility into the system to be used under conditions of extreme stress. The commodity price spike in 2007 and 2008 would be a good example. Many countries took emergency measures, including price and export controls, to protect the poorer members of their countries. Similarly, if foreign competition threatens to dramatically increase unemployment in some large sector, the affected country may want to cushion the blow by having a transition period in which exposure to external competition is introduced only gradually.

In principle, this kind of flexibility can be built into a rules-based system. In practice, negotiating the circumscribed areas of flexibility and discretion while containing the potential for abuse is much more complicated. More generally, there are asymmetries across countries in their ability to comply with rules. Enforcing intellectual property rights, for example, a priority for the developed countries (for obvious reasons), is difficult in some developing countries that may lack the legal and enforcement infrastructure.

This tension between fixed and clearly understood rules and systems, on the one hand, and flexibility in responding to changing conditions and divergent stages of development, on the other, is perfectly evident in the international trading system. Addressing these competing objectives in a balanced way remains a challenge for the WTO.

The WTO does not mainly address issues relating to capital and financial flows and capital-account management; but it or another organization could in the future. In the capital-account area, the variations across countries are significant. Capital controls, exchange-rate management, and convertibility all vary across countries and according to the state of development of their economies and financial systems. These policies are adapted to local conditions but have external effects. For the major emerging countries, the era when the external effects were small enough to safely ignore has come to an end. The challenge of developing a new rules-based system that accommodates divergent conditions and stages of development, but which safeguards global stability and ensures equitable outcomes, is entirely before us. It is one of the main design challenges facing us if a reasonably cooperative process of globalization is to be maintained.

28. Legacies of the Crisis: Slow Growth and Sovereign-Debt Issues in Advanced Countries

The run-up to the economic crisis in the United States was characterized by excessive leverage in financial institutions and in the household sector, inflating an asset bubble that eventually collapsed and left balance sheets damaged to varying degrees. The aftermath involves resetting asset values, deleveraging, and rehabilitating balance sheets—resulting in today's higher savings rate, a significant shortfall in domestic demand, and a sharp uptick in unemployment.

So the most immediate question the United States now faces is whether continued fiscal and monetary stimulus can, as some believe, help to right the economy. To be sure, at the height of the crisis, the combined effect of fiscal stimulus and massive monetary easing went a long way toward preventing a credit freeze and limiting the downward spiral in asset prices and real economic activity. But that period is over.

The reason is simple: the precrisis period of consuming capital gains that turned out to be at least partly ephemeral led, inevitably, to a postcrisis period of inhibited spending, diminished demand, and higher unemployment. Countercyclical policy can moderate these negative effects, but it cannot undo the damage or accelerate the recovery beyond fairly strict limits.

As a result, the benefits associated with deficit-financed boosts to household income are now being diminished by the natural propensity to save and rebuild net worth. On the business side, investment and employment follow demand once the inventory cycle has run its course. Until demand returns, business will remain in a cost-cutting mode.

The bottom line is that deficit spending is now fighting a losing battle with an economy that is deleveraging and restructuring its balance sheets, its exports, and its microeconomic composition—in short, its future growth potential. That restructuring will occur, with or without deficit spending. So policy needs to acknowledge the fact that there are limits to how fast this restructuring can be accomplished.

Attempting to exceed these speed limits not only risks damaging the fiscal balance and the dollar's stability and resilience, but also may leave the economy and government finances highly vulnerable to future shocks that outweigh the quite modest short-term benefits of accelerated investment and employment. Demand will revive, but only slowly.

True, asset prices have recovered enough to help balance sheets, but probably not enough to help consumption. The impact on consumption will largely have to wait until balance sheets, for both households and businesses, are more fully repaired.

Higher foreign demand from today's trade-surplus countries (China, Germany, and Japan, among others) could help restore some of the missing demand. But that involves structural change in those economies as well, and thus will take time. It will also requires a complex coordinated set of moves negotiated under the auspices of the G20. It is too soon to tell whether that will bear fruit, but there are reasons to be skeptical at this stage.

Moreover, responding to expanded foreign demand will require structural changes in the U.S. economy, which will also take time. This is not to say that rebalancing global demand is unimportant. Quite the contrary. But achieving that goal has more to do with restoring the underpinnings of global growth over a period of three to five years than it does with a short-term restoration of balance and employment in the advanced economies, in particular the United States.

Today, the best way to use deficits and government debt is to focus on two things:

- The first is addressing distributional issues, particularly the unemployed, both actual and potential. In an extended balance-sheet recession of this type, unemployment benefits need to be substantial and prolonged. The argument that this would discourage the unemployed from seeking work has merit in normal times, but not now. Today's unemployment, after all, is structural, rather than the result of perverse incentives. Benefits should be expanded and extended. When structural barriers to employment have diminished, unemployment benefits can revert to their old norms. Doing this would not only reduce the unequal burden now being carried by the unemployed; it would also help to sustain consumption, and perhaps reduce some precautionary savings among those who fear losing their jobs in the future.

- The second consists of a set of public-sector investments and reforms that are needed to support longer-term growth. These would include infrastructure, education, and programs designed to create incentives to reinvigorate the export sector and to make the United States more competitive in the tradable portion of the global economy.

Monetary policy is a more complex and difficult balancing act. An aggressive policy of raising interest rates would likely reduce asset prices (or at least slow the rate of appreciation), increase adjustable-rate debt-service burdens, and trigger additional balance-sheet distress and disorderly deleveraging, such as foreclosures. All of this would slow the recovery, perhaps even causing it to stall.

But there are consequences to abjuring this approach as well. Low-cost credit is unlikely to have a significant impact on consumption in the short run, but it can produce asset inflation and misallocations in the longer run. Much of the rest of the world would prefer a stronger dollar, fewer capital inflows with a carry-trade flavor, and less need to manage their own currencies' appreciation to avoid adverse consequences for their economies' competitiveness. In short, the sort of monetary policy now being practiced for fragile advanced economies, like that of the United States, will cause distortions in the global economy that require policy responses in many other countries.

From a political point of view, the crisis has been portrayed as a failure of financial regulation, with irresponsible lending fueling a rapid rise in systemic risk. That leaves the rest of the real economy populated with people who feel like victims—albeit victims who, prior to the crisis, bought a lot of houses, vacations, TVs, and cars.

Unfortunately, this perception pushes the politics of the policy response in the direction of too much remedial action, even when the marginal returns are low. What we most need now is support for the unemployed, stable government finances with a clearly communicated deficit-reduction plan, some truth-telling about medium-term growth prospects, and an orderly healing process in which balance sheets are restored mostly without government intervention.

The counterargument to this approach holds that the recovery is clearly difficult and fragile. An early withdrawal of fiscal support could produce a return to the downward spiral we experienced in the crisis itself. The short version of this is deflation. The simple prescription is spend now and save later. This challenge is sometimes put in terms of escape velocity, by analogy with rockets escaping the gravitational pull of the earth. The idea is that the economic equivalent of gravity pulling the economy down is still strong enough to overcome the natural forces that generate growth in the private sector. In this view, the likely outcome of a withdrawal of support would be a recurrence of the downward spiral.

This disagreement comes, in part, from a different set of judgments about timing. Presumably all agree that there comes a time when one has to let the patient heal more or less on his own, recognizing that the healing process could take some time, and that the patient won't be running marathons any time soon.

Strong and varying views are held on this issue of the timing of the withdrawal of fiscal stimulus, and there seems to be no straightforward way to settle the issue. Some who advocate more immediate fiscal rebalancing admit that there is some risk of deflation but argue that the risk of a loss of confidence in government debt is more dire.

Europe has recently experienced a crisis in the eurozone and Greece managed to dig itself into a deep fiscal hole. Restoring fiscal balance could reduce growth so much as to be self-defeating. Thus the hole may be deep enough that there is no way out of it without some form of partial default on the debt. Other countries (Spain, Ireland, Portugal) have suffered fiscal damage as a result of the crisis and are viewed as higher risk.

Why are the fiscal problems in a few countries a problem of the eurozone as a whole? First, markets bet against Greece and some of the other peripheral countries. Investors started exiting, selling the bonds carrying heightened risk. Then external investors holding euro-denominated assets (not just periphery bonds) noticed the decline in the euro and began to exit too, producing a broader sell-off of euro assets and causing depreciation of the euro. The latter is not necessarily a bad thing, from a growth standpoint. Industrial companies that export or face import competition are quietly celebrating.

The banks in Europe are holding substantial amounts of periphery sovereign debt. Risk to the latter creates risks to bank balance sheets, and that, as we know from the crisis, causes many problems in the area of credit availability and cost. This risk is serious enough that the European Central Bank reversed itself and broke its own rules when it started buying periphery sovereign debt from the banks in June 2010.

The longer-term issue for Europe is whether fiscal discipline, a crucial underpinning of a major currency, will be restored and maintained. That is the reason the problem is not just in the periphery. Europe is decentralized fiscally but until recently was relatively homogenous with respect to perceived sovereign debt risk. The fiscal-discipline mechanism that went along with the creation of the common currency—the Maastricht rules—has failed. It was too rigid. It needs to be replaced by rules that are flexible enough to allow for a countercyclical response to shocks—and these rules must be enforced. One way or another, Europe will have to learn to live with a higher degree of fiscal centralization if it is to maintain stability in the eurozone.

In the meantime, the response across countries in the eurozone has been an increased focus on fiscal balance. That plus the sovereign debt risk is slowing growth in most of Europe. Germany is a notable exception, because it had restructured its economy for competitiveness earlier in the decade. The slower growth is spilling over to other advanced countries and increasing the headwinds for developing economies, too.

29. Periodic Systemic Risk and Investment Behavior

This chapter is devoted to investment behavior. It will, thus, be a little more specialized, and perhaps more technical, than the rest of this book. Readers whose interests do not lie primarily in the lessons of the crisis for investment behavior may want to skip ahead to Part IV. I include this chapter because the lessons learned and the adjustments made in investment strategy and behavior could have a strong influence on the self-regulatory properties of the system—along with, of course, a new set of regulations for the financial system.

Most market participants were caught off guard by the unanticipated system risk. Pension funds, university and foundation endowments, and others experienced declines in their assets of 20 to 25 percent, some larger. With a 25 percent decline, you need a return of 33 percent to recover. It takes perhaps three years to get back to where you started. Think of it as taking a four-year vacation with zero returns on investment. Budgets are being cut across a broad array of institutions, with all kinds of side effects, including a further drag on growth.

Learning from this experience will affect investment behavior and the performance of the system, as the latter is determined in large part by the combined effect of the investment behavior of millions of participants. Reviews of investment strategy are ubiquitous, though the long-run effects are uncertain.

Investors have a renewed or heightened sense that risk is dynamic and far from stationary as the conventional framework held. My main aim here is to raise some investment-strategy issues that are brought to the forefront by focusing on two things: the presence and dynamics of systemic risk, and the presence of illiquid assets in the portfolios of many large investors. Failure to attend to these two aspects of investment strategy probably contributed to greater balance-sheet distress than was necessary.

Investors have been hit hard by the current crisis. From peak to trough in the present crisis, global equity values declined by 50 percent— that is, $25 trillion. Regardless of whether or not one views the peak with hindsight as inflated, this is an enormous loss of wealth. Since the bottom in March of 2009, there has been a large rebound almost everywhere in advanced and developing countries. The advanced-country markets appeared to be valuing assets on the basis of quite a sharp recovery. Many observers, including this writer, view the valuations as excessive. Government support, both financial and fiscal, is still in place; unemployment is very high; deleveraging and household balance-sheet restoration is far from complete; and important sectors in small and medium-size business lack access to credit. The federal income statement and balance sheet is stretched, and thus far there is no detailed plan for restoring balance over the next few years. Housing prices have stabilized some, but distress remains. This suggests that the recovery will be protracted and difficult and that postrecovery growth might very well not match precrisis levels.

Much of the postcrisis analysis and commentary is focused, as it should be, on regulatory reform that leads to greater stability and a lower probability of periodic shocks of this type. But that is not the whole story. The crisis was not just a regulatory failure. It was also a failure of self-regulation. What is self-regulation? It is the presumed ability of the participants in the markets to detect shifting patterns of risk and to react defensively on a sufficient scale so as to reduce the magnitude of leverage and the asset bubble. If self-regulation had happened, it would have reduced the height of the bubble, the amount of leverage, and the violence of the downward spiral.

This self-regulatory defense mechanism failed quite completely in the current crisis, a signal that the models that we use to assess risk are incomplete and not sufficiently dynamic.

Much in the future will depend on investor behavior and on reassessments of risk. We are in the early stages of that reassessment now. Lessons are being learned and investment strategies revised. The effects on investment behavior and global capital markets are likely to be substantial.

The core of this learning process has to be the rethinking of models of risk. It seems to me that the central lesson is that risk is not static. It evolves in a way that is not yet completely understood. Static risk models are thus not so much wrong as incomplete.

The possibility that risk in the system as a whole can rise in a way that is difficult to detect is important. When it happens, it causes the "normal" correlations of returns among asset classes to shift rapidly upward, even as asset values rise (usually to unsustainable levels) and then fall (sometimes very suddenly). That shift, which is normally accompanied by rising levels of debt, causes the diversification and insurance models and risk mitigation strategies to malfunction.

A subset of large investors, including universities, foundations, and pension funds, has income or payout requirements. So do people who are nearing retirement. The crisis highlights the question of how much volatility in income is tolerable or desirable. The rules governing payouts may need to be adjusted in light of the crisis experience and the possibility that short- and medium-run returns are misleading signals about long-run returns owing to rising systemic risk.

In this and other areas of decision making in complex environments, choices are strongly influenced by implicit models that we carry around with us without knowing it. A model in this context is just a set of assumptions that we use to translate choices into predicted outcomes. These models have complex origins: typically they are learned initially from others and then adapted in response to experience. Debates and disagreements about strategy and policy choices often have their origins in differing assumptions about the underlying reality, while the model differences remain unstated. The meaningfulness of the debate and the quality of choices can be materially improved by taking time to be explicit about the underlying assumptions and models.[1]

Non-Stationary Components of Overall Risk

Experience and a growing body of evidence and research indicate that risk may have two distinct parts: a nonsystemic and stationary component, and a systemic and nonstationary one.[2] On the systemic side, the intertemporal dimensions are important. Major systemic disruptions do not occur every year. Rather, instability builds up and then the system is shocked and resets, the exact timing being still quite unpredictable.[3] As a result, wrestling with systemic risk requires a reasonably long time frame, longer than that associated with the stationary risks, which generally get the lion's share of attention.

In Table 1, below, I take a ten-year period and assume that there are nine years of normal average returns at various rates followed by a "bad year" caused by the systemic risk component. On the left side are the average returns in the nine normal years. The top is the percentage decline in the year of the shock, running from 0 percent to 25 percent. The table shows the average returns for the ten-year period with the shock factored in.

Table 1			Percentage Shock				
		0	5	10	15	20	25
	6	6	4.84	4.28	3.69	3.06	2.40
	8	8	6.62	6.05	5.44	4.81	4.13
	10	10	8.40	7.81	7.20	6.55	5.87
Normal Return	12	12	10.17	9.58	8.95	8.29	7.60
	14	14	11.94	11.34	10.70	10.03	9.33
	16	16	13.71	13.09	12.45	11.77	11.05
	18	18	15.47	14.85	14.19	13.50	12.77
	20	20	17.23	16.60	15.93	15.23	14.49

Table 2 (on page 178) contains essentially the same information, but with some alterations. It shows, for each combination of normal return and shock, the amount by which the average annual return over the ten years is reduced by the shock. For example, with a 16 percent annual return in normal times, a large shock of 20 percent has the effect of reducing the average returns over the ten years by 4.23 percent.

Insofar as these tables reflect the kind of environment we live in, they have a number of implications. Long-run investors should probably think of their returns as more like those depicted in Table 1 rather than the unadjusted normal returns. An endowment might consider basing its payout decisions on long-run average returns (more like Table 1, above) than a simple trailing weighted average of past returns or ending asset values, the normal practice now.[4] Of course, there are competitive and other

Table 2				Percentage Shock			
		0	5	10	15	20	25
	6	6	1.16	1.72	2.31	2.94	3.60
	8	8	1.38	1.95	2.56	3.19	3.87
	10	10	1.60	2.19	2.80	3.45	4.13
Normal Return	12	12	1.83	2.42	3.05	3.71	4.40
	14	14	2.06	2.66	3.30	3.97	4.67
	16	16	2.29	2.91	3.55	4.23	4.95
	18	18	2.53	3.15	3.81	4.50	5.23
	20	20	2.77	3.40	4.07	4.77	5.51

consequences of adopting this more conservative approach, and they will vary across institutions. The point here is not to suggest that there is one right answer, but rather that thinking about the longer time-horizon dimensions of risk is a material consideration in investment strategy, as well as in spending rates and decisions.

A different but related way to think about this is as follows: if your return in normal times is 7 percent and you experience a 30 percent negative shock, you will need a total return of almost 43 percent to get back to where you were before the shock, and at preshock annual returns that will take over five years. That is equivalent to thinking of the "real" returns being those in Table 1. You just get there later.

This is not necessarily an argument against the high-return strategies. Investors may very well take the position that the strategies that generate the higher normal and postshock average returns are worth it. (I will say more about this presently.) But the high-return choice should be accompanied by a thoughtful companion decision about the need for, and the pattern of, payouts and the use of the returns. You have to be able to withstand the volatility.

It is also an argument for being cautious about the use of leverage in investing. That includes the leverage implicit in the investments that are being held in corporations, mutual funds, and private equity investments. Leverage, as we have seen, compounds distress when systemic disruptions strike. Further debt is unavailable, or only at very high cost, when it is needed most during these periods, leading to further loss in asset value via forced distress selling.

There will be investors (a minority, I suspect) who do not have payout or income requirements and can focus almost exclusively on the long-run returns. For these investors, insurance options that smooth returns, but at some cost, may be of less interest. Even then, the issues having to do with liquidity and flexibility (discussed below) are relevant in that they impact long-run potential returns.

One can think of all this as an inherent tendency toward mean reversion. There are long-run returns associated with various investment strategies and capabilities. The short- and medium-term returns can deviate considerably, and for extended periods, from the expected long-run returns. Put another way, when returns seem abnormally high for an extended period, they probably are, and something is likely to bring the returns down, even if we don't know in advance what it will be.

This observation is particularly relevant for large investors who cannot totally segregate themselves from the macroeconomic fundamentals without abandoning a reasonable pattern of diversification. Traders can do better than that. The trading superstructure is partly about market-making, and deepening, and value creation. But a lot of it is a zero-sum game in which some win and some lose. High returns in that part of the system do not therefore generalize or add up to the potential for high returns in the whole economic and financial system.

Successful value investors may enjoy some degree of protection by virtue of an unwillingness to invest in what they consider to be overvalued assets (absolutely overvalued rather than relatively). They are, in effect, shifting their portfolios away from "overvalued" assets as they become more numerous in the run-up to a crisis. Nevertheless, they are not invulnerable to systemic risk. Fair valuations and undervaluations are not exempt from the downward pressures of a crisis, or from the resetting of asset values after a buildup of systemic risk.

Responding to Periodic Systemic Risk

If one accepts that periodic bouts of systemic risk are likely to be a feature of our future as well as our past, what can be done to mitigate the impact of the shocks that occur? First, if an investor thinks that he is able to detect a pattern of rising systemic risk, then that investor can take action in the form of portfolio adjustments and/or the addition of insurance-type holdings (tail-risk insurance) that have the effect of mitigating the shock.[5]

Done successfully, this will have a significant effect on long-run returns. Of course the insurance side is dependent on the counterparties not failing—not necessarily a safe bet in the event of a large shock, unless one can expect government support, in the case of extreme distress.

There is a wide variety of views on this subject. Some say bubbles are undetectable before the fact. Others argue that all relevant information is priced in—and detectable—at any point in time. Still others disagree and make their reputations and returns in part on anticipating trouble in the form of instability or lack of sustainability.

My view is that while the current theory of financial market dynamics and the evolution of its risk profile are far from complete, there are useful indices, and there are investors and analysts who pay particular attention to systemic risk. In the crisis we have just been experiencing, the rising aggregate-debt-to-GDP ratio, the rising ratio of real estate prices to rental rates, and the abnormally low risk spreads, though not definitive, might have nudged investors into a more cautious posture. It therefore seems to me that investment and portfolio strategy should include a careful monitoring and evaluation of these external inputs. (Think of them as assessments and warnings from those with a track record of focusing on the stability of the macroenvironment.) Action can be taken when the weight of the arguments is persuasive, if not definitive.

Depending on the liquidity properties of a portfolio, defensive action in the form of portfolio adjustment may be more or less restricted. As to tail insurance, the costs tend to rise as the evidence of imbalance rises. Early anticipation, to the extent that it is possible, has potentially great value.

Another possibly complementary approach is the purchase of insurance as a routine matter and not conditional on the correct or incorrect anticipation of rising systemic risk. Table 2, above, would give some idea of the maximum amount one should be prepared to pay in terms of forgone annualized returns.

A sensible approach could be to insure against intermediate-level shocks. That would also mitigate the impact of larger shocks, and, depending on the annualized cost, could increase the net annualized return in the upper half of the shock range. Of course, it would also lower the annual average return in the lower half of the shock range, too.

Finally, insurance, because it has annual costs, has the added feature of lowering the differential between annual and long-run average returns and takes some of the pressure off the spending-rule side of the equation for those institutions for which it is relevant and at times internally politically challenging.[6]

Regulatory Reform

A major focus of postcrisis regulatory reform has to do with detecting and limiting systemic risk. Since we are in mid-process, it is difficult to say how it will come out. One could take the position that this will eventually solve the problem of periodic rising systemic risk, and that we will return to the more comfortable world of relatively stationary risk without the periodic imbalances.

In my view this is not a good bet, for a variety of reasons. The historical evidence suggests that the problem is persistent and resistant to previous attempts at management. Financial innovation will proceed along with regulatory arbitrage. The dynamic sources of systemic risk probably lie, in part, in the evolving network structure of financial markets. These are subjects of intense interest and active research. But it is unlikely that dramatically enhanced understanding will occur overnight and then be reflected in effective regulatory systems. Finally, the international contributors to systemic risk, such as global imbalances, are increasingly material, and we have only limited if any demonstrated capacity for dealing with them.

Individual investor behavior will continue to create systemic risk. The simple truth is that individual investors chase returns and have varying but often limited capacities for assessing risk, particularly periodic systemic risk. That seems unlikely to change. Of course, they often invest through agents who are sometimes more knowledgeable. But that doesn't necessarily solve the problem. People have a choice of agents, and those who are either hedging or taking a conservative posture are likely to have lower average returns in normal times. They will experience an outflow of assets under management. I remember an experienced asset manager telling me, before the crisis struck in full force, that if you are managing other people's money, you can be a contrarian for two quarters, and then the funds start to flow out. It is a slightly dramatic overstatement, but the idea is right.[7]

Asset markets are driven to some extent by individual investors. At the height of the Internet (or high-tech) bubble, many of the stocks were dominantly held by individual day traders whose level of understanding of the business models of the companies whose assets they held could be charitably described as limited.

In Italy, where I live part of the time, nominal returns on bonds were high prior to the arrival of the euro, because inflation was relatively high. Italy periodically devalued to remain internationally competitive, and as a growth strategy it worked quite well. It did take away some of the pressure for structural change in the economy, and the price for that is now being paid. Individual investors liked the high nominal returns and got used to them. The run-up to the euro forced inflation down, resulting in nominal returns. So financial institutions, mainly banks responding to investor desires, went looking for higher-return fixed-income assets. And they found them, in Argentina and in a few companies like Cirio and Parmalat, both of which were indicted for fraud and resulted in spectacular bankruptcies. These are examples of chasing yield or return while paying insufficient attention to risk.

In short, it is possible that non-stationary systemic risk will become a feature of the past. But that's not a sure thing at this stage. Even if it happens, in order to be certain that it has, we will need an extensive period of stability in order for confidence to rise.

Liquidity and Risk

The present crisis has caused distress across a wide range of institutions with respect to the cash-flow aspects of liquidity management. For relatively illiquid portfolios, an unanticipated shift in the parameters of the cash-flow models (reduced distributions, increased capital calls, and collateral or margin calls on various instruments) created an extreme lack of liquidity. The effects were multiple. Distressed sales of assets were required, exacerbating the negative returns. Borrowing was sometimes possible and needed, but borrowing changes the leverage and hence the risk profile of the overall portfolio. Further, with illiquid assets, and large shifts in asset prices, portfolios can become unbalanced with respect to asset-class targets and are not rebalanced easily in the short run.

In these dimensions, the lessons of the crisis have not been missed, in part because the distress was so widespread. The focus, I think it is fair to say, has been appropriately on the cash-flow challenges that come from a combination of large percentage allocations to illiquid assets and large systemic shocks.

There are two other aspects of liquidity management that deserve attention. One is that illiquid investments place limits on the investor's ability to respond to early warnings of a shift in systemic risk of the type discussed above. It does so by limiting the ability to adjust the portfolio. Presumably this lack of adjustability is what is priced into the differential returns relative to liquid investments with similar underlying properties. Whether this pricing adequately reflects the cost of inflexibility in the presence of systemic instability is an open question. But it seems reasonable to guess that illiquidity premia are set to rise at least for a period of time.

Even with an illiquid portfolio, there is still the tail-insurance option. Careful analysis of the relative costs of these two possible responses to rising instability (tail insurance versus asset allocation adjustment) should be an important input to the basic liquidity choice for the portfolio. It may vary across institutions, as well as by size and sophistication, such that there is not necessarily one right answer.

The second important strategic issue is that liquid portfolios create investment opportunities in times of widespread distress. These result from distressed prices or downward overshoots in asset values, combined with the capacity to invest while others cannot or will not. Liquidity therefore has potentially significant option value that rises with systemic problems. Conceptually this value needs to be added to the return that is normally attributed to various classes of liquid assets in "normal" times. That will affect the relative value attractiveness of liquid and illiquid assets and hence influence the target-asset allocation choices made by various classes of investors.

So you have three underappreciated (at least until recently) virtues of liquidity: avoidance of cash-flow distress; flexibility in adjusting to overvaluations and signs of rising systemic risk; and option value in the aftermath of crises, or after a major resetting of values and the trajectory of the system.

What Does This Mean for Investment Strategy?

Periodic increases in systemic risk are likely to be a recurring feature of the world we live in. It should influence investment strategy in a number of ways. Short- and medium-run returns, especially when they are high, should not be taken as accurate signals of long-run returns when there is a component of risk that is periodic and systemic. Analytical effort and institutional capability should include regular assessments of systemic risk, utilizing outside expertise and inputs in combination with in-house evaluation. When the evaluation dictates, defensive action in the form of portfolio adjustments and tail insurance should be undertaken.

Asset allocation needs to have a dynamic component, and value needs to be attached to flexibility. For illiquid investments, a complementary part of the portfolio needs to be liquid and relatively less vulnerable to cor-related asset movements of the type that occur when systemic risk causes an abrupt asset-value reset. Liquidity should be valued for avoidance of cash-flow distress, for flexibility in adjusting asset allocation in response to rising systemic risk, and for the option value it creates in the aftermath of a crisis or a systemic resetting of asset values.

Asset pools with payout requirements should make payouts based on short- or even medium-run returns, even if they choose to retain strategies that are relatively more exposed to systemic risk, and they should adjust the payout rules to match the capacity of the operating entity they support to withstand income volatility.

Investment strategies should not be based on the properties of the system in normal times on the implicit assumption that periodic insta-bility is abnormal. The complexity created by the challenge of assessing systemic risk and the unpredictability of the timing of instability are just that—challenges, not reasons to ignore these phenomena.

PART FOUR

The Future of Growth

30. Can the Emerging Economies Sustain High Growth?

Over the past two years, industrial countries have experienced bouts of severe financial instability. Currently, and partly as a result of the crisis-response measures, they are wrestling with widening sovereign-debt problems and high unemployment. Their growth will not provide the same kind of tailwind for the developing economies as in the precrisis boom.

During the same period, emerging economies, once considered much more vulnerable, have been remarkably resilient. They have mounted large fiscal and monetary responses to counteract the dramatic falloff in trade. With growth returning to pre-2008 levels, the breakout performance of China, India, and Brazil are important engines of expansion for today's global economy. But the emergency responses cannot be carried on forever. So the question is whether they can transition to a different but sustainable pattern of high growth while the advanced economies struggle. It is a matter of great importance to developing countries, and to the global economy more broadly.

High growth and financial stability in emerging economies are helping to facilitate the massive adjustment facing industrial countries. But that growth has significant longer-term implications. If the current pattern is sustained, the global economy will be permanently transformed. Specifically, not much more than a decade is needed for the share of global GDP generated by developing economies to pass the 50 percent mark when measured in market prices.

So it is important to know whether this breakout growth phase is sustainable.

If you had asked this question under similar circumstances ten years ago, the answer would have been: clearly not. But now is different. These economies are larger and richer. The range of things they consume is wider because of the higher per capita income. The early-stage limitations of the domestic market (as an engine of growth) are beginning to recede. These economies trade with each other and the aggregate market size is very substantial.

The answer to the question of sustaining long-term growth comes in two parts. One depends on the ability of emerging economies to manage their own success; the other relates to the extent to which the global economy can accommodate this success. The answer to the first question is reassuring; the answer to the second is not.

While still able to exploit the scope for catch-up growth, emerging economies must undertake continuous, rapid, and at times difficult structural change, along with a parallel process of reform and institution building. In recent years, the systemically important countries have established an impressive track record of adapting pragmatically and flexibly. Accommodating structural change on both the demand and supply side of the economy has become deeply embedded in many emerging economies. That underpins the basis for their potential growth.

With government policy remaining on course, we can expect a gradual strengthening of endogenous domestic-growth drivers in emerging economies, anchored by an expanding middle class. As trade among them increases, the future of emerging economies is one of reduced dependence on industrial-country demand. Reduced dependence, however, does not mean a complete decoupling.

Distribution, as well as growth, matters. Emerging economies still need to manage better their growing domestic tensions due to rising income inequality and uneven access to basic services. A failure on this front would derail their domestic and regional growth dynamics. Among emerging economies and their governments, this is better understood today. Distributional aspects of growth strategy are firmly placed on emerging countries' policy agendas.

While emerging economies can compensate for and adapt to the economic slowdown in industrial countries, the financial-sector transmission mechanism is more challenging. Today's low-interest-rate environment is causing a flood of financial flows to emerging economies, raising the risk of inflation and asset bubbles. The continuing capital problems in Western banks have served to disrupt the availability of trade credits, and, if amplified, could destabilize local banks.

These risks are real. Fortunately, several emerging economies continue to have cushions and shock absorbers. Having entered the 2008–09 crisis with sound initial conditions (including large international reserves, budget and balance-of-payments surpluses, and highly capitalized banks), they are nowhere near exhausting their fiscal or financial flexibility—nor, hence, their capacity to respond to future shocks. In this respect, there is a sharp contrast with the advanced economies, as evidenced by the fiscal challenges and sovereign-debt risks.

Overall, emerging economies are well placed to continue to navigate successfully a world rendered unstable by crises in industrial countries. Yet, again, the decoupling is not complete. A favorable outcome also requires the ability and willingness of industrial countries to adapt to the growing size and prominence of emerging economies. The risks here are significant and point to a wide range of potential problems.

The flow of knowledge, finance, and technology that underpins sustained high growth rates in emerging economies is closely linked to an open, rules-based, and globalized economy. Yet this global construct is coming under pressure in an environment in which advanced countries have stubbornly high unemployment and experience bouts of financial volatility. Growth in the global economy comes to be seen as a zero-sum game, leading to suboptimal protectionist reactions.

As a result, the continued openness of industrial-country markets cannot be taken for granted. Political and policy narratives are becoming more domestic and narrow, while the international agenda and those voices advocating collective common global interests are having greater difficulty being heard.

These challenges will grow in the years ahead, at least for a period of time. Deleveraging, restoring fiscal balance, and establishing a new basis for longer-term growth will take time in Europe, America, and Japan. And then there is the issue of global institutions and governance.

Managing a growing and increasingly complex set of transnational connections in a multispeed world that is being turned upside down is an even bigger challenge than it was when the G7 dominated the global landscape. Such a world requires better global governance, as well as the implementation of overdue institutional reforms that will give emerging economies proper voice and representation in international institutions.

In the absence of such changes, the global economy may bounce from one crisis to another without a firm hand on the rudder to establish an overall sense of direction. The result is what economists call a "Nash equilibrium," a series of suboptimal and only quasi-cooperative outcomes.

Emerging economies will be called on to play an even larger role in a multispeed global economy characterized by protracted rehabilitation of overextended balance sheets in industrial countries. Left to their own devices, they are up to the task; but they do not operate in a vacuum. The ability of emerging economies to provide the growth lubrication that facilitates adjustment in industrial countries is dependent on two things. One is a willingness to accept, and even insist on, a larger role in global policy priority setting even as their domestic growth and development agendas remain a source of preoccupation. The other is the willingness of the advanced countries to accommodate tectonic shifts in the operation and governance of the global economy.

The G20, which includes the systemically important developing countries, is the epicenter of this effort to balance and integrate domestic and international objectives. The G20 countries are attempting to carry out this mission under extremely challenging circumstances. It would be an understatement to say that the future of developing country and global growth depends on a pattern of increasingly effective coordination of policy setting and structural change in this arena.

31. China and India

The future of growth in the global economy will be very heavily influenced by the two most populous countries in the world, China and India. Earlier we spent some time talking about the high-speed growth dynamics in these and other countries, and on the internal policies and external opportunities that have made them possible. If, as seems likely, the growth continues in the future, China's and India's and these other countries' share in the global GDP will rise, and along with it all their economic power and influence. How these two countries and the rest of the world respond to this shifting configuration of size and influence will have a major effect on global growth, and on the growth of various countries in the developing world.

Perhaps it is easiest to start with the arithmetic. As China and India grow, their size will tend to raise global growth because their share of global GDP is increasing. Eventually, as their incomes rise and begin to approach those of advanced countries, two things will happen at the same time. They will be the largest countries in the world, and their growth will slow down. As it does, global growth will slow because by then a substantial majority of the world's people will live in advanced countries. And as we have seen, advanced countries do not grow at 6–10 percent a year.

On the journey between now and then, much will depend on these two countries and on their integration into some system for managing the global economy. For example, if their economies are reasonably open to imports, their markets will be a major opportunity for lower-income developing countries to export and grow.

Because of their populations (China 1.3 billion and India 1.2 billion, together about 40 percent of the global population) and with China in the lead, they will become large and influential in the global economy while still having relatively low per capita incomes. One can see the growing impact in many areas. Climate is one. Others are: prices and consumption of food; energy and other natural resources; and the volume and composition of trade and capital flows.

China holds over $1.5 trillion worth of foreign currency reserves. In late May 2010, when the euro was under pressure as a result of sovereign-debt issues in Greece and other countries, there was a report in the *Financial Times* that the People's Bank of China (PBC) met with multinational banking firms to express concern about losses on their estimated €630 billion asset holdings, the implication being that they might consider reducing their holdings or limiting future purchases. That report caused immediate and dramatic downward pressure on the euro.

My response to that report was that it was crazy. Downward pressure on the euro would cause further appreciation of the yuan relative to the euro, reduce the value of the reserves, and cause additional competitive problems for China's export sector. In no conceivable dimension was it in China's interest to add to euro volatility. Within a day or two, the State Administration of Foreign Exchange (SAFE), the division of the PBC that handles foreign-exchange investment, stated that they had no intention of dumping euro-denominated assets (mainly bonds) or of withdrawing their long-term commitment to euro assets.

This episode illustrates several things. Interdependence is remarkably high. Mistakes and accidents are possible. In an earlier era, with less sophistication, SAFE might have remained silent, leaving a huge and uncertain overhang on the euro. The results could have been quite chaotic and volatile. In the event, the turbulence proved temporary and that potential source of downward pressure was eliminated. But the general point is clear: interdependence is significant, and increasing, and the major emerging countries are important players. The maintenance of system stability requires sophistication and appropriate policy responses if accidents are to be avoided.

The domestic growth and development agendas in China and India will, quite naturally, take precedence, in part because they remain challenging and in part because habits of thought and patterns of behavior are, of course, products of the past. It will not prove either natural or easy to absorb a growing set of global responsibilities, and then to integrate and balance them against a full domestic development agenda.

This situation is without historical precedent. Perhaps one could argue that the United States became large in the then global economy in the late nineteenth and early twentieth centuries (remember that the "developing countries" then were mostly poor and didn't add up to much in terms of GDP). One could also argue that America arrived without a lot of background or inclination to shoulder international responsibilities, including economic ones. But by the time it became influential, it wasn't really a low-income country. It seems safe to say that this is uncharted territory for China and India, and for the global economy.

Part of the transition is already under way. As a result of the financial and economic crisis, the G20 replaced the G7/8 as the principal body for setting international priorities with respect to global issues. As yet there is not a long track record to rely on. Whether this grouping, which for the first time includes the major developing countries and reflects more accurately the size and influence of the major nations, can be effective in achieving coordination in major policy areas remains to be seen. A lot will depend on the way that India and China engage with this process.

32. China's Structural Challenges

The per capita income in China is about $3,500 at today's exchange rates, and approximately double that when adjusted for purchasing power and price differences. It has weathered the present financial crisis better than most countries, for a number of reasons. It reacted very quickly to the collapse of external demand with a domestic stimulus package of 9 percent of GDP in each of the two years, 2008 and 2009. This package was implemented in November 2008—the U.S. stimulus bill passed Congress in late February of 2009, that much later in part because of the coincidence of a crisis and a presidential transition. The stimulus package in China was heavily weighted toward investment, especially in infrastructure, which is something they know how to do. To some extent, the Chinese relied on past experience in the '97–'98 currency crisis in Asia, a storm they weathered without depreciating the currency but instead with what was then a large domestic stimulus program. China also eased credit quickly, and used their massive reserves to stabilize the currency. The relatively controlled capital account meant that credit did not tighten to the same extent as in most other developing countries when foreign capital started to flow out, running to the aid of damaged balance sheets at home.

The result is a rapid transition to high growth, with projections for 2010 in the 9 percent and above range. This growth is a major factor in the return of growth to Asia generally. On the other hand, as with other countries, the stimulus and other dimensions of the emergency response are not a permanent solution. There is a growing concern among knowledgeable Chinese policy makers and academics with regard to two things. One is a return to the old ways, meaning the strategies and policies of the past thirty years that focused on investment and labor-intensive exports, policies that worked well but have outlived their usefulness. The influence of those in government and in the labor-intensive sectors that are set to decline is still substantial. Their hand has been at least temporarily strengthened by the crisis.

The other is a deep concern about overconfidence in the economy's resilience in the face of some daunting short- and medium-term challenges. Managing to bounce back in the worst global crisis in eighty years—and by far the largest in the history of the PRC—is impressive. But, then, the hallmarks of Chinese growth have been rapid learning, a long time horizon, a willingness to support and encourage constant change, and a pragmatic problem-solving approach to a long process. These will likely reassert themselves and displace any short-term tendency toward triumphalism. Nevertheless, the risk is there.

China is entering upon a complex set of transitions that will build the base for its path to advanced-country status in the next twenty-five years. After three decades of sustained high growth and a remarkably successful, rapid, and effective policy response to the crisis, confidence is justifiably high.

China faces several parallel and related rebalancing challenges that are crucial for its internal growth and development, as well as for its relations with the rest of the global economy. Among them are

- The middle-income transition, entailing a major microeconomic restructuring of the economy
- A macroeconomic shift to a higher level of household income and consumption and a more rapid expansion of the middle class
- Reversing the pattern of rising income inequality
- Lowering the very high savings level relative to investment and thus reducing the current account surplus
- Reducing the energy and carbon intensity of future growth
- Assuming growing global responsibilities as its size and global economic impact become steadily larger

In this last respect China is unique. It has arrived at a point where it has systemically important global impacts, but at a much lower per capita income than any predecessor. The reason is that it is by far the largest country in terms of population to have sustained very high growth for thirty years. Global impact and responsibility have therefore been added to an already complex domestic growth-and-development agenda at a point where most countries can be excused for maintaining a largely domestic focus. It will require balancing the domestic and international policy priorities with very little historical experience to provide guidance. India should follow in about a decade in this respect.

With a rising per capita income, important urban segments of the Chinese economy are in or are entering the middle-income transition. It is a difficult transition, one where many countries have lost growth momentum and experienced a stalling-out of the structural transformation process. Labor-intensive exports sectors that have been a major contributor to growth are losing competitiveness and have to be allowed to decline or move inland and then eventually decline. They will be replaced by sectors that are more capital, human-capital, and knowledge intensive.

Services will grow. Higher-value-added sectors and functions upstream and downstream from the processing industries will need to grow. Global brands should start to appear, and government ownership of enterprises will continue to diminish to facilitate the shifting engagement of the private sector with the global economy. Public-sector investment will shift toward education and R&D. The market (global and domestic), not the government, will increasingly drive the transitions. Targeting of sectors will decline. The domestic market and a growing middle class will assume greater prominence in driving growth and guiding the structural evolution of the economy. Urbanization—an important supporting parallel process in development, modernization, and the middle-income transition—will accelerate with supporting public-sector investment.

I noted earlier in discussing rebalancing of global demand that household disposable income is about 60 percent of national income and the household savings rate is close to 30 percent of disposable income. These numbers are, respectively, low and high as compared with other countries, both advanced and developing. To empower the domestic market to drive income growth, and to accelerate the growth of the middle class, these numbers need to shift. Household income needs to rise; and, as more ample provision of social security, insurance, and services is made, precautionary savings should fall. Both will support the middle-income transition by expanding the domestic market as a driver of growth. They will help sustain growth in the face of prospectively weaker global demand, as the stimulus expenditures are withdrawn. But, most important, rapid growth of the domestic market, especially the service sector, needs to largely replace the export sector as the employment engine driving the rural population's entry to the modern economy. The export sector will move into higher-value-added sectors and will no longer serve this function as effectively.

The corporate sector has financed a large fraction of its growing investment out of retained earnings without having to raise capital from the household sector. The government continues to owns in excess of 50 percent of the large state-owned-enterprise sector but does not use or need the income. The government is fully funded by tax revenue sources without resort to dividends from this ownership position. While there are a number of different ways to do it, the bottom line is that a portion of these two income streams (corporate and government) needs to be redirected to the household sector.

Reducing excess savings by increasing consumption while holding productive investment up will contribute to a reduction in the current account surplus and hence materially help with the restoration of global aggregate demand. China is not the only systemically important surplus country, but the elimination of its surplus could restore about a third of the missing global demand. Exchange-rate appreciation and rising incomes will help drive the needed transitions, but rapid expansion of domestic demand is needed to sustain growth.

High growth and urbanization have caused rapid rises in incomes in urban areas, with smaller increases in the rural areas. Rural residents suffer from inferior education and health care. A large group of migrant workers and families (on the order of 150 to 200 million people) are officially considered residents of rural areas, but in fact are marginal urban residents with constrained rights and access to services. Serious social tensions have arisen as a result. They are being addressed by expanded provision of rural services, by rapid urbanization with supporting investment in infrastructure and service provision, and by a regularization of the status of the migrants.

The government has put in place an aggressive set of plans and policies to accelerate the reduction of the energy and carbon intensity of the economy consistent with sustaining growth. Much of this is in fact pro-growth. Some initiatives create growth opportunities: for example, alternative energy sectors like solar. Notwithstanding these programs, overall energy consumption and carbon output will inevitably rise in the short and medium term because of growth. This creates additional sources of tension with advanced countries in the context of the climate-change discussions.

China has faced daunting challenges in the past and has generally outperformed the predictions of the skeptics. In this sense, the present is not all that different. But now, to these challenges has been added a set of global pressures, impacts, and responsibilities. These latter come in part from the sheer size of China's population, but also from an occasionally hostile external environment that doesn't like the form of government, doesn't always place much value on the rising incomes and opportunities of a people who used to be very poor, and tends to see the game as zero-sum and to attribute the economic success to noncooperative policies in areas like exchange-rate management.

Meeting the challenge of the domestic restructuring to sustain growth, asserting the right to develop and not to be penalized purely for being large, while taking on increased responsibility for global balance, stability, and governance and representing the interests of less-powerful developing countries are major new mountains to climb. China's success or failure will, in any event, have a significant impact on the rest of the world.

33. India's Growth, Diversification, and Urbanization

India's future growth looks to be high. It is operating on an open-economy model that has been tried and tested. The foundations in a functioning democracy in an enormously complex environment have been painstakingly built over several decades. I have to confess that I somewhat expected China's growth rebound but was more surprised and impressed by India's resilience in the crisis, and by the speed of the restoration of growth. There is evidently deep managerial skill and adaptability in both the public and private sectors.

India's challenges in sustaining growth are not insubstantial. As in China, they are well understood by political leaders and policy makers. Infrastructure investment on a steady sustained basis is one of them. It has to be accomplished with a central government budget that does not have the space to finance all the required investment. India has adopted and is evolving a public-private partnership model in which private capital, supplemented by incentives, will make up the public-financing shortfall. The needed infrastructure is in process and covers a wide range of territory, including roads, ports, upgraded rail systems, airports, and electricity-distribution systems with sufficient capacity to keep up with the growth.

The leading item on the infrastructure list is urban infrastructure. India has 1.2 billion people, 70 percent of whom still live in rural areas and villages. The country is set to experience a massive process of urbanization over the next twenty years. To support it, housing, transportation, sewage, water, and electricity systems are needed to make the new and growing cities work. The McKinsey Global Institute estimates that this will entail $1.2 trillion of investment in urban settings. Just in terms of construction, the need in each year of the next twenty is roughly equal to the total residential and commercial real estate in Chicago now. This is reminiscent of China, which I have occasionally described as needing to build Los Angeles every year in order to accommodate the flow of 15 million people a year to the cities. The scale is truly hard to comprehend.

Crucial services like education are delivered unevenly across the states of India. For the lagging ones, including several in the north of the country, significant improvements, primarily in quality and effectiveness (and output), are needed.

India's growth has followed an unusual pattern in one important respect: relative to other high-growth economies, the service sector is large, given the level of income. An important high-growth part of that sector is trade in services; we associate this with outsourcing of a variety of kinds. Trade in services is expanding rapidly in size and in scope. From its origins in IT outsourcing, it has added business processes, expert medical services, film editing for television, grading exams for teachers in advanced countries, and writing political speeches for inarticulate politicians. The rapid expansion of this sector has been enabled in part by an earlier heavy investment in postsecondary education, initiated by Rajiv Gandhi, who foresaw the economic potential of computers and information technology for India.

Important as it is, this engine of growth and the domestic economy are unlikely to be powerful enough engines to employ those in the rural-to-urban migration that occurs in all sustained-growth and development cases. It is likely, in my view, that the manufacturing sector will need to continue to expand domestically and in the export sector to generate the needed employment. Powerful additional employment-generating engines are critical, not just to sustain growth but also to deliver on the inclusiveness dimension—important in a democratic setting, where broad-based support is needed to support the reform and transformation process. India is open to foreign direct investment. Infrastructure and education will support the economic diversification. Some rigidities in labor markets will require reform in order to compete for an expanding place in global supply chains.

Reform in India is a continuous process, and it is difficult. For example, the government in July of 2010 increased the consumer price of oil, triggering countrywide protests. It was the right move, though not easy politically. The economy needs to adjust to a more fuel-efficient path (as do many other countries) and the government needs the tax revenue to finance investments in growth supporting tangible and intangible assets.

There remain in India's government residual elements of the old days—of the license or permit raj—when government had its hand in everything and starting a business was a mini-nightmare of complexity, relationships, payments, and the like.

India, like the other major emerging economies, has both its size and high growth as a major attraction to foreign investment and businesses. The potential future market is formidable.

It is a very densely populated country. That, combined with its democratic structure and the rule of law, ensures that people are treated fairly. But it does make shifting things and people around difficult and complex. Building almost anything—roads, new power lines, expanded airports— all requires relocating people. Frequently the occupants and the owners of land do not coincide, complicating and lengthening the process.

The financial system is well developed for a country with India's income level. The government continues to own a majority share in most of the major banks. That configuration makes it possible to finance the government, even when its deficits are relatively large. There is some risk of crowding out of private investment. The overall savings rate has historically been high, so that most domestic investment is financed domestically. Recently, however, the current account deficit has risen. That is okay, provided that the growth keeps the external debt as a percentage of GDP from rising rapidly. Like other major emerging markets, India is having to carefully manage international capital flows for stability and consistency with the overall growth objectives. In the postcrisis period, with low advanced-country interest rates, the immediate challenge is to maintain control over the size and composition of the inbound capital flows that tend to be flooding into the higher-growth economies.

This might seem a huge agenda, and indeed it is. Is it manageable? Without a track record of growth acceleration, reform, and success, one might be inclined to think not. But the feeling one gets in India is a sense of confidence that the capacity and commitment of both the private sector and the government are up to the task. That kind of confidence is an intangible asset that is easy to underrate.[1]

India is by far the largest democracy to set out on this lengthy high-speed journey. Its continued success will demonstrate that democratic governance and rapid growth and development are compatible and mutually supportive. And it will ensure that democratic values are represented as the emerging economies move to a position of dominance in the global economy. There are a lot of people who very much want it to succeed.

34. Brazil's Growth Reset

We saw in Part II that Brazil was one of the countries that grew at 7 percent a year for more than twenty-five years. That growth actually came early in the post–World War II period, starting, along with Japan, in about 1950. Then a remarkable thing happened. The growth dropped dramatically around 1975 to roughly the rate of population growth so that per capita incomes stopped increasing—and remained constant for the next twenty-five years.

By 1975, Brazil had become a middle-income country. One might be tempted to attribute the subsequent deceleration to the challenges associated with the middle-income transition. That's certainly part of the explanation, but Brazil is in fact a surprisingly complex case.

The slowdown was accompanied by regime changes, from democratic to military dictatorship and back. It was linked to fiscal over-extension leading to several bouts of damaging hyperinflation that was eventually conquered in the 1990s. Policy also turned inward and away from the global economy with a focus on import substitution as a way to sustain growth. This can, and did, work for a while, but the disconnect from the global economy eventually results in rising costs and lower productivity. Growth eventually slows down.

Brazil is rich in natural resources, and these helped to sustain growth. But as we have seen, natural-resource wealth by itself does not sustain growth indefinitely. Long-term growth is associated with deepening of human capital and the structural evolution of an economy. Natural resources can (but often do not) help if the income streams are used to make the investments that facilitate and underpin the structural transformation.

That did not happen in Brazil until recently. Brazil, like much of Latin America and parts of Africa, has one of the highest levels of measured income inequality in the world. That reflected a pattern of underinvestment in the education of a large part of the population. As agriculture modernized, this group moved to cities. Too uneducated to participate in the modern economy, these families ended up in slums or shantytowns (called *favelas*). Brazil evolved into a dual economy: a relatively rich one whose growth is constrained by the normal forces that constrain the growth of relatively advanced economies, and a poor one where the early-stage growth dynamics that we have discussed just didn't start, owing to its separation from the modern domestic economy and the global economy.

By the late 1990s, Brazil had, in effect, become a middle-income country by taking an average of a relatively rich and a relative poor economy within the same boarders. This was fundamentally the result of a massive failure of inclusiveness in the growth dynamics.

In the late 1990s, and for the past decade, under the leadership of Presidents Cardoso and Lula da Silva, the growth accelerated again. The positive impact of effective macroeconomic management and stability was undoubtedly an important reason. But more fundamentally, the country and its leaders added important elements to the policy mix by redistributing income, improving access to basic services, and investing heavily in the underinvested part of the population—the "second economy," if you like. The result is that the economy has recovered much of the structural dynamics of sustained high growth, including the absorption and productive employment of underutilized human resources. In other countries, this is associated with a parallel process of urbanization. In Brazil, the population is largely already urban. The underinvested part of the economy lives in cities and in slums, and so the government has expanded the investment in the *favelas* in parallel with its commitments to income distribution and access to quality education.

The consensus view, which I share, is that these changes have largely restored the underpinnings of sustained high growth to the economy. Success has helped embed the more inclusive approach into the political and social culture. One can reasonably expect Brazil to navigate a path toward advanced-economy status in the next ten to fifteen years. With a population of 200 million, it will become one of the largest economies in the world and a significant driver of growth in all of Latin America.

As a footnote, Latin American growth more broadly has returned or surpassed precrisis levels, aided in part by growing trade linkages with Asia (and, of course, Asia's size and growth rebound).

35. Energy and Growth

Are we going to run out of oil and come to a screeching halt? Probably not. But energy and environmental issues could slow us down.

Oil in the ground is an asset. It can be taken out and sold or left in the ground and taken out later if the price is expected to be higher. If it is be taken out now and sold, the proceeds should be invested in a financial asset, say a bond. The expected return to taking either action should be about equal: otherwise all the holders of the asset would either leave it in the ground or take it out. The resulting excess supply or demand would cause the price to adjust. This is known as Hotelling's rule: the price of an exhaustible resource like oil should go up at a rate that is similar to the rate of increase in the value of other assets.

But there are complications. There are supply disruptions and supply and demand surprises. It seems fairly clear, for example, that the extent of the growth in emerging-market demand was a market surprise. Otherwise, if anticipated, prices would have risen sooner and more gradually, rather than spike up in 2007 and 2008 as they did. Also, turning the spigot on and off is not a costless exercise. So the Hotelling forces operate with frictions that cause deviations from the predicted frictionless outcome.

To explain the history of declining real oil prices up to the mid 1970s, and then again after, up to the price spike in 2007, you have to assume, I think, that there were a long sequence of positive supply surprises. That is, we discovered that we had more oil than we thought.

What can we expect in the future? The demand from the emerging economies will probably outrun the supply increments, and the price of oil will rise. But there are moderating forces that will constrain this rise. First, experience tells us that rising prices will reduce the rate of increase of consumption, though not immediately. It takes a little time for consumers to adjust their behavior and the equipment they use. But surely, economies will become more energy efficient. Second, the developing countries have had energy subsidies on a widespread basis, and these are now known to be uniformly bad for long-term growth. The subsidies are in the process of being eliminated in the major emerging economies and much of the developing world. Brazil is in the forefront of the effective use of biofuels.

Third, and quite important, a wider array of alternative energy sources become economically viable without subsidization as the price of oil increases. As oil prices rise, economies will diversify to some extent away from oil, and that will diminish demand and the upward pressure on the price while at the same time expanding the supply of energy.

Fourth, emerging economies become less energy intensive as they get richer. Advanced countries consume a lot of energy, but not a lot in relation to their output. The short way of saying this is: energy intensity declines with rising income levels. Energy consumption will still rise as a result of emerging economy growth, but not in proportion to the increase in incomes and output.

If you add this all up, with known sources of energy and their costs, and with the likelihood of technological innovation in response to rising energy costs, energy will become more expensive but not to a level that will materially diminish the growth potential of the global economy.

Policy will have a significant effect on the path, the transitions, and the environment. Natural gas is cleaner than oil. Coal has a high output of both particulates and CO_2 per unit of energy produced. If oil and natural gas prices rise, some emerging economies will use coal for the generation of electricity. This substitution process could therefore have significant adverse environmental impacts. To avoid these adverse effects, we will need environmental regulation. A global price for carbon-dioxide emissions would help create the right incentives.

Generally the rising price of oil, while much complained about, is a friend, in that it creates a broad-based incentive for energy efficiency and investment in technology that is energy efficient and environmentally friendly. Sensible, forward-looking energy policy consists of elevating the prices now via taxes and deploying the proceeds to support investment in technologies that solve energy efficiency and environmental challenges. Doing the latter without the rising prices makes no sense, because the prices are needed to create the appropriate demand-side incentives.

Europe, which is heavily dependent on external sources of oil, has followed this kind of approach to energy policy and pricing. The United States has thus far not taken this route. It is time for the laissez-faire approach to energy in the United States to change, though shifting course is more difficult in the aftermath of the crisis. Ken Rogoff, an influential economist and policy thinker, has suggested that the BP oil spill disaster in the Gulf of Mexico may turn out to be a catalyst for a major shift in U.S. policy with respect to energy and the environment. We can all hope that he is right about this.[1]

36. The Challenge of Climate Change and Developing-Country Growth

Global warming is probably the most complex challenge to our capacity for global governance today. After many years of careful work by dedicated scientists and environmentalists, a majority of people believe that there are significant risks of climate change associated with the production of greenhouse gases by humans. A growing majority of governments and nations is taking the problem seriously in various different ways.

There is some controversy, but it does not yet seem to have overwhelmed the emerging consensus, even in the midst of a difficult economic crisis. Some skeptics claim that the full range of scientific views has been suppressed and that the problem has been overstated. Others admit there may be a warming problem but argue that it is too soon to know. The problem with this last approach is that waiting until we know more increases the risk.

Thoughtful commentators agree that in slowing down or reversing the trends in greenhouse gas emissions, we are "buying insurance" rather than averting a sure thing. But that feature of the challenge makes it much more difficult to address. We just don't have a lot of practice buying fat-tail insurance on a global basis. But if we are going to do it, we have to do it together. No single nation or small subset can solve the problem. A low-carbon environment is a public good.

It is widely understood that human activity has contributed in the past few decades to an increase in the stock of greenhouse gases in the atmosphere. But there is considerable remaining uncertainty about the magnitude of the impact on temperatures and climate. The temperature ranges remain wide.[1] And there is uncertainty about the impact of any given level of carbon in the atmosphere on average temperatures.

Notwithstanding recent controversies about scientists "overselling" the risks, the science community has, on balance, been quite honest about the uncertainties and the limits to their forecasting abilities at this stage. From scientists, one gathers that a lot will depend on what happens to cloud cover as a result of warming. That turns out to be notoriously difficult to predict because of the complexity of the climate system.

In the past three to four years, we have entered a new phase in dealing with climate change—from persuading people there is a problem to doing something about it. This second phase is a huge challenge, and much bigger than we thought, in part because a combination of scientific, technological, and economic inputs are required to devise a long-term strategy that may succeed and that will accord with the values, needs, expectations, and goals of a wide variety of people and countries.

A brief word about terminology as it has emerged in the global-warming discussion of the past years may be useful for those of us who are not part of the day-to-day discussion. (Apologies to those who already know this.) Responding to potential and actual climate change involves two kinds of action: mitigation and adaptation. "Mitigation" refers to actions that lead to the reduction of net greenhouse gas emissions. They include increasing energy efficiency, reducing energy consumption (through public transportation, the design of cities and buildings, etc.), reducing emissions from known sources, and increasing the rate at which carbon is removed from the atmosphere; examples of the latter would be reforestation and afforestation. Mitigation could also include activities that increase the reflectivity of the outer atmosphere so that less heat-generating radiation enters the atmosphere.

"Adaptation" refers to actions that people, countries, and societies take to adjust to climate change that has actually occurred. It would include changing the crops that are grown, changing irrigation techniques, building levies to protect against rising ocean levels or moving away from low-lying coastal areas, buying air conditioners, making adjustments in medical care in response to changing disease patterns—in short, a huge range of responses to shifts in climate and average temperature and their impacts.

To a first approximation, mitigation is undertaken to reduce the chances that significant adaptation and its associated costs will be required. The two are clearly linked because the options and costs for adaptation partially determine the payoffs to buying insurance in the form of mitigation.

I am going to focus on mitigation because reconciling effective global CO_2 reduction and accommodating developing-country growth is the core of the climate challenge and by far the hardest problem to solve. By focusing on mitigation, I am not suggesting that adaptation is secondary in importance. Indeed, in some possible scenarios where mitigation fails or is too late, adaptation may become the dominant approach. And its distributional aspects are of great human and moral importance.

"Cross-border" mitigation efforts are mitigation activities undertaken in one country and financed and paid for by an external (foreign) entity (a government, a public utility, or an oil company) that has a mitigation obligation or target in its home country. The accounting, rules, and processes of cross-border mitigation in the Kyoto Protocol are called the Clean Development Mechanism, or CDM. In discussions and legislation in various countries, cross-border mitigation is sometimes referred to as "international offsets." Domestic offsets are similar but apply to two entities within the same country. Both kinds of offsets occur automatically in a global carbon-trading system.

Developing Countries

The high-growth developing countries include more than half the world's population. In Part I, I argued that by mid-century, or shortly thereafter, many of them will be approaching advanced-country levels of income with associated patterns of consumption, energy use, and carbon emissions. That is about the same time scale on which CO_2 stocks in the atmosphere will become perilously high and risky. What those patterns of growth will be and how we get to them is the central issue before us. If those patterns are like the present ones, the climate change battle will have been lost.

The G20 accounts for close to 90 percent of global GDP and about two-thirds of the world's population. The lion's share of the economic and technological aspects of the mitigation challenge falls within the purview of the G20, which includes the advanced countries and a few other potentially high-growth and populous countries like Egypt, Nigeria, and Mexico.[2] The share of GDP attached to the high-growth developing countries will rise, and with it their share of global emissions.

In the next five decades almost all the increase in CO_2 emissions will come from high-growth developing countries. This is the result of their size (3.5 billion people) and projected growth.

One way to solve the problem would be to limit the developing-country growth. Early mitigation proposals did this implicitly. This won't work. It is neither fair nor acceptable to the developing world. Imposing it would involve tariffs and trade sanctions and eventually the undoing of much of the progress in creating the global economy over the past half century.

The central question, at least as I see it, is this: Is there a path for developing countries to follow on their way to advanced-country status (allowing for increasing energy consumption and carbon emissions for some years along the way) that will arrive at what are viewed as safe levels of global emissions in about fifty years? The answer is maybe, and the challenge is to begin to head down such a path.

In my view, the only way to get to a global agreement on a mitigation strategy is to start with a shared understanding of what such a path might look like. Without it, it will be difficult, at best, to define roles and responsibilities for various classes of countries that are consistent with the overall intertemporal pattern of CO_2 emissions. Right now we do not have the requisite shared vision.

The Data

The United States and Canada emit annually about twenty tons per person at present. The data for a variety of countries are shown in the graph opposite. Other advanced countries are in the range of 6 to 12 tons per person. France, at 6 tons per person, is at the low end because of its extensive use of nuclear power for electricity generation. The global average (4.8 tons) and the safe level (2.3 tons) are also indicated to the left of the graph. The developing countries are generally below 2.3 tons per person, and substantially so—except for China, which weighs in at 4.8 tons.

But that is just the status quo. Without a substantial mitigation effort, the future looks worse. If the high-growth developing countries approach the European average of 10 tons per person in fifty years or

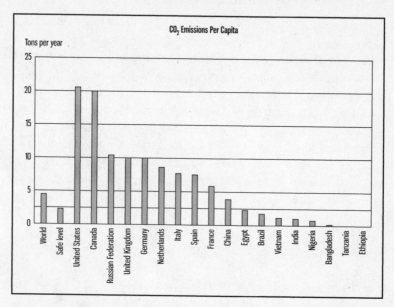

less, then global per capita emissions will go from 4.8 tons to almost 9 tons per person—a near doubling, and four times the Intergovernmental Panel on Climate Change's (IPCC) "safe" level of 2.3 tons. And if the developing countries overshoot the E.U. average and start to look more like the United States, Canada, and Australia, then we are talking about per capita emissions in the high teens.

Why might this happen? Well, as discussed earlier, coal is abundant in China and India, and it is a cheap source of energy for electricity. It is also "dirty." It produces particulates that cause local pollution and acid rain, though these can be scrubbed, at some cost. But it also produces a lot of CO_2 per unit of energy, more than oil and much more than natural gas. With a lot of coal-fired power plants, we are going to need to capture the carbon and store it. Otherwise CO_2 emissions will rise dramatically.

The growth in developing countries is going to account for almost all of the increase in CO_2 emissions in the next half century. Without a complex, intertemporal global-mitigation strategy, CO_2 emissions are set to double (or perhaps rise even more, depending on how pessimistic you are). Emissions from high-growth developing countries would exceed the safe levels. Therefore, aggressive mitigation in the current advanced countries by itself cannot solve the problem.

Now, suppose that there is in place an aggressive mitigation strategy in the advanced countries—the details we will get to shortly. In the near term (the next twenty years), the race between developing-country growth and affordable low-carbon technology will be won by the growth. Global carbon emissions will rise, not fall. But then it can reverse as the developing countries approach advanced-country income levels and as they absorb, use, and start to develop low-carbon technologies. International policies and burden sharing can affect the absorption rate, and that will have the beneficial effect of reducing the rate of growth of developing-country emissions. Let me turn now to the time paths that go with this general description.

How Do We Get to Safe Levels Over Time?

The principle of "common but differentiated responsibilities," established in the United Nations Framework Convention on Climate Change (UNFCCC) and the Kyoto Protocol, recognizes that solutions that have any chance of being acceptable will involve asymmetric roles for advanced and developing countries in various categories. For the higher-growth developing countries this will mean that the roles in the climate-change effort will evolve continuously and eventually become coincident with the other advanced countries that they will be joining at "graduation." The challenge is to define the differentiated responsibilities in such a way as to create a path to hit safe emissions targets without undermining developing-country growth.

Working out such a time path is a slightly complicated exercise. The target in the exercise is to get to roughly 2.5 tons per person globally in fifty years. That is not precisely the currently estimated safe level, but it's very close. In reality, it doesn't matter what exact target you set now because it will be revised many times in the coming decades in response to new information about risks, technology, and costs. The object is getting started on the right path and not peering into a distant future that we cannot know without making the journey.[3]

The path to hitting long-run targets has several phases. The advanced countries need to engage in mitigation strategies that get them to the target in fifty years. To accomplish that involves many elements, including increasing energy efficiency, pricing energy so as to create incentives for efficiency, and developing new energy-efficient and low-carbon technologies.

To keep the costs of meeting the targeted reductions down, advanced countries should get credit for mitigation that they carry out and pay for in developing countries. This cross-border system requires the cooperation of the developing countries.

Developing countries will grow, and as they do, they will increase energy consumption and carbon emissions. But they will eliminate energy subsidies and increase energy efficiency—a step that is pro-growth rather than the reverse.[4] As time passes, the developing countries will absorb new technologies from advanced countries. Emissions growth will decelerate and then reverse. Incentives will be needed to get the developing countries to absorb this technology. They could be provided by keeping the cost of the technology low, and by aiding the natural technology-transfer process in the cross-border mechanism.

Eventually, as these countries grow, their emissions will start to look more and more like the advanced-country emissions that are coming down. The growth will drive them toward graduation, as the developing-country per capita emissions paths will merge with that of the advanced countries.

It is a bit complicated because it has to contain asymmetries that shift over time in order to accommodate developing-country growth. But when you think about it, there really isn't any alternative. Emissions paths that are significantly below what I just described for developing countries have a high probability of reducing their growth. Developing countries won't accept them. Advanced countries might try to impose them, and then economic conflict would ensue, with quite unpredictable results.

The Copenhagen meeting in November 2009 is widely viewed as a disaster. It failed to reach binding agreements on emissions paths for various groups of countries. That was no surprise. There was no shared understanding of what the feasible paths forward might look like. Just as important, all countries view long-term binding targets as wildly risky, since no one has any solid idea what the economic and social costs of meeting them will be in the out years. And we won't find out what they are except by setting out on a sensible path in the near term and discovering them as we go. Long-term binding targets sound good, but in truth they are a poor way to solve a complex intertemporal problem that involves considerable uncertainty and learning along the way.

The good news is that despite the perception of failure, there are signs of major progress. Numerous countries, as well as subnational units, companies, and just ordinary people like us, are in the process of changing their policies and behavior in such a way as to move in the right direction. This includes the systemically important large countries like China and India and Brazil, where aggressive plans to deal with energy efficiency, local environmental issues, and carbon emissions are under way.[5] China and India have both set in motion policies to minimize the energy and carbon intensities of their economies, consistent with growth. They acknowledge that energy consumption and carbon emissions will rise in the short and medium run; but they expect them to eventually reverse course and start to decline.

Prime Minister Manmohan Singh of India probably captured the spirit of the enterprise best when he foresaw that India would not need to exceed the per capita emissions of the advanced countries at any time on its growth and development path. If advanced countries drive down per capita emissions and developing countries agree to stay under the advanced-country levels, we just might get there.

It is important to understand that on a successful long-term path, global emissions will not fall and are very likely to rise for as much as twenty years. It might be tempting to conclude that the mitigation efforts are a failure. That would be a mistake. The progress in the advanced countries combined with a developing-country commitment to participate in the cross-border and technology-transfer programs, and eventually to line up with the advanced-country standards (however they are implemented), will form the basis for achieving the long-range targets.

Implementation

To get started on the path described above, one needs the advanced countries to adopt mitigation plans that cause carbon emissions to decline, in real numbers, over time. These plans should have the following characteristics:

- They need to recognize that there are different starting points in terms of per capita emissions.

- They need to be reasonably coordinated so that countries and regions do not suffer competitive disadvantages.
- Incentives such as a price on carbon or alternative regulations should be created to stimulate investment in low-energy and low-carbon technologies. These incentives need to be long term and stay in place to be effective.
- Advanced countries need to make use of and be given credit for cross-border mitigation efforts, as these may be low-cost compared to the domestic ones. This will keep the costs down in the short and medium term.

Likewise, the developing countries need to take the following steps:

- Remove energy subsidies and create incentives for energy efficiency. This is supportive rather than antagonistic to growth.
- Support the cross-border mitigation programs.
- Participate in and support a global monitoring system for carbon emissions.
- Adopt new technology as it becomes available, utilizing international financial support and the cross-border mechanism.

The good news is that despite the pessimism surrounding Copenhagen, the direction of movement by individual countries and groupings like the E.U. appear to be entirely consistent with these requirements.

Carbon Credit Trading

There is much interest in carbon-credit trading systems for dealing with mitigation. And there is a reasonable chance that we will eventually have one.

The use of tradable credits to deal with environmental issues is not new. The theory was worked out forty years ago, and successful tradable credit systems have been used in several countries to reduce sulfur dioxide emissions in an efficient manner. So we have some useful experience.

How does a tradable credit or license system work? A carbon credit entitles its holder to emit one unit of CO_2. If you emit one unit and don't have the credit, you have to buy it. If you hold more credits than you need, you can sell the excess. There is a market in these credits, and credits have a common price—one credit is just as good as the next.

Now, consider some entity that is emitting CO_2 and has enough credits to cover it. It can cut its emissions at a certain cost, and if it does, it can sell the credits. It will do this if the cost of cutting is less than the value of the credits it can sell. If you think about it for a moment, this means that the price of carbon will be the marginal cost of cutting emissions for all sources, since the price is the same. That means that with a tradable credit system, the mitigation is accomplished at least cost.

That is one of the big advantages of a tradable credit system. It minimizes the cost of achieving any level of emissions reduction. It also establishes a price for carbon. That price provides an important signal to investors in new energy-saving or carbon-reducing technologies because it establishes what the emission reductions are worth. Of course, there are prices for various kinds of energy, too. In addition, financial markets will develop to provide future prices for carbon, just as they do now for energy.

A global carbon-credit trading system is essentially a large version of the same thing. It allocates carbon credits to countries, who then must arrange for emissions to be at or below the level of the carbon credits that the country holds. The carbon credits are traded on a global market. Countries that need more credits to cover their emissions can buy them, and countries that have a surplus of credits can sell them. Each country can then sell (or give, or both) credits to people and organizations internally and they can buy or sell them. Or they can just regulate emissions and buy and sell the credits at the government level.

The global version has the same characteristics as the more local version. The price of carbon is the marginal cost of mitigation, and costs are minimized globally if the system is working properly. The total global carbon emissions will depend on the total number of credits that are allocated across all countries. The total would be expected to change over time. If the earlier analysis of feasible time paths is right, then the total would not change much; it might even expand for a while before coming down. These choices about the time path are best made in steps, because we learn a lot about the costs of mitigation from the operation of the system and the incentives it creates for new mitigation technologies.

The question, then, is who pays for the mitigation. Remember that the location (by region and source) of the mitigation is determined entirely by the total, and by the cost-minimizing character of the system. This is important—and a source of much confusion. What actually happens in terms of the global pattern of mitigation is *not determined by the allocation of credits to countries*. It is determined entirely by efficiency criteria.

The allocation of credits across countries determines who pays for the mitigation. It is therefore of central interest to everyone. In the context of a global credit trading system, accommodating developing-country growth consists in allocating enough credits to developing countries so as not to impose costs on them.

Unfortunately, a large problem pops up right at this point. It is the question of how many credits to allocate to developing countries. The goal is to allocate enough credits to each developing country to avoid imposing costs that would damage growth but not so many as to give them a large and profitable surplus. Developing countries would reject an underallocation. Advanced countries would reject an overallocation. The problem is, you don't know, and cannot know in advance, what the right allocation is. To calculate the number of credits needed to "make a country whole," you need to know all the information about costs in the various locations that the system is designed to determine. Before the system is up and running, you don't have that information. And you can't get the system up and running without an initial allocation of the credits.

This sounds like a minor technical glitch but is actually a very serious problem. Take an example. If you allocate credits so that the per capita allocations are equal, developing countries will experience, in the short run, an enormous windfall profit. India has 18.5 percent of the world's population but accounts for 5 percent of total emissions. If credits were allocated on a per capita basis, India would receive 13.5 percent of the total credits that they do not currently need. With total emissions of about 31 billion tons currently, India could be selling in excess of 4 billion tons of credits, the funds coming largely from purchases by advanced countries that would need them.

I think the point is clear. Simple formulas for allocating credits like the one just described are quite likely to produce massive transfers of income from advanced to developing countries, and these would have very little to do with mitigation costs. This fact is known (sort of), and any such scenario would be totally unacceptable to the advanced countries as a group.

The solution to this problem is not to try to modify and complicate the credit-allocation system. It won't work. The solution is just to leave the developing countries out of the credit-trading system and to rely instead on the cross-border mechanism to bring them back into the system for efficiency purposes. Leaving them out will have the effect of accommodating their growth. A functioning cross-border mechanism will bring them back into the system in order to lower total mitigation costs, but without imposing growth-constraining burdens.

Adding the details of how this works would take me beyond what is reasonable to cover here.[6] But one *can* implement a credit-trading system for advanced countries where the issue of potential massive transfers of income is less likely to arise. Developing countries would then join the system when their growth, over several decades, brings them to the graduation point. The timing of this last part of the process will obviously vary across countries.

A tradable credit system in advanced countries combined with an effective cross-border mechanism will reproduce the efficiency characteristics of a fully global system, without the attendant income-transfer issue.

A goal over the next ten years should be to establish such a system for advanced countries.

What is happening now is the development of national or regional credit-trading schemes in a number of advanced and developing countries. Eventually these may be integrated into a larger system, but at the moment the national credits carry location tags. They can, and do, have different prices. But over time a functioning cross-border mechanism will tend to cause these prices to come together, because it will tend to cause the marginal cost of mitigation to equilibrate across countries. At that point it will be easier to drop the location tags and integrate the systems.

This piecemeal approach is probably inevitable, however, and not at all a bad process. Feasible steps can be taken, ones that are much easier to accomplish than global agreements.

There is a secondary issue created by the asymmetric roles of advanced and developing countries. It has to do with energy- and carbon-intensive industries that produce tradable goods, and hence are geographically mobile. If the global approach to mitigation "exempts" the developing countries, so as to accommodate their growth, then there will be an incentive for mobile carbon-intensive industries to migrate to developing countries. That would reduce advanced countries' emissions, but not the global total. This pattern would not only not represent real mitigation, but it would also badly distort location decisions. Neither advanced nor developing countries would benefit.

The implication, clearly, is that for such industries the mitigation system has to be global. Probably the best way to restore the appropriate incentives is to agree to impose a carbon tax on the output of such industries, regardless of their location. The tax would be the carbon price in the advanced-country credit system or an estimate of the marginal cost of mitigation in advance of the implementation of the credit-trading system. But it would require a fully global agreement.

The bottom line seems to me to be that there is a conceivable path that accomplishes the dual objectives of mitigation and developing-country growth. We cannot know if the costs of getting all the way to the end of the path will be tolerable, because we can't know now what the costs in the last couple of decades will be—the technology doesn't yet exist. But the path we are starting on seems consistent with the longer-term path.

To progress further, we need to do three things:

1. Create a competent institution under the auspices of the G20 that will collect and evaluate the best ideas for moving forward, with due attention paid to issues of efficiency, fairness, and asymmetries across nations, and which will give the results to the G20 leadership in an understandable form.[7]
2. As part of the assignment under point 1 (above), to generate a credible time path for emissions patterns across the full range of countries as a basis for evaluating mitigation proposals.
3. Stop trying to reach global agreements on long-term mitigation goals and enthusiastically endorse a step-by-step approach.

37. Information Technology and the Integration of the Global Economy

In 2009, the number of cell phones in the world went above 4 billion for the first time. That's almost two-thirds of the world's people. The number is probably now closer to 4.5 billion.

Fixed and Cell-Phone Penetration

Mobile-phone penetration is very high in many developing countries and is rising rapidly in the rest of them. Rural areas are being reached with telephone and related communications and information services of the type we associate with the Internet, for the first time in history. In a few countries like Italy, there are more cell phones than people. It is a question of function and fashion. (It is gauche to take your BlackBerry to the opera.)

In achieving connectivity in the developing world, it is cell-phone technology that is solving the connectivity problem. A telephone system based on landlines is highly capital intensive, and for many developing countries, the capital cost proves to be simply too great. Mobile phones require capital, but much less than landlines. Mobile phone service has therefore become affordable to hundreds of millions of people.

But what makes this trend so interesting, and so important, is that it doesn't concern only phone service. The cell phone is rapidly becoming, for many, the access point to the Internet and to the world of digital communication. The Internet and the World Wide Web, an invention by and

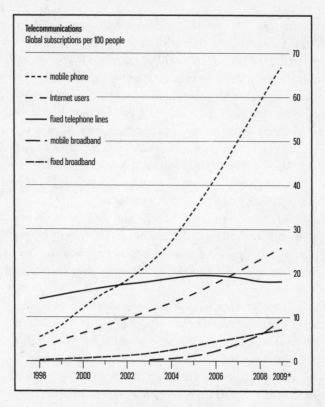

Telecommunications
Global subscriptions per 100 people

- - - - mobile phone
- - - Internet users
——— fixed telephone lines
—•— mobile broadband
—·—· fixed broadband

70
60
50
40
30
20
10
0

1998 2000 2002 2004 2006 2008 2009*

Source: International Telecommunication Union
*Estimate

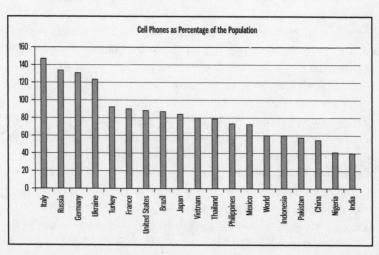

Cell Phones as Percentage of the Population

160
140
120
100
80
60
40
20
0

Italy, Russia, Germany, Ukraine, Turkey, France, United States, Brazil, Japan, Vietnam, Thailand, Philippines, Mexico, World, Indonesia, Pakistan, China, Nigeria, India

for scientists, started to spread in the industrialized countries in the late 1980s, initially with e-mail, then with broadband or higher-speed access throughout the 1990s. The technology then started to migrate to the mobile phone in the latter part of the nineties and accelerated dramatically in the past decade. Mobile access to the Internet became a reality.

Meanwhile, the costs came down, in part because that is what happens pretty much automatically with new technologies, but also because costs decline with volume, and accumulated volume (the learning curve), and, perhaps most important, because they had to in order to gain access to the huge potential market in the developing world. All of this is an emerging reality, and a process still under way.

As recently as six years ago, an ongoing worldwide debate was in progress under the heading of "the digital divide": a world in which the few had access to a growing array of information and transaction services, while the many did not. The *McKinsey Quarterly* reported that

> Only a dozen years ago, for example, authoritative predictions for the coming decade envisioned no more than a few million mobile-phone users throughout Africa. Local income, consumption, technology, infrastructure, and regulatory conditions seemed to hold little promise for significant growth. Less than ten years later, though, Nigeria alone had 42 million mobile subscribers—80 times more than initial forecasts predicted—as growth skyrocketed, largely as a result of the interaction between just two trends: improved income levels and cheaper handsets.

The two-world scenario, the connected and the disconnected, has not come to pass. Technology seems to have largely outrun that older discussion. The focus has shifted to making sure that the potential that is within reach is realized by ensuring that remaining obstacles, including regulatory ones, are removed.

It is a striking feature of the mobile-phone revolution that it largely occurred flying below the radar of telecommunications regulation and without the regulatory structures and constraints that had grown up around the older system of fixed phones and landlines. That old landline regulatory structure came into existence mainly because there are "natural" monopolies embedded in the older system. It makes no sense to have multiple sets of wires running along streets and into houses in order to achieve connectivity. One set is expensive enough. That part of the network is called the "local loop," and it is a natural monopoly. Regulation emerged to prevent abuse of that monopoly power in pricing and access to services. Quite often the state owned the system. In fact, in many countries, the "telephone" monopoly became a profit center and a source of government revenue. Not infrequently the government's regulator forgot that it was supposed to exist to ensure access via high-quality, reasonably priced services and instead engaged in profit-maximizing monopoly-pricing practices. Bureaucratic, inefficient, and high priced would be a better description of the result in many cases.

The mobile phone/networked digital device mostly escaped regulatory oversight. Its growth was largely unanticipated, and hence was either unregulated or lightly regulated. It grew in a highly competitive environment with beneficial effects on cost, price, and the growing array of services.

It is almost impossible to overstate the long-run importance of these emerging trends. It is seen by many to be one of the most significant elements of inclusiveness in the connectivity of the global economy.

To understand why this is important, we need to focus for a bit on the economic impacts of modern information technology.

History

The modern electronic digital computer is a creature of World War II. Thomas Watson, the former CEO of IBM, famously estimated in the early postwar period that the long-run demand for computers would be about three a year. In fairness, the existing computers, which by today's standards were considerably less powerful than your cell phone, were physically huge, they bristled with vacuum tubes that kept burning out in spite of the massive air-conditioning systems that were deployed to keep them cool, and they were very expensive. But Watson's estimate was wrong mainly because he (along with many others) didn't anticipate what would happen to costs, and to computing power.

With U.S. Defense Department funding, the semiconductor device was invented, and it successfully replaced vacuum tubes. The main objective really wasn't cost so much as portability and durability. DOD wanted computers in airplanes, missiles, and tanks, not just on a full floor of a large office building. A major driver of growth and productivity was created for reasons that had nothing to do with either. This is not uncommon.

Moore's law (the number of transistors that can be placed inexpensively on a semiconductor device doubles every eighteen months) took over, and the costs of digital information processing and computing began a long and rapid downward march, one that is still going on.

Cost reductions were therefore achieved mainly by making the devices smaller and smaller, and at the same time faster and faster. Reduced size and portability came along with the cost declines. So you could put the device (call it a computer) in an office, and then a home, and then a briefcase, and then in a handheld device.

As computers proliferated in offices and then on desktops and then in homes, one might have expected some fairly broad-based (across sectors of the economy) productivity gains to show up in the economic data. It didn't. Notwithstanding the declining cost and size, and rising investment by businesses, and eventually by regular people like us, economists' attempts to measure the impact on productivity yielded disappointing results: essentially there wasn't any effect for many years.

Then the pattern changed in the 1980s, when the productivity effects started to show up. They rose in the nineties and are very significant from the mid-nineties to the present. We now know that the big gains in productivity are associated not with powerful computers per se but with the network.

The Internet was developed within the Department of Defense to provide researchers and scientists with the ability to communicate electronically and to transfer data—another example of a key innovation not motivated by its potential economic impact. In fact, the latter was largely unanticipated.

Commercial access to the Internet was allowed for the first time in 1988, and with the introduction of Netscape, a user-friendly piece of software to access the World Wide Web, business and personal use of the Internet and the Web took off. Internet service providers (ISPs) provided access initially over telephone lines. Broadband came with a lag as the chicken-and-egg problem of applications creating demand and broadband access creating incentives for broadband service worked its way through.

It turns out that it was the connectivity that created the large and growing economic (and, indeed, social) impact of networked computers and information technology. The mundane day-to-day activities of acquiring information and completing transactions or interacting and coordinating activity are costly and use up a lot of time. And at some very basic level, all the network did was lower the costs and increase the speed of performing these functions. It sounds mundane, but it is not. The reductions in time and cost are so large that they are changing the informational structure of markets and the world in which we live.

The Economic Impacts of Network-Based Information Technology

In a network-based system, computers talk to computers. Information is stored digitally in electronic databases, and because the computers are connected, this means that every electronic database (numbers, documents, Web pages, libraries) in the world is, in principle, accessible from anywhere else in the world by anyone with the authority to access it. All this happens at very high speed, so there are only insignificant lags. It really doesn't matter where the person and the data are located. In this "virtual" part of the world, the information and communication layer, proximity doesn't matter anymore, and delays are minimal. Increasingly we live in a world in which the binding constraint is not how much information we can find, but how much information we can process.

Network-based information technology makes possible dramatic reductions in the costs of day-to-day activities—what economists call transaction costs. A simple example will illustrate. We Californians own a lot of cars, and we drive a lot. It is not uncommon for a household to own two (or more) cars so that couples can get to work. Cars are required to get just about anywhere, including to buy a loaf of bread. These cars are registered once a year at the Department of Motor Vehicles. Pre-Internet, this required a one-to-two-hour trip to the DMV office, one for each car, and only on a weekday, meaning a workday, because that is the only time the DMV is open. You can still do it that way. But the alternative is about two minutes on the Internet after receiving an access code in the mail, and can be done anytime, including weekends.

It is pretty easy to see that the productivity gains from this one relatively minor application of the Internet and the Web, in this case in delivering a government service, are very large. Then, if you start to multiply them by the thousands of areas in which the process involves information, data, and communications, the elimination of wasted time and loss of productivity is breathtakingly large. Even the subcomponent and side effects—namely, the reduced use of gasoline and the resulting positive effect on air quality, the environment, and CO_2 emissions—are large.

Lying behind this is a feature of networks that has to do with the number of people, or, in the case of the Internet, the numbers of people and computers, connected to the network. (Remember that computers talk to each other.) It is called Metcalfe's law.[1] It says that the value of a network is approximately proportional to the square of the number of users (people plus machines) connected to it. This creates something close to a tipping point: at a certain number of users, the value exceeds the cost for the majority of potential users, and they start multiplying rapidly, increasing the value in total, and to other individual users.

This phenomenon was observed with telephones, and then with faxes. The rate of growth of Internet users was extremely rapid, in part because of the original base of scientific, defense, and academic users, a group that was essentially subsidized. But the other main driver was that the computers and servers and related databases also counted as users, from the point of view of value creation. The result was that within a period of ten to fifteen years, every major organization on the planet was connected to the Internet and the World Wide Web, providing information and access to data and services.

The economic impact of network-based computers came in overlapping, but different, trends. They can be thought of as the following:

- Automation of information and data processing, initially within firms, and then extending out to supply chains.
- The migration of information acquisition activities, search and transactions to the Internet and the World Wide Web as the databases and other stores of information were connected to the network.
- Accessing valuable human resources (regardless of where they are located) and productively employing them in the market processes and supply chains that interconnect the global economy.

Automation

Before the Internet started to spread to businesses and the general public, companies realized that a large fraction of their human resources were devoted to storing and processing information. With computers, the data shifted from paper to electronic storage, but the necessary storage facilities (databases) were scattered geographically. These were updated manually.

As soon as computers were networked, innovators in this field realized that for much of the required information processing and storage activities, the human component wasn't needed. Over time it was just eliminated.

The elimination of manual processing of information reduced labor, time, cost, and errors. The aggregate effect was, and is, enormous. It is what economists call labor-saving technological change. Its anticipation caused distinguished economists like the late Wassily Leontief (Nobel Prize in Economics, 1973) to speculate that the productivity gains and the reduction in employment would be so large that there could be an extended unemployment problem. This did not materialize because the resultant growth and absorptive capacity of the economy turned out to be sufficient, and also because the automation process didn't happen overnight.

Three things become clear when you look at this process from a strictly economic point of view, ignoring the details of the technological underpinnings. This first wave of automation was a productivity-enhancing form of technological progress that was massively labor-saving. This is not an unfamiliar concept. In the course of industrialization, incomes rise and labor gets expensive. Innovators create technologies that substitute capital for this more expensive labor. The value added per worker rises, and the displaced workers do other activities where their added value is also higher, activities that require judgment and analysis.

But before the network-based computers, this hadn't happened much in the portion of the economy that processes information. This layer came to be called the information layer, or the virtual part of the economy. Whatever you call it, it is the essential part that coordinates and controls the underlying economic processes, the production and movement of goods. The productivity effect of the Internet and the automation process was large because the coordination and control functions are required in every industry and sector and company in the economy. A major innovation in the chemical industry may increase productivity in that sector by a lot, but it is only 3 percent of the economy. If you have a major productivity gain in a horizontal function that runs across every vertical sector, then the impact is much larger. That is what happened in this case.

The economic impact of networked computers ultimately came from a dramatic reduction in transaction costs. These are mundane costs that go along with and are required for an economy to function. Economic theory assumes that buyers know the various products on offer, their characteristics, and their prices. For understanding market resource allocation and pricing, there is nothing particularly wrong with this assumption. That's what we teach in intermediate price theory and microeconomics. But in reality people don't magically know products and prices; they have to expend time and effort to find them out. This is just one example of transaction costs. They are everywhere, and as long as they don't change much, they may be safely ignored (well, almost). Oliver Williamson received the Nobel Prize in Economics in 2009 for his research on organizations and markets. When is resource allocation best done by markets and when are nonmarket allocation mechanisms within companies to be preferred? How does the boundary between firms and the market get set? Traditional theory assumes that that boundary is predetermined. In fact, it is endogenous and is determined by competitive pressure to reduce transaction costs of a variety of kinds.

But transaction costs cannot safely be ignored when they are changing rapidly, because, as we shall see, those shifts cause not only large macroeconomic effects on productivity and incomes but also major changes in the microeconomic structural composition and connectedness of the global economy.

Search, Information, and Transactions

For those whose jobs were unaffected by the automation wave, that trend went largely unnoticed. Information processing, coordination, and control are rather like plumbing: as long as it works, one doesn't pay it much mind. The second trend was different. It was noticed by, and affected, everyone directly. The World Wide Web was created by scientists with the goal of publishing academic papers quickly and efficiently. A related benefit was that the papers would be easier to find as well. It turned out that this second part was the main event. You can publish anything on the Web: newspapers, analyst reports, annual reports and financial filings, catalogues, books, articles, journals, music, films, medical information. The volume of "stuff" published electronically grew exponentially and at unheard-of rates. And the central challenge became *finding* things in this mass of information—institutional websites, online stores, books, papers, numerical data, pictures, films. The core technology required to realize the benefits is search. It is a service, and the delivery mechanism is the search engine. This is a rapidly evolving and sophisticated technology and field, and the business models that generate revenue and profits for providing the service are also in a state of rapid change.

With this rapid evolution, the Web became the platform for a range of services that are knowledge intensive and which do not require proximity to be carried out. It turns out that the list of activities that fit this description is incredibly long and comprehensive: e-banking, e-bill pay, e-investing, e-government, e-learning, e-research, e-procurement, e-commerce, e-business, e-citizenship, e-politics, e-publishing, e-news, and e-commentary, to name just a small subset.

What drives all of this is the dramatic reduction in the costs of finding information, communicating, and transacting—that is, in transaction costs, broadly defined. The aggregate effect is staggeringly large in two dimensions. One is the reduction in the time required to do these things. Before the Internet, the costs of doing many of these things were so high that they simply didn't get done. So while in formal economic terms it is correct to say that what we are seeing is the result of reduced transaction costs for information-intensive activities that do not require physical proximity, the practical effect is to increase knowledge, access to information, the power of consumers (via the knowledge effect), and the efficiency and effectiveness of decision making.

I briefly mentioned the business of renewing car registration above. Let's now consider another example, one close to home. Many economists, myself included, need data and information to carry out their research. I would guess that pre-Internet, we would spend on average more than half our research time (maybe 70 percent) locating information and data, and the rest of the available work time on analyzing it. Post-Internet, the percentages are roughly reversed. What is that worth?

Well, I suppose the answer depends on what you think of the quality of the research. But what is indisputable is that the wasted time spent on the cumbersome mechanics of gathering information has been reduced tremendously. For example, if you are interested, in about five minutes you can find out the population, GDP, and incomes for every country in the world. If you pick a specific country and spend another ten minutes, you can find out its size, the major industries in its economy, and its energy consumption and carbon emissions. Over time, low-cost access to relevant information about the global economy and landscape will enable most people (and not just specialists) to become increasingly knowledgeable. The hope (and at this stage it is just a hope) is that broader understanding will eventually result in an informed public and form one of the building blocks of a more effective system of global governance.

Can we measure all these effects? Well, the automation trend that started earlier does produce measurable benefits in the form of reduced labor costs in the information and control layer of the economy. In the second category of search, information acquisition, and transactions, the truth is that we do not know how to measure the effects quantitatively, at least not yet. The likelihood is that pieces will be measured, but adding them all up will be a challenge. Farmers in developing countries will increase their output with better market and weather information, for example. Schoolchildren in much of the world will have access to a library for the first time. It is hard to know how to quantify these effects. Broad areas will remain resistant to quantification, but that does not diminish their importance. If less time is spent on what might be called the mechanics of life, it can be spent on reading or study or sports or interacting with friends—in leisure. Income data won't capture very well these shifts in the quality of life.

Is There a Downside to All This?

There is. Pretty much anything can be made more efficient with these powerful informational tools, and that includes money laundering, terrorism, snooping, coordinating criminal activity, and identity theft. In the early days of the growth of public use of the Internet, a young professor at NYU referred to the potential privacy-loss effect as the result of the "collapse of inconvenience." Privacy is threatened not just because of "hacking" but more importantly because the costs of collecting information are so much lower than they were before. You can find out where I live, how many houses I have, what they are worth, and so on, with very little investment of time, and without breaching any "private" databases. In principle, pre-Internet, you could collect this same information, but in practice the costs were prohibitive. Hence the collapse of inconvenience.

Misinformation can be propagated and disseminated at low cost. Some people worry that there are few mechanisms beyond the laws related to liability and slander to "edit" the information and commentary for bias. Others celebrate the democratization of the world of comment and analysis. All of us who are the consumers of information are on a learning curve, upping our skepticism and revising the filters we use to sort out reliable information from that which is unreliable, and at times plain malicious.

There is a sense among many that the constant connectivity is a burden, not a boon. I cannot count the number of times I have heard people say the main benefit of flying is that the cell phone and the BlackBerry don't work "up there"—at least not yet. The walls of the last refuge from bits and bytes may come tumbling down soon. As with filtering information, managing time and controlling constant connectivity so that it doesn't take over your life is a learning process (individual and social) that takes time. One hopes that, in time, etiquette will make it rude to read your e-mail while talking over lunch. All of this is so very new.

The Internet Bubble

When investors (and, more broadly, people in general) started to see the potential scope of the impact of this technology, a moment of temporary irrational exuberance occurred. Business and engineering students with venture-capital backing started just about every imaginable type of Internet company. Some of these start-ups would, it was said, put traditional retailers out of business: brick-and-mortar retailers would be a thing of the past. Others would increase the quality and efficiency of search. Many failed, but not all. Some new enterprises, like eBay, Amazon, Yahoo, and Google thrived and became important companies. Meanwhile the suppliers of computers and networks that are the nervous system of the network came about as close as you can get in business to printing money. But at the time, investors and the markets didn't discriminate very well among the new ventures. Prices were set by individual investors and day traders, many of whom would have flunked a quiz on what the companies actually produced or did, if such a quiz had been administered. Valuations escalated into the stratosphere. Conventional valuation approaches, based on earnings and growth, could not provide an underpinning that made any sense. In fact, they were not even close.

Many companies never produced a profit, and a nontrivial fraction never produced any revenues; nevertheless, at the height of the enthusiasm for this new world, they managed to "go public" with an IPO. Selling the future without a track record of any kind actually worked for a while. Because it was a new world, historical data didn't apply. It was an environment in which imaginations unconstrained by data could soar—again, for a while. But with the passing of months, and then a few years, data did start to come in. The valuations were evidently too high and the markets plunged.

To much of the general public this signaled that the whole enterprise had been a gigantic mistake, another tulip bubble: that the lofty visions of transformation of business, knowledge, consumer power, supply chains, and the global economy were just that—visions, and not much more. This is, to be sure, the simplest interpretation of the bursting of the bubble. But it is probably not the right interpretation. In fact, the visions, while somewhat exaggerated, were in many respects accurate, and the unfolding reality over the longer term is not all that dissimilar to the forecasts. The problem with the valuations wasn't the vision. It was, as is so often the case, a misunderstanding of the time scale on which revolutionary change occurs. The investors predicted months, while the reality is that transformations take years, even decades. People and organizations don't change their behavior overnight. Implementation is hard and faces a host of technical obstacles. Thousands of legacy systems had to be integrated to achieve the full set of envisioned benefits. There are embedded interests in any system that are threatened by change. Aunt Millie may not be bowled over by Steve Jobs extolling the virtues of the Internet, but she does respond to her nieces' and nephews' pressure to get on e-mail or Skype.

It is important not to lose sight of both lessons. Revolutionary change takes time, and that time is commonly underestimated, to the regret of investors. But the fact that it takes time doesn't mean it won't happen.

Accessing Human Talent Globally

The defining characteristics of the Internet are connectivity, speed, the irrelevance of location, and asynchronous communication (like e-mail and fax, and unlike the telephone and surfing the Web) when needed or desirable. The "participants" on the network are people and computers, and the latter are talking to each other all the time. On one level, this means that databases are linked; activities that are scattered geographically can be controlled and coordinated and made efficient. Global supply chains have the advantage of using low-cost resources around the world—that is not new. They have historically also had the disadvantage that management and control over a geographically distributed domain used to be costly and prone to delays, miscommunication, errors, time-zone issues, and inefficiency. Much of that disadvantage is in the process of disappearing. Of course transportation costs have not disappeared (though they have declined), and when things have to be moved around, those costs have to be factored in—unless, that is, what is being moved around is information.

This brings us to perhaps the most significant long-run effect of the spread of the Internet. Human potential is scattered around the world pretty much randomly. In an increasing portion of the world, that human potential is being turned into valuable talent by combining it with education and the learning that goes with productive employment. But much of that human talent is inaccessible. In the global economy, goods and capital are quite mobile, but labor (that is, people) is much less so. To make use of human talent, jobs can move to people or people can move to jobs. In most healthy national economies, both happen. But in the global economy, people face high barriers when it comes to moving to jobs: the more important process is jobs moving to people. And that is what has been happening.

There is an important set of services that people uniquely provide, and these are both information processing and knowledge intensive. By definition, of course, they are labor intensive. With the need for physical proximity removed by information technology, the markets for these services (and the labor markets that support their provision) are becoming global. The jobs are moving to the people, wherever they are located. Because the delivery of the service involves bits and bytes, the disadvantage of remoteness is negligible. Human resources that formerly were inaccessible because of the need for proximity have joined the labor market. To put it differently, for this class of information (knowledge- and human-capital-intensive services), the geographic boundaries of labor markets are collapsing and the formerly disparate geographic markets are integrating and becoming global.

Outsourcing is a part but certainly not all of this. Many of these services are provided inside organizations (business, government, and non-profit). This subgroup is sometimes referred to as insourcing. We have outsourcing and insourcing in a growing array of service sectors: management of IT systems, software development, business processes, customer service and support. And the list is getting longer. Functions in the medical area such as analysis of X-rays and MRI scans are being carried out remotely. Surgery with remote expert input is also being experimented with. Editing of video for TV is a new area. The expanding scope also includes surprising, and even funny, areas: writing political speeches for semiliterate politicians, grading exams for teachers who are too lazy to grade their own, and so on. As the list lengthens, the volume is growing at 30 percent a year. It is probably the fastest-growing area in international trade. It is surely one of the primary drivers of growth in India, which has been in the forefront of this trend, in part because English is an official language.

Interestingly, the origins of the remote provision of services were not international but domestic. Before international trade in services blossomed, banks and credit card companies in the United States and Europe were performing services from states and provinces with educated, but remote, and therefore relatively inexpensive, labor. These initial forays tended to be customer service centers. One might object that customer service centers require only phone connections, and have nothing to do with the Internet. Actually, that isn't true. For service to be high quality, the service providers require real-time access to the corporate customer databases so that they actually know with whom they are talking and what they are talking about. That access is made possible at low cost by the networked databases and the Internet.

It is interesting that the first major impact of network-based information technology was automation and labor-saving technical change. There were of course other benefits in speed, accuracy, ability to coordinate activity over great distances, and the like. The third category, accessing valuable human resources, brings people back into the picture and in a sense is the opposite of the first category. It is about functions and activities that are inherently labor intensive, because there is no known substitute for people. Rather than replacing people, this trend is about finding and utilizing highly skilled human resources all over the world for what are inherently labor-intensive activities. The markets in highly skilled labor are becoming more global as technology brings down the costs that formerly made proximity important. There are limits to this. As noted earlier in thinking about urbanization, the value of proximity has not declined to zero. What those limits are we do not yet know. But we are on a journey in which they will be discovered.

The Distribution of Benefits

Is this trend toward the globalization of a subset of labor markets good for everyone? Not necessarily, in the short run. It certainly benefits educated people in developing countries who were formerly remote from the jobs. Opportunities increase and incomes rise. But when a labor market is protected by barriers, whatever their origin, and those barriers are removed by policy or technology, there will be more competition on the supply side, and the incumbents (the ones formerly protected by those barriers) will probably experience declines in incomes or loss of jobs, or both. How long this "short run" lasts really depends on the growth rate of the formerly protected economy, its flexibility, the structural evolution of the composition of the outsourcing economy, and the speed with which it creates new jobs.

Ultimately the question that gets asked is the following: "If highly educated scientists, engineers, doctors, and others are similar in their abilities regardless of their location, and if they can add value without much impediment in the form of a disadvantage on account of remoteness, then where does the comparative advantage of the advanced countries lie?" For much of the recent past, our belief, in Western countries, was that our comparative advantage lay in knowledge, research, and human-capital-intensive activities, including education. But that is precisely the territory in which the markets are becoming global. It may still be true that the comparative advantage of advanced countries lies in these areas, but there is more competition, and arguably the degree of differentiation and comparative advantage are diminished. It is possible that an important part of the comparative advantage of advanced countries in the future will lie in precisely these areas, but only the ones that do durably require proximity to perform at the highest level. There is a reason why there are major global financial centers and why advanced economies are largely urban. Proximity still matters, and that could continue to be a basis for differentiation in value creation and disparate income levels. But it may also not be enough to sustain employment and incomes in the future.

The truth is that we are in the middle of a rapidly evolving global economic structure, and we do not know, and probably cannot calculate, what the medium-term destination will be. It is not that the principles and forces aren't understood. It is rather that the system is too complex to lend itself to forecasting.

One can think of these powerful forces in the upper skill end of the labor market as similar in impact to a large-scale relaxation of immigration policies and restrictions, but with the proviso that these new "immigrants" are confined to fields in which the services can be performed equally effectively remotely, given the state of technology. That proviso, of course, is what makes the analogy imperfect. As a legal and practical matter, advanced countries probably can't have immigration with labor-market restrictions attached. Some countries, however, do have immigration with educational and professional qualification requirements.[2] Further, what is globalizable is a moving target as innovation in the technology and managerial underpinnings shifts the boundaries, adding to the complexity. I strongly suspect that a colleague of mine was at least partly right when he referred to education once as a "body contact sport"— that is, it's more effective with proximity. I have similar suspicions about venture capital and other important parts of finance, and about a host of functions in which learning, judgments about people and capabilities, and trust are important ingredients.

Nevertheless, this is the right time for honesty about what we do and do not know about who benefits in the process of globalization, and who loses. Globalization was sold initially as benefiting everyone. When that didn't turn out to be the case, the formulation was modified to "potentially benefiting everyone," where the "potentially" part involved compensating losers through redistribution of income. This proposition is based on static welfare analysis and the gains from trade. That modified principle probably still is true, provided the unit of analysis is the global economy. To be more specific, it is valid provided one can redistribute income across the global economy. But it isn't necessarily true for individuals or subgroups, or for nations, which nevertheless remain the primary political and social decision-making units. The distribution of benefits across subunits of the global economy is an empirical, not a theoretical, problem. Redistribution within nations is feasible and normal, though it does not always take place. It is much more problematic transnationally.

To say that everyone benefits in principle is therefore somewhat misleading, because what makes the "in principle" part valid is potential redistribution. In the global economy, that potential is pretty remote once you get outside of nation-states.

Globalization has been and is of enormous importance to developing countries for the reasons discussed in Part II. It is also true that if you add up all the benefits in terms of rising incomes, the number is very large and positive and rising over time, and if there is a bias in the distribution of benefits, it surely runs in the direction of at least a subset of developing countries—the ones that have succeeded in finding a productive engagement with the global economy. All of this would strike most people as benign. And their argument would be based at least in part on distribution, and not just on total income and output.

Furthermore, no advanced country has yet experienced extended periods of negative real growth, or even low growth, since World War II. So it is not possible to argue that globalization thus far has produced actual losers at the level of nations—there aren't any.

You could object by saying that isn't the right question; your argument might be that globalization has lowered the growth rates in advanced countries. I doubt it, though, and suspect that most economists would agree. But it would be very hard to prove either way. It is one of those counterfactual questions to which we will probably never have the answer.

Nevertheless, looking to the future and to the trends in the direction of globalization in the high-end labor markets, it is possible that the distributional impacts will be greater and more adverse with respect to advanced countries. If that were to happen, I expect their response would be policy choices that have the effect of slowing down the globalization process by re-erecting partial barriers. The result of these policy responses would be a slowing down of the structural evolution of the global economy, and a slowing down of the rate of change of relative prices. That may be the cost of sustaining support for the openness of the global economy.

The welfare propositions we have about trade and the global economy come from static models. By "static," economists mean that if we compare the pre- and post-trade equilibria, benefits are higher in the latter when you add them all up. How they are distributed is a different question. Subunits can lose in this static analysis. Loss in advanced countries tends to occur when developing countries experience big increases in productivity in sectors where the advanced countries have a comparative advantage.[3] That abstract description fits with the globalization of knowledge and human-capital-intensive service sectors.

But the most important point to understand is that the bigger and longer-term effects have to do with the dynamics. We do not have powerful models and theories that tell us what the intertemporal welfare effects of growth in the global economy will be. We have data. Advanced countries seem to grow at quite acceptable rates, except in crises; and a subset of developing countries has grown at heretofore unimaginable rates. Thus far in the postwar period, the overall results look benign.

We also know that the medium- and longer-term impacts depend on mobility of resources and on structural flexibility. This is clearly true for the developing countries and is easy to see because of the high growth rates and the overall speed of the process. But it is equally true for advanced countries. The benefits are higher and the costs are lower with flexible labor and capital markets and an entrepreneurial and dynamic private sector.

Beyond that we should stop making assertions based on static models about the distribution of benefits, not because the assertions are wrong in a static context, but because they are irrelevant. The important effects are the intertemporal ones. For these, the current state of theory is not advanced enough to permit confident statements about the distribution of benefits.

The best defense of globalization thus far is that millions of people are materially better off and have the prospect of having grandchildren who will live in an advanced country. The advanced countries have done just fine, and are slowly getting used to the idea that as the developing countries increase their share of the global economy, advanced countries are not exempt from structural transformation. Perhaps we are getting better at adapting our policies to the shifting external need to protect people and help them in transitions.

We can also admit that it is possible in the future that the patterns may shift enough that the distribution of benefits and costs will make it harder to sustain support for the openness of the global economy. If that happens, we have two possible avenues to pursue. One is to slow the process down. That is the most likely avenue, but it is also the noncooperative one. If it will occurs, if it will be because the political costs of sustaining support for the cooperative outcomes becomes too high.

The other possibility is more remote, but still imaginable. It is that we have built the institutions of global governance to the point that distributional issues can be dealt with internationally as well as within countries. I have to admit that I think this second possibility is a long way off, but one can at least hope to be wrong about that.

Cell Phones and the Developing World

I began this discussion with a look at cell phones in the developing world: 4 billion phones worldwide and rising—some people with more than one in the advanced countries, some sharing a phone in the developing world.

It looked for a while as if the powerful forces for change and empowerment through access to information embedded in the Internet would play out over time in a subset of the world's countries and people and simply bypass the rest. In business, banking, commerce, social interaction, access to information, and connectivity to global supply chains, poor countries and poor people in remote areas would simply not participate. But we underestimated technology and entrepreneurial incentives in search of large markets. What appeared a few short years ago as a digital divide (more like a chasm) seems to be in the process of collapsing. Mobile phones are now commonly digital devices connected to the Internet. A growing array of by now familiar information, communication, and transaction services are available to people of all income levels and at all locations, at very low cost. True, services that require large screens and/or high-speed connections are a continuing challenge. But the trends in costs of equipment and network speed are favorable.

It is hard to overstate the economic importance of this trend. The low-cost availability of information increases productivity, efficiency, and market awareness. Fifty percent of the world still lives in rural areas—and until now in relative isolation. But increasingly financial transactions and banking can be conducted with mobile phones. Payments, savings, credit—the most fundamental financial enablers of commerce and business—are becoming accessible to the vast majority of people. For some of these basic services often the technology required is nothing more that a secure SMS transmission.

It is estimated that the flow of remittances to developing countries each year is at (or above) the flow of foreign aid for development purposes. Remittances are funds sent (mostly by citizens of developing countries living in another country) back to the home country, usually to family. The total is somewhere near $100 billion per year.

What of the transaction costs associated with these massive (and growing) private transfers? The World Bank has estimated recently that for individual transfers in the range of $200 to $500, the transaction costs are not uncommonly in the range of 10 percent of the transfer, and can get as high as 15 percent, including foreign-exchange transaction fees. Thus, somewhere around $10 billion a year disappears on the trip from the source (the wage earner in a foreign country) to the destination (the family back home). These very high costs result from a variety of sources: local monopoly power and uncompetitive pricing, poor regulation, and very inefficient multistep processes with every step in the chain collecting a fee.

These costs are set to come down dramatically via mobile-phone-based electronic banking and the additional infrastructure to facilitate efficient international electronic transfers. There is nothing in the evolving cost structure that would justify these historically high costs. It is just a matter of filling in the financial supply chain.

This is just one example, but repeated often enough, the aggregate effect becomes quite transformational. What we feel in advanced countries as a huge increase in convenience, access to information, and economical use of time in transactions and commerce is for many in the developing countries felt as access for the first time to essential services: safe savings channels; access to credit; expansion of potential markets beyond traditional geographic boundaries; job opportunities; relevant and timely information about market prices, weather, and health issues; access to books and periodicals; communication and social interaction; support groups and systems; and low-cost access to government services.

Knowledge and access to information are the underpinnings of much of the value creation in the modern world. Without them, productivity, potential output, and incomes are seriously constrained. Such a constrained environment characterizes the way in which many people in the world have lived for generations. And that is about to change. It may be the most egalitarian aspect of globalization. We can look forward to a period in which the opportunities and incomes of poor people in many parts of the world expand substantially.

Access to information and connectivity in the transaction systems will not remove all the obstacles to growth. No one views these technological developments as a substitute for basic education, for example. But the capacity to leverage the human capital created by basic education via connectivity, access to information, and the removal of isolation is extraordinary. We are in the early stages of this mini-revolution. It may turn out that the most important long-run human impact of the constant drumbeat of Moore's law will be a form of inclusiveness. People may still live in environments in which the physical infrastructure is deficient by advanced-country standards. It takes many years to build all that. But the gap in knowledge, information, transactions, and connectivity in the virtual world is closing faster than anyone could have believed possible even ten years ago.

38. European Integration and Transnational Governance

After World War II, Europe began a process of economic and then political integration that is still in process sixty years later. It will likely require another fifty years to complete, if it is ever to be fully successful. It is a very large-scale attempt to build a functioning supranational unit with economic, political, and governance dimensions. The goal is a deep level of integration. If it succeeds, there will be authoritative governance structures functioning above the level of the nation-state. In many ways it is a massive real-time experiment in transnational governance. As I write, Europe is at a crucial crossroads, dealing with sovereign-debt issues in the periphery and spillover effects to the eurozone and its currency.

The scope and depth of the interdependencies in the global economy have run well ahead of global governance structures. Maybe the governance structure (the tortoise) will catch up with the economy (the hare). But it is not a done deal, nor a sure thing. It may not even be a good bet. But how this comes out is likely to have a profound effect on the future of growth—not only of the developing world but of the whole global economy.

This mismatch between governance and the market creates, at the very least, tensions. It is unlikely that the march of globalization can be sustained if the gap continues to widen. And if it is sustained, it will be along a volatile and bumpy path, with the risk of accidents along the way. A central issue for the next few decades, and a couple of generations, is whether that gap will widen or close.

This matters to millions of people in the developing world because, as we have seen, the global economy is what enables very rapid growth in developing countries. Economic integration has its limits without a parallel process of building effective and legitimate supranational political institutions. I use the term "political" here to refer to processes in which we make collective choices.

The dominant political-economic formula, or model, that prevails in most of the world involves a division of labor and behavior. In that model the economy is the domain of the pursuit of self-interest while the government and the political process are supposed to take charge of making collective choices in pursuit of the common interest. To be sure, there are modifications and qualifications to this overly simple formulation. Shared values such as honesty undoubtedly increase the efficiency of the economy. A financial system in which the participants understand and take seriously their collective responsibility for stability of the system in addition to the regulators isn't a bad idea, but it is slightly at variance with the notion of pure narrow self-interest. Individuals internalize environmental concerns and reflect them in their purchasing behavior. As a complement to regulation and more formal incentive adjustments such as pricing effluents or carbon, this is likely to be a powerful and beneficial force, in part because it is cheaper than regulation.

But by and large, the economy remains the domain of self-interest and decentralization operating in an evolving framework of laws and policies designed to enable contracts and investment and to constrain, influence, and adjust market outcomes to make them socially desirable and acceptable.

The picture painted above is not the global economy at present. The economy remains the domain of self-interest, but the political structure is not unified and consists of groups of people, called nations, pursuing their individual collective self-interest. There is no evidence or theory that suggests this structure will work, either in economic or political terms, or that it will produce good results. On the economic side it may turn out to be unstable, or incapable of protecting the relatively more vulnerable people and nations. Also, within this structure it may be too hard to reach collective decisions where some large common interest is at stake.

The genius of the market system is that it doesn't require micro-level intervention and coordination to work. The noncooperative equilibrium (in which every individual and every legal entity pursues its self-interest and in which everyone is doing as well for themselves as they can, given what others are doing) sounds bad. But it is actually good, provided there is credible governmental entity that pursues, perhaps imperfectly, the common or collective interest. The government does this in a variety of ways. It provides for enforceable contracts. It identifies externalities and modifies the behavior, or the incentives of the players, to take them into account. It identifies problems in markets that come from informational gaps and asymmetries and intervenes to close the gaps or constrain the misuse of informational advantage. It invests in public goods that tend to be underprovided with private incentives alone.

In the global economy, the piece that is largely missing is the global effective government pursuing the common interest. I say largely because there are ongoing attempts to pursue genuinely common global interests in a number of areas—liberalizing trade is one example. But the dominant political forces remain national. So we have a system in which the global economy functions much like a domestic economy, but in which the pursuit of the collective interests is replaced by a noncooperative equilibrium, with the players (nations) pursuing their self-interest.

Will nations pursuing their self-interest on top of an increasingly dynamic and integrated economic structure work? For those who think it will not, the natural question is: "What supranational governance structures are needed, then, and can they be created?" And for those who think the answer to this last question is either "no" or "not for a long time," what would be the consequences: deglobalization, partial globalization, lower growth, more risk, environmental disasters?

That is why the European experiment is so important. It is important in itself, for those who live there and for the global system. At the very least it is a very big economy. As such it changes the balance of power and influence. But it is also a huge pilot project in building supranational governance capability. The issue is whether people—that is, citizens—whose collective identity is deeply rooted in their nations and languages and cultures will be willing to cede control to supranational entities.

On the optimistic side, the global economy was built in part by far-sighted cooperative action.

39. Global Governance in a Multispeed World

The global economy is resetting after the traumatic 2008–09 financial crisis that shook the banking system, disrupted growth, raised unemployment, and increased tensions among and within countries. The crisis exposed big gaps at virtually every level of national societies—from individuals who bought homes they could not afford using exotic mortgages that they did not understand; to firms that had inadequate risk-management systems, poor incentives, and partial disclosures; to governments that failed in their regulatory responsibilities and prudential supervision.

These consequential breakdowns occurred in multiple national jurisdictions—most critically in the highly finance-dependent economies of the U.K. and the United States. Yet they do not constitute the whole story. They were also accompanied by amplifying failures at the global level. More than ever before, the crisis exposed the damaging inadequacies in the governance of a global system that has become highly interdependent while lacking in prudential redundancies and circuit breakers.

In contrast to the national level, where large parts of society were caught unaware by the extent of the underlying vulnerabilities, recognition was less of an issue at the global level. After all, there were many analyses of the persistent and well-publicized payment imbalances, unfair country representation at the international financial institutions, and the general legitimacy deficit in global governance. There were, and continue to be, concerns about an international exchange-rate regime that is a mixture of floating and managed exchange rates with little effective oversight and management balance and stability in the whole system.

High recognition did not give way to meaningful action until the global financial crisis imposed a "sudden stop" on trade, contaminated economic activity, and fueled a surge in joblessness. The global reaction that followed was key to avoiding a global depression. And rather than be coordinated through the long-standing mechanisms of the G7 and the IMF, this crisis-management exercise brought to the fore a relatively new grouping, that of the G20, which involves a more sensible representation of both industrial and emerging economies.

Despite this critical success of the global crisis *management* response—and despite the even more evident prior failures in global crisis *prevention*—the focus on better global governance is already dissipating. National and (in the case of Europe) regional issues are again becoming much more dominant, and not only in absolute terms, but also in a fashion that is undermining recent gains at the global level.

If this phenomenon continues—and it will continue if left to its own devices—it will reverse some of the achievements and make the resetting of the global economy an even bumpier, lengthier, and less comprehensive process. The result will be a global economy that retains a significant element of instability that, regrettably, will again prove problematic over the medium term.

The purpose of this chapter is threefold. First, to summarize the manner in which failures at the global level contributed to the financial crisis; second, to show how the subsequent enthusiasm for globally coordinated policy responses has already given way to conflicting national and regional initiatives; and, third, to explain why, in the absence of corrective steps, weak global governance will remain a hindrance to medium-term growth and financial stability.

Global Governance in the Run-up to the Global Financial Crisis

It is widely recognized today that many factors contributed to the global financial crisis. One of these multiple factors was the persistence of global imbalances—the seemingly endless willingness and ability of surplus countries to run persistent surpluses, and of deficit countries to run persistent deficits.

By "willingness" I mean a reflection of national beliefs that the status quo was in the interest of individual countries, be they in surplus or in deficit. Among the surplus countries, led by China, the initial driver was a desire to accumulate large stocks of international reserves for prudential (self-insurance) reasons. This purpose was soon overshadowed by the reality of how a dynamic net-export orientation facilitates massive job creation, income generation, and poverty alleviation. In the deficit countries, led by the United States, it was hard to resist the temptation to maintain consumption well above levels warranted by national-income generation. This was particularly the case when appreciating asset prices appeared to be continuously increasing the wealth of households, businesses, nonprofit institutions, and even governments.

How about the "ability" of surplus and deficit countries to stay the course or change course? Two elements were in play here that asymmetrically impacted surplus and deficit countries: first, the ability to control one's destiny, and, second, the ability to change course.

Surplus countries maintained much greater ability to maintain their chosen course. Unlike the deficit economies, they did not need to rely on others to fund consumption. And the longer the imbalances persisted, the greater the improvements in their international financial balance sheet.

By contrast, deficit countries relied on external borrowing to cover the inadequacy of their internal savings and, with time, incurred a growing cost of servicing that part of the debt. The extent of their reliance varied, depending on whether they could borrow in their local currencies, how far they could extend maturities, and the extent of their overall stock of debt.

There were also variations across countries in the extent of net borrowing by households and governments. For example, in the United States, both rose rapidly in the run-up to the crisis. The same was true of the U.K. and Spain. Many other E.U. countries, however, did not experience a significant expansion of household debt.

The ability to change course was also material. It was not easy. At the very root of the analysis, the persistence of the imbalances reflected structural (and not just pricing and exchange-rate) issues. As such, policy adaptations faced complex design and implementation challenges. The sociopolitical narrative required considerable attention, which was mostly lacking or badly handled. Moreover, as tends to be the case with structural reforms, short-term political considerations often clashed with the required longer-term economic and financial reorientations.

This combination of willingness and ability factors fueled increasingly unstable conditions at both the national and the global levels. Too large a range of activities was enabled by a system that lacked the needed national and international infrastructures. The system built to a critical state.

By early 2007, the growing excesses were starting to give way to instability. Initially, the cracks were within specific sectors at the national level (e.g., the subprime segment of the U.S. housing market). But the combination of deep-rooted excesses and faulty circuit breakers fueled a morphing crisis that first went national, then global. The world witnessed a cascading series of market and policy failures, resulting in the major global financial crisis that put large segments of populations at risk, and set the world on the verge of a great economic and social depression.

At that stage, policy makers scrambled, adopting a "whatever it takes" mode. The policy response abandoned careful planning and conventional tools in its well-intentioned attempt to stabilize the situation at any cost. And policy makers had no choice but to risk a combination of collateral damage, unintended consequences, moral hazard, and incentive misalignments, while at the same time eroding the long-standing integrity of key institutions.

The Global Crisis Response: Effectiveness

As policy makers gathered in Washington, D.C., in early October 2008 for the annual meetings of the IMF and the World Bank, they quickly recognized that their national narratives were replicated in other countries. It became evident that they were all in the midst of a major global crisis that required a global response.

That response essentially came in two steps. The first, which was led by the United Kingdom at the October annual meetings, involved a coordinated multicountry approach to stabilizing the banking system and, within that, the functioning of a range of funding mechanisms. The second, which emerged from the April 2009 meeting of the G20 in London, involved a multicountry effort to arrest the collapse in economic activity using massive fiscal and monetary-policy stimulus.

Both policy reactions were successful. The banking system slowly regained its footing, helped by massive injections of capital, guaranteed borrowing, and steep yield curves. Funding markets started to normalize. However, the sheer size and distributional aspects of bailing out the banks left a large residue of anger that impacted political outcomes, with consequences for subsequent reform directions.

On balance, we suspect that this historical episode will be viewed as an impressive example of economic global coordination. A lot of it was designed on the fly. The catalyst was a sinister crisis that was lurching from bad to worse. And, particularly when it came to substance, the response essentially bypassed the long-standing institutions that had stood for years at the center of the international monetary system (most notably the IMF and the G7)—illustrating once again that the global architecture was in need of urgent reform.

The question then turned to whether global coordination could also prevail in the postcrisis phase. Could such coordination help clean up the collateral damage and the unintended consequences of the emergency measures? And could the coordination develop deep institutional roots that would ensure perseverance and long-term effectiveness?

Postcrisis Global Policy Response: Dilution

Unfortunately, it did not take long for national and regional considerations to dominate once again. This was most evident in the United States and Europe.

Pushed by internal political pressures, the United States and certain European authorities announced a series of unilateral policy measures that effectively preempted the discussions that were taking place at the multilateral level. Examples included U.S. announcements on taxation, the regulation of banks, and financial-sector reform. They also included the United States' bilateral dealing with the Chinese on exchange-rate policy. Additionally, the low-interest-rate monetary policy of the Federal Reserve in the United States complicated the management of capital flows, asset prices, and inflation in the emerging economies.

Some European countries also moved independently. Witness the initiatives to regulate hedge funds and, in the case of Germany, the dramatic announcement on the banning of naked short selling.

Many of these items were on the agenda of the G20. Yet when push came to shove, national authorities showed little interest in returning to the collaborative mechanisms that had worked so effectively in the immediate aftermath of the global financial crisis.

All this led to more than just recriminations and heated multilateral discussions; it also sent confusing signals to the markets and to businesses, providing an additional headwind to investment activity and, more generally, the sustainable level of final private demand needed to make a meaningful dent in the high unemployment rates prevailing in many industrial economies.

Europe had an additional problem. The collateral damage from the 2008–09 "whatever it takes" policy responses manifested itself in the form of huge budgetary deficits that the weaker members of the eurozone could no longer fund in an orderly fashion. Greece was the poster child, having run persistently high deficits even before the global financial crisis. Portugal also faced market pressures.

Spain did not enter the crisis with huge fiscal deficits. But it soon became evident that its fiscal situation was tentative, the product of a leverage-fueled real estate bubble whose collapse caused government revenues to fall and social insurance payments to rise. A difficult lesson relearned in many countries and subunits is that financial and economic imbalance causes fiscal imbalance; and fiscal issues can quickly translate into pressures on the banking system.

Facing a quickly amplifying crisis of its own, Europe responded dramatically, if less than sufficiently. Europe's reponse included agreement on large fiscal stabilization funds, a complete turnaround in the European Central Bank's attitude toward asset purchases, and a series of national announcements on fiscal austerity.

Interestingly, this dramatic response was formulated at the regional level, with little global coordination. This was most vividly illustrated by the initial strong aversion expressed by European policy makers to having the IMF involved in regional issues—a stance that was reversed in a humiliatingly public fashion. Indeed, Europe went from insisting that it needed no IMF help to counting on the institution for over $200 million of the $1 trillion "shock and awe" package aimed at safeguarding and stabilizing the eurozone and the euro. Europe also looked to the IMF for technical expertise in managing the conditionality of the package.

It mattered little in Europe that the IMF was in no position to pre-commit such an amount to a region. It mattered little that the issue had not been properly discussed by the board of the IMF, which represents its 186 member countries. And it mattered little that the announcement went against the long-standing principle that the IMF treats its individual member countries on a case-by-case basis and adopts a uniformity of treatment when it comes to assessing financing needs and policy conditionality.

Europe's initial exclusion of the IMF, abruptly followed by the co-option of the IMF, sent a signal that goes beyond the subservience of global considerations to national and regional ones. It also highlighted the persistence of representation and legitimacy deficits in global governance.

Looking Forward

The global financial crisis demonstrated that our globalized world has reached a level of international connectivity that far exceeds the reach of national policies and the effectiveness of the global architecture. It also demonstrated the extent to which the system as a whole lacked the redundancies and circuit breakers necessary for a degree of systemic resilience.

Initially the crisis forced national governments to coordinate their policy responses and to abandon representation mechanisms that made sense sixty years ago but no longer do so today. Yet the postcrisis period is already seeing a dilution in this trend toward greater cooperation.

Should we worry about this reversal, and can something be done? Yes, and yes.

The postcrisis world requires a multiyear resetting of the global economy. Elsewhere, we have likened it to a journey on an uneven road, through unfamiliar territory, to an as-yet-unknown destination. Importantly, this "bumpy journey to a new normal" is being undertaken with most of the spare tires already used up, resulting in a very limited capacity to accommodate any additional market accidents and policy mistakes. Political accommodation is also in short supply, given the trend toward greater polarization and anti-incumbency.

Postcrisis, we are looking at a world of more muted growth in industrial countries, reregulation, partial financial deglobalization (as a way to diminish the impact of disruptive financial transmission channels), and, more generally, a shift in the balance between unfettered markets and government involvement. It is also a world where systemically important emerging markets can probably maintain their development breakout phase, provided they are properly accommodated within the international financial system.

This type of world urgently needs steady hands at the helm of global governance. It also needs fundamental reform in a number of areas. Yet, as argued above, the trend is going the other way.

Management of the Global Economy in the Past Twenty-five Years

Part of the challenge is to identify the problem correctly. The global economy for much of the past twenty-five years has been running in dual mode. With priorities and policies set largely by the advanced countries via the G7/8 mechanism, the advanced countries oversaw a steady opening of the economy and the financial system. Exchange rates floated and were set by markets and global financial flows. Capital accounts were mostly open, and monetary policy was pursued independently, with inflation being the primary target.

Meanwhile, the developing countries, responding to a more complex set of growth and development priorities, took a different path. Capital controls were retained and phased in and out as the perceived need changed. Exchange rates were managed via the capital controls and the accumulation and shedding of reserves.

On the real economy side, most developing economies opened markets at a measured pace with the goal of keeping the job creation and destruction forces in reasonable balance. Interventions in the form of subsidies, tax concessions, special export zones with preferential tariffs, and priority infrastructure development were commonly used to jumpstart export diversification. Some were more successful than others.

Standing back, one can see that on a global basis we ran a hybrid system with different de facto rules and practices for advanced and developing countries. It worked remarkably well for the final quarter of the twentieth century. It did so in part because the developing countries' practices, while deviating from advanced-country and international norms, served them well in managing change and growth through complex transitions with incompletely developed market, legal, and regulatory institutions. But it also "worked" because while the external effects of the developing countries' practices were present, in the aggregate, these countries were not large enough to cause major distortions and imbalances in the global economy or potentially large negative effects on their larger, advanced-country trading partners or each other.

The steady and rapid growth in the developing countries caused these external and systemic effects to grow. We are now at the point where they are big enough to have major effects throughout the whole system. The old hybrid system—in which the developed countries operated according to a set of rules that in principle were designed to allow the whole system to function (and in which the developing countries mainly experimented their way along a path with a focus on domestic growth and development)—won't work anymore. The major high-growth developing countries are big and impactful, and they (or at least some of them) need to be part of a new international system that maintains stability and accommodates the growth and structural changes in both advanced and developing countries.

This is why we now have the G20. It will evolve to include the economies that have major impacts on other countries and on the system. The process is in its very early stages. The challenges are enormous because of the diversity of the major players in terms of income and state of development. The old hybrid was easier. Coordination occurred largely among developed countries, where a reasonable degree of homogeneity prevailed.

Right now the progress is slow. Bilateral disputes dominate, and so reform of the whole system takes a backseat. To advance beyond this, we are going to have to develop the capacity to see the world though the eyes of all the players as a basis for constructing a system that supports their various needs. This applies symmetrically to advanced and developing countries. The former are going to have to get better at understanding and responding to development challenges while the latter will need to better understand and internalize the external and global impacts.

In specifics, we need a different exchange-rate regime than the current hybrid. The new one has yet to be constructed, but it will almost surely need to retain the concept of built-in asymmetries because of the diversity in states of financial-sector development across the systemically important players. But the old model, in which the external effects of developing country policies were ignored because their size was such that the distortions were limited and manageable, has to be abandoned.

Similar adaptations will be required with respect to real-economy interactions and trade. Trade-offs between rules and the flexibility needed to manage economic growth and development will have to be made, with guidelines driven by the magnitude of the external impacts of these policies.

I strongly suspect that we will eventually arrive at a new hybrid. The advanced-country framework of the past quarter century will be replaced and the G20 countries will have to commit to a set of principles designed to avoid suboptimal noncooperative outcomes, ones that make the global system stable and balanced, but which recognize the asymmetries and growing diversity within the systemically impactful group. Other countries will join this grouping as their growth and size dictates. The remaining countries (and here is the hybrid) can, and I believe should, continue to be largely exempt. The argument is that, collectively, they represent less than 15 percent of global GDP. Their systemic effects will be de minimis for some considerable period of time. This is probably the best way to deal with the development and flexibility challenge. It is not a new idea. It is, in effect, just a continuation of the past hybrid system minus the large and rapidly growing countries.

The alternative would be to try to construct frameworks and principles that recognize and accommodate the full range of developing-country diversity and the related challenges. My view is that this is too difficult and is doomed to fail. Better to focus effort on the group with large external systemic effects and fold in the others as they achieve that status.

The reader will have noticed similarities between these structures and frameworks and those that seem to be required to deal successfully with the global carbon mitigation challenge. Both require somewhat complex evolving systems with built-in asymmetries designed to recognize diverse sizes, income levels, and stages of development.

How Can We Make Progress on the New Architecture?

First, the G20 needs to succeed in addressing its two main challenges: first, coordinated financial regulatory reform, and, second, restoring and rebalancing global demand. Its main supporting institutions in these efforts—namely, the Bank for International Settlements (BIS), the Financial Stability Board (FSB), and the IMF—need to be more effective. They have to be; and they must be seen to be governed in a way that is consistent with the evolving economic and financial standing of the participants—the global economy of today and tomorrow, rather than that of yesterday.

Second, politically, for the international agenda to get the attention it urgently deserves, a pattern of sustained growth needs to be restored and unemployment brought down in the industrialized countries. Some of this requires patience as the deleveraging process has further to run. Trying to accelerate that process by overusing the government wallet will negatively impact an already risky drift toward fiscal imbalance and sovereign debt risk in the industrial countries, ultimately damaging growth. Accordingly, governments must do a much better job at communicating realistic assessments of the time horizons and the sacrifices required to restore sustainable growth.

Third, major emerging economies need to become more comfortable with their increased global responsibilities, and that includes accepting their roles in helping to manage the international economic and financial systems, and engaging more forcefully in the reform processes referred to above. Because this comes at stages of development where per capita incomes are still very low by historical standards, this will not be easy. A delicate and sophisticated balancing act will be required between purely domestic growth and development agendas, and international priorities.

Fourth, restoring balance to the global economy and maintaining it along with growth requires structural change in many economies, industrial and emerging. International policy coordination efforts need to reflect this reality and the timelines that are implied.

As part of that effort, exchange-rate regimes need to be brought back into the sphere of international coordination. The present configuration, which dates back to the 1970s, reflects a shift away from managed exchange-rate regimes toward floating rates and market-determined outcomes in the industrial countries. That was never workable in the developing world, where exchange rates have generally been managed for years. This latter group is now larger, and the hybrid system, as noted earlier, is breaking down and adding to potential instability.

The present configuration is a diverse set of unilaterally determined approaches to the exchange rate, interspersed with periodic bilateral negotiations and threats. The result is inevitably likely to be suboptimal uncoordinated equilibria. The system needs to be rebuilt with a view to accommodating the growth, development, and structural-adjustment goals of all countries.

Fifth, the E.U. governance structures are broadly acknowledged to require institutional reform. As one of the two largest economies in the world, its stability and that of the euro have important global implications. While views on the right direction for reform vary, there is agreement that a stable common currency requires fiscal discipline. The shared and deep interest in fiscal discipline is simply inconsistent with complete fiscal decentralization.

That was recognized in the original Maastricht rules. Whether these rules and oversight procedures can be modified so as to accommodate responses to shocks, structural adjustments, and countercyclical policies while maintaining discipline is subject to analysis and debate. The alternative is a greater degree of fiscal centralization, though there remain questions about the political feasibility of moving in that direction.

The G20 appears to be sidetracked by relatively short-term cyclical issues. In part this reflects the fact that a serious discussion of structural change and growth is not yet occurring in the United States. Perhaps there is an implicit presumption that if the shorter-term deleveraging process is completed with a little patience, then growth will return under the influence of private-sector dynamism, with or without a boost from rebalancing of global demand. Perhaps also the present very high unemployment is creating a sense of urgency and causing the political system to look for quick fixes. But here we start again to write public investment out of the script. Properly analyzed, there is a massive deficit in education, human capital, and infrastructure in the United States that must be addressed if growth is to return on a sustained basis so that unemployment can come down. These require the government and the citizens to make a collective commitment to the future and future generations. The starting point with large government deficits makes it all the harder. We dug ourselves into a pretty deep hole. It will take short-term sacrifice to dig out. Whether there is the political capacity and will to do it is an open question. We seem still to be looking for the quick fix or the silver bullet.

The Global Economy at a Crossroads

The global economy is at a critical juncture. It has emerged from the 2008–09 financial crisis weakened, and is still subject to a lengthy process of resetting and rebalancing. It is operating with little room for error, at a time when unemployment in industrial countries is unusually high, the credibility of the banking system very low. Moreover, public debt and deficits have exploded, and the credibility of central banks is being questioned.

It is natural for countries to look inward in such circumstances. Yet this would be a big mistake. The global economy is too interconnected to be subject to orderly national solutions. Proper global coordination and governance must also play a critical role.

Both the run-up to the global financial crisis and the subsequent crisis management process carry important lessons about global governance. Sadly, it appears that some of these lessons are already being forgotten, and others are being negated. Let us hope that this pattern can be changed so that the global economy may reduce the probability of even more economic and financial volatility in the years ahead.

40. The G20, the Advanced Countries, and Global Growth

The G20 is a group of countries, advanced and developing, that has assumed the responsibility for setting priorities in the global economy. It is attempting to address issues of financial reform, fiscal stimulus and balance, and global demand. It asserted after a June 2010 Declaration that its long-run and most important priorities are growth and inclusiveness in the global economy: "The G20's highest priority is to safeguard and strengthen the recovery and lay the foundation for strong, sustainable and balanced growth, and strengthen our financial system against risks." But on the growth part, it is failing. Not, as many assert, because there are deep disagreements about fiscal stimulus and consolidation and other issues, but rather because the basic growth-oriented building blocks at the national level are not in place. Without them, policy coordination will almost certainly fail. The reason is that in the absence of a clear set of commitments (which, I argue below, will entail considerable short-term pain) to five-to-seven-year growth strategies at the national level, none of the major players will know what the global economy will feed back in response to their own commitments. Yes, finding the right combination of fiscal stimulus and restraint is relevant to growth, but it is just part of the story. In all countries, developed and emerging, there are important structural changes, that are needed to sustain growth. *The New York Times* reported in June of 2010 that financial markets are getting nervous about the implicit assumption in developed economies and policy circles that restoration of fiscal balance is the major policy priority with respect to the growth agenda and that the private sector will take care of the rest in terms of growth.[1] That kind of view is widespread in developed countries, but it is not supported by evidence from the history and evolution of either developed or emerging economies. To the contrary, public-sector investment and continuous adaptive policy reform are important elements in facilitating structural change and in sustaining growth and employment.

Growth and Employment Problems in Advanced Countries

The most important single economy is the United States. It is more than twice the size of the second-largest economy, which is now China. Its structural evolution over the past fifteen years has been driven in large part by excess consumption enabled by debt-fueled asset inflation. The crisis put a stop to the excess consumption, but the structural deficiencies and imbalances remain. The export sector is too small and underdeveloped. The financial sector became outsized and is downsizing. A systemic pattern of underinvestment in infrastructure has left the economy less competitive than it should be, despite the continuing private-sector dynamics and innovativeness.

Energy prices have remained low, causing underinvestment in urban infrastructure and in intra- and interurban transportation.

The education system has many strong sectors but continues to have well-known widespread problems with efficiency and effectiveness. While expenditures per student are relatively high, the output of cognitive skills that can be matched to the labor-market needs of a high-income, advanced, and open economy are deficient. To put it bluntly, a significant subset of the population is ill-equipped for productive employment in the rapidly evolving domestic and global economy.

State budgets are in distress as a result of the crisis and insufficiently conservative initial positioning. When times were good, they didn't put away sufficient reserves for a large downturn. Because budget balance for most states (unlike the federal government) is a requirement by constitution and convention, investment supportive of growth will decline rather than increase.

The fiscal side requires long-term balance and a delicate and difficult short- and medium-term trade-off between the benefits of short-run stimulus and the costs of rising sovereign-debt risk (and its associated costs). There are understandable disagreements, internally and internationally, about how to strike this balance, some related to initial conditions and others to different assessments of the risks of deflation and fiscal stability.

Even with a fiscal strategy that balances short-term stimulus and longer-term stability, the United States must still address the composition and size of expenditures, investments, and revenues. To finance growth-supporting long-term investments, domestic private consumption has to shrink. This means higher taxes. In addition, existing government expenditure must be shifted away from consumption and toward investment, meaning fewer government services. Restoring fiscal balance in a way that supports longer-term growth will therefore be painful.

But even that is not enough. The real issue is employment: not just stubbornly high unemployment, but a bigger problem described recently in a thoughtful article by Andy Grove, the longtime chief executive of Intel.[2] He argued that manufacturing is vanishing in the United States, a trend that must be reversed. The question is how.

There is little doubt that America's social contract is starting to break. It had on one side an open, flexible economy, and on the other the promise of employment and rising incomes for the motivated and diligent. It is the second part that is unraveling.

Incomes in the middle-income range for most Americans have stagnated for more than twenty years. Manufacturing jobs are moving offshore. Globally, the set of goods and services that is tradable is expanding, but the United States and other advanced countries are not competing successfully for an adequate share of the tradable sector.

The employment effects of these trends over the past fifteen years have been masked by excess consumption and the overdevelopment of sectors such as finance and real estate. The latter are now set to shrink, as multinational companies grow where they have access to high-growth emerging markets in Asia and Latin America. Such companies will locate their operations where market and supply-chain opportunities lie. In the tradable sector, in manufacturing, and in a growing group of services, that means, increasingly, outside the advanced countries.

The availability of low-cost, disciplined labor forces in developing countries reduces the incentive for these companies to invest in technologies that enhance labor productivity in the tradable sectors of the advanced economies. As a result, the evolving composition of advanced economies is increasingly weighted toward the nontradable sector, combined with a set of high-end tradable services where both human capital and proximity matter. The rest of the tradable sector is shrinking. This is not a market failure in the conventional economic sense. The markets are doing what they are supposed to do: searching for and employing valuable human (and other) resources on a global basis. The problem is rather a distributional one for advanced countries. The global market forces and competition may result in the creation of too few employment opportunities at adequate income levels in these countries, and in particular in the tradable sector. Remember that the set of goods and services that is practically tradable is expanding because of transportation and information-technology innovations.

The shrinkage in the tradable sector creates several problems. Overspecialization could threaten independence and national security. Spillovers between R&D, product development, and manufacturing will be lost if manufacturers leave, a point that Grove emphasizes. Employment will stagnate. Income distribution will move adversely, and the social contract will erode further.

Solutions to these problems are not easy to find. The unequal distribution of income can be dealt with through the tax system, although this does not attack the underlying problem. Protectionism could alter the pattern of out-migration of manufacturing, but only by imposing costs on domestic consumers and risking the breakdown of the open global-economy model.

To avoid an outbreak of protectionism, there has to be an alternative. First, the United States and other advanced countries may need to accept a period of lower income growth in order to restore competitiveness in the tradable sector. Germany did this as part of its restructuring in the period 2000–05, and is now competing more effectively in exports and the tradable sector than other advanced countries. Second, we need new technology investment with public support. A broad public-private partnership to invest in the development of technology in parts of the tradable sector where there are opportunities to make advanced countries competitive could help restore competitiveness and growth. The goal must be to create capital-intensive jobs that have labor-productivity levels consistent with advanced-country incomes.

Would this damage developing countries? Clearly not. The United States does not have hundreds of millions to employ (nor do all the developed economies combined). A targeted program would leave the vast majority of labor-intensive manufacturing right where it is now: in the developing world. With new, credible growth strategies in place in America (and in other advanced countries), developing countries may even be willing to play an important complementary role in restoring global demand through, for example, the reduction of excess savings.

I have gone into some detail on this challenge not to try to provide a complete answer but rather to highlight the importance of comprehensive strategic thinking about growth in the United States (and in other advanced countries, where the details vary but the challenges are similar). Getting the medium-term macroeconomic balance issues right is not sufficient. Growth strategies are needed to get the required public-sector contributions to long-term growth in focus. They are also an important underpinning to the G20's attempt to coordinate the efforts to restore and sustain global growth.

Global Coordination

The major emerging economies and the entire developing world has a large stake and an intense interest in the restoration of growth momentum in the advanced economies, as well as in the maintenance of the openness of the global economy. If the advanced countries developed credible growth strategies, the emerging economies may very well be willing to play an important complementary role.

As implied in the last remark, the United States and the developed countries could use some external help. Armed with a fairly fully developed plan to restore growth while maintaining an open economy, the United States could reasonably go to the surplus countries and ask them as part of a larger bargain to help restore global demand by making, over time, the structural shifts that would lead to a maintenance of growth and openness and a reduction in the excess savings. The plans will differ across the surplus countries because of different initial conditions, stages of development, and structural challenges. But they should all be similarly specific with respect to timing and content.

China, as a result of an active internal debate (albeit with outside input), is well along in developing the policies that will shift the demand and supply sides of the economy, increase household income, reduce household and overall savings, and drive more growth from the domestic market. As in the United States, these structural changes are complex to implement in a way that sustains the growth momentum. And the reforms are by no means complete.

Similar plans from other surplus countries should be formulated (some are already in place or in process), and merged into a global plan for restoring balanced growth.

The major developing countries have displayed remarkable resilience in the crisis and its aftermath. Growth is returning and is already approaching precrisis levels in Asia (East and South) and in Latin America, the latter helped in no small measure by the tailwind provided by Asian growth. I argued earlier that this growth is sustainable even in the event of slow medium-term growth in the developed countries. The reason is that the size of the emerging-market economies taken together is large and growing. Trade within the group is substantial and growing, and perhaps most important, incomes are rising, so that the composition of demand is better matched to the productive capabilities of these economies. In addition, macroeconomic management in the developing countries is sound and conservative, and the commitment to reform and structural change is deeply embedded. In short, the ingredients for sustained high growth are in place.

The ability to sustain high growth with a slow developed-country recovery would not have been true ten years ago. While the structural change was in place, the aggregate demand and the income levels would not have been sufficient to compensate for the shortfall on the developed-country side. It is also true that while the emerging economies can probably sustain high growth in the context of an extended slow-growth restructuring in the developed economies, a major downturn or crisis in the latter is a different story—the proposition about sustaining growth would not hold.

The persistence of growth in the emerging markets is a major positive for the global economy in terms of overall growth and because of the positive impact it will have on the smaller, poorer developing countries. In addition, it will help lubricate the structural adjustments in the advanced economies.

If the G20 is able to agree that a coordinated and coherent strategy for restoring and sustaining balanced global growth requires these concrete national growth strategies as building blocks, then it should ask for them. Its supporting institutions—the IMF, the World Bank, the BIS, and the FSB—should then be tasked with determining whether they add up in terms of consistency. Adjustments will undoubtedly be needed, as national level assumptions about external conditions on both the supply and the demand sides for any given major country may not be consistent with the plans and projections of the others. A process of negotiation and reconciliation would be needed to make sure that the adding-up constraints are satisfied.

In order to carry out the task of assessing the viability and coherence of the component growth strategies, the supporting organizations will need to have broad and deep knowledge of the structural dynamics that underpin growth in a wide range of countries at various income levels and stages of growth. It is useful but not sufficient to have expertise in the macroeconomic and monetary management spheres. Building that deep understanding is an important underpinning of the process of supporting the implementation of G20 growth goals.

Absent a reasonably disciplined bottom-up process of this type, rebalancing global demand and restoring the conditions for balanced growth will most probably remain words and concepts: goals without a path to get there. Every country will have legitimate concerns that this or that country's contributions, which by assumption will be vague, will fall short of adequate and that some will be free-riding on the investment, structural change, and growth of others.

A workable set of understandings about coordinated growth policy will enable the G20 to address the specific issues on its agenda. These include the following:

- Restoring and rebalancing global demand with the twin goals of growth and sustainability.
- Restarting the WTO process with an agenda guided in terms of priorities by the growth targets of various classes of countries. Completion of the Doha round is important to developing countries, and hence to G20 credibility. A substantive step toward restoring openness in the global economy should be a high priority.[3]
- Coordinating financial reform to achieve stability and sufficient consistency (to avoid regulatory end runs). Ensuring that financial flows are free enough to support the financing component of the growth strategies is important. A set of understandings about in-

vestment behavior on the part of the major holdings of reserves and sovereign wealth funds is a critical part of achieving stability. This behavior needs to be consistent with the surplus- and deficit-reduction transitions that are agreed on.

Currencies and exchange rates will also need to be addressed in a more systematic way, and not just on a contentious bilateral basis. The post–Bretton Woods system that we have now is a hybrid. Developed countries by and large have floating exchange rates, independent monetary policies, and no reserve accumulation. (Japan is something of an exception.) The emerging economies never followed the same rules—for good reason, we now understand. Exchange rates are managed, capital controls are in place (both inbound and outbound, for different reasons), and, after 1997–98, significant reserves have been accumulated. These exchange rate policies were undertaken as part of a set of overall growth strategies. Judgments clearly have to be made, and that implies that occasionally, mistakes are made too.

As we saw earlier, in developing countries, it is now fairly well understood that an undervalued currency is not a basis for long-term sustained growth. Pursued too aggressively, or for too long, it damages domestic suppliers of the domestic market, locks in the export sector to a low value-added configuration, and stalls structural change. But as an interim strategy for jump-starting export diversification in the context of a surplus labor environment and managing volatility that otherwise would add risk and would damage foreign direct investment, it has merits as well as the aforementioned risks. This is why we have ended up with the hybrid system.

This system more or less worked for an extended period of time (about twenty-five years) because it met the needs of diverse economies, and, importantly, because the external impacts of emerging countries on overall global financial and economic balance were small enough to ignore. That time has passed. The divergent needs are still present but the systemically important external effects of emerging-country policies are too large and important to ignore. This is the direct result of their increasing size. The emerging countries need to understand and accept this. For G20 countries, exchange rates are not just domestic issues anymore. The old hybrid won't work because of these growing external effects and because floating exchange rates in a relatively volatile capital market environment won't either. For the G20 core, we will need a new system that accommodates these diverse needs but balances them against system-wide balance and distributional issues. The non-G20 group countries, large in number and small in economic size (less than 15 percent of global GDP), can probably usefully function under the old hybrid model. Adding them in will probably only create unnecessary complexity.

The G20 Declaration from the recent June 2010 meeting in Toronto is quite lengthy. Lots of words blanket the outstanding issues. But apart from the barely hidden disagreements, what is missing is not scope or intent; rather, it is a meaningful sense of what it will take to bring all parties toward a concrete set of longer-term growth-oriented agreements, with some reasonable degree of confidence that each is contributing adequately according to his ability and to some extent receiving according to his needs.

This is a cooperative game on a giant scale that we are trying to learn how to play, a complex one because of asymmetries among the players. The chances that asynchronous moves and separate agreements on distinct issues will lead to a fully cooperative outcome are very low. More likely is a noncooperative outcome with attendant suboptimal results and instability. A bumpy road to a new and not very attractive normal.

National growth-oriented strategies in this context are building blocks that can be thought of as potential commitments, ones that recognize divergent initial conditions and capacities but that bring specificity to the contributions to the overall outcome.

Underpinning such an effort, there is a need to recognize that growth entails continuous reform, adaptation, and structural change. This framework seems to have been thoroughly internalized in the emerging economies and their governments. But not in the developed countries.

Let me go back to the *New York Times* article on the policy focus on fiscal timing and balance, with the private sector picking up the rest of the growth challenge. Though probably the majority view, it has several problems. It is probably not right. The private sector is clearly critical. But the structural evolution and competitiveness of an economy comes from the interaction of public-sector policies and investments and private-sector incentives and dynamism. The advanced countries should not fall into the trap of implicitly adopting a narrowed-down version of the Washington consensus.

More to the point, the successful emerging economies don't believe it, based on lengthy and at times painful experience. If the debate in the West focuses exclusively on fiscal stimulus or consolidation and timing and on financial regulation, unemployment and incomes will continue to be a problem. Protectionism will seem an increasingly attractive option. It will be impossible to produce credible growth-oriented strategies (as viewed from an emerging-economy perspective). That in turn will undercut the G20 process. Thus, part of the process has to be a more serious discussion of longer-term growth in the developed countries.

Perhaps the mutual assessment processes that are under way under the auspices of the G20 will move things in the right direction. Much is at stake. The future of cooperation and global growth rest in the balance.

41. Sustaining Growth: The Second Half Century of Convergence

Much of our growing awareness of sustainability has to do with the environment. We use more energy and water, create more waste, emit more particulates and gases, and negatively impact biodiversity via land use, climate change, and in other ways. The addition of billions of people to the high-income ranks, with its attendant high consumption patterns, increases the pressure enormously.

But the issue of sustainability is not confined to the environment. We have seen developing countries grow and then stop because the structural underpinnings had built-in natural brakes. In the years preceding the 2008 crisis, advanced economies were sustaining growth with asset bubbles and excess consumption. That turned out to be unsustainable, and the rebuilding of a sound basis for employment and growth is now the central economic challenge, and is proving to be difficult. It will require short- and medium-term adjustments that are not yet fully understood or internalized within the political and policy-making choice matrix.

I have long thought about sustainability in terms of balance sheets. The idea is that our economies and lifestyles are underpinned by a set of assets, not just the conventional ones like infrastructure, but a broader set that includes the ecology of the planet and the knowledge base on which we function. If we run those assets down over time, then one way or another, material well-being and quality of life will suffer. We will have damaged the opportunities of future generations, possibly in several different dimensions. At the very least we will have imposed costs on future generations that we ourselves did not have to bear to the same extent. Most of us think that there is a moral imperative not to do that.

If we accept this moral constraint, then individuals, corporations, and governments need to internalize these values and to adopt guidelines that place some emphasis on preserving the assets that affect economic well-being and opportunity and quality of life. It should motivate us to think harder than we perhaps normally do about what those assets are. All this would be a step in the right direction.

But it won't be enough. The answer is more complicated than preserving the status quo by not damaging the tangible and intangible asset bases of our economies. The challenges of the transformations coming in the next fifty years require more than preventing "balance sheet" degradations, and sustaining the future of growth will require more than preserving the status quo. To accommodate the massive changes in the global economy that are before us, the old asset base of institutions and knowledge will not be sufficient. We will need new things: governance structures, technologies, incentive systems, institutions, even values— things that will enable us to navigate through uncharted territory as the asymmetries between advanced and developing countries systematically decline, and as the powerful participants in governance, with all their diversity, multiply. Part of this evolution will surely involve understanding and accepting the newcomers in the structures of governance.

In this context, sustainability is likely to require not just operational attention to maintaining, or at least not diminishing, the opportunity set of our grandchildren (the "balance sheet," if you like). It will require much more than that, something more akin to creative adaptability. We need to be able to solve problems that are new, some that we can see from our current vantage point and others that will appear later, that are presently over the horizon. The experience of developing countries is hugely relevant in this respect. As a framework, developing countries accepted the importance of decentralization, market incentives, and entrepreneurial capitalist dynamics. Also, clarity of goals and persistence in pursuit of them, combined with a problem-solving mind-set in a complex and rapidly shifting internal and external environment, has served these countries well. It will serve the global economy well, too.

Are we on the right course? As Zhou Enlai, the first premier of the People's Republic of China, said when asked about the impact of the French Revolution, "It is too soon to say." It is probably fair to say that we are on a steep, long learning curve and have a very substantial distance to go. On the positive side, awareness of global issues among politicians and the general public seems to be growing, along with expanding knowledge of the circumstances of people in other countries. Perhaps this will form a firmer foundation of international cooperation and governance as time passes. Growth in the developing world appears to be expanding in scope.

But there are headwinds. Among them are major challenges to be dealt with in the industrialized countries, including adapting to the growing impact of the global economy on their own economies. Grappling successfully with growth, employment, and structural change will increase the likelihood that the openness of the global economy will not start to erode. It will also make the advanced countries more inclined to provide effective leadership in achieving cooperative policy choices in the context of the G20.

Getting there from where we are now will be difficult. Political, business, and academic elites have lost credibility with the populace in many countries. We have been wrong about important characteristics of the economy that affect people's lives, and relatively insensitive to distributional issues. The benefits of global openness have been oversold and the potentially adverse distributional impacts brushed aside. Being wrong does not seem to have been accompanied, however, by the expected increment in humility. The loss of trust in the elites has left a vacuum that is being filled by an increasingly confrontational politics, one in which shared goals are few, and investment in the world that future generations will inherit is well below optimal, nor does it seem to be a high priority.

Rebuilding an inclusive, centrist, pragmatic agenda, with a cooperative problem-solving approach to addressing it, will take time and effort, and it is important. The challenges ahead to sustaining growth and expanding opportunity in the final fifty years of a century of convergence are large. So also is our capacity for creativity and adaptation. But to unleash it, we need to be firmly committed to inclusiveness globally and to be willing to set aside overly simple and somewhat ideological prescriptions of the one-size-fits-all sort, regardless of where on the political spectrum they emanate from.

These problems we have been discussing are hard, because they are global and new. People will disagree on the road to experimenting with, and finding, solutions. In this context, those who disagree with a particular point of view are not necessarily morally or intellectually deficient, and to characterize them in this fashion will do little for forward movement.

Given the magnitude of the shock from the recent crisis, the difficulty of restoring employment, the incentives for protectionist solutions, and the potential for divisive politics, it would be easy to be pessimistic. But I am an optimist at heart. Yet even optimists think it reasonable to expect a bumpy and volatile road ahead for the next few years. But then, the newfound dynamism of the developing countries, combined with a righting of the advanced-country ships, will likely set us on a new sustainable course. It will be a multispeed world, and a hard one to manage. And although the stakes are high, the problems are not beyond the scope of human ingenuity. Past experience and conceptual tools will be useful but not sufficient. We, and future generations, will have to invent our way through and around the potential roadblocks along the way.

Notes

5. Economic Growth

1. Jonathan K. Nelson and Richard J. Zeckhauser, *The Patron's Payoff*, Princeton University Press, 2008.

2. There is an Indian inventor by the name of Kanak Gogoi who has produced a host of interesting technologies and products. Among his numerous inventions are a gravity-operated bicycle and a car that can run on air. He steadfastly refuses to commercialize his innovations, though he has no problem in having others do so. See "Techie Builds Air-Car! Refuses Commercialization," *Silicon India*, November 23, 2009.

6. Common Questions About the Developing World and the Global Economy

1. The idea to class together Brazil, Russia, India, and China (the BRICs) originated with a talented economist at Goldman Sachs named Jim O'Neill. His early insight was that the very large and potentially high-growth countries would have an increasing impact on the global economy. Interestingly, the BRICs didn't really think of themselves as part of a group until O'Neill's work. Now they perceive themselves as having this identification with overlapping common interests and a pattern of regular interaction.

7. The High-Growth Developing Countries in the Postwar Period

1. *The Growth Report: Strategies for Sustained Growth and Inclusive Development*, the main report of the Commission on Growth and Development, May 2008, published by the World Bank Group on behalf of the Commission. All Growth Commission publications can be found and downloaded without cost at www .growthcommission.org.

9. Knowledge Transfer and Catch-up Growth in Developing Countries

1. Mohamed El-Erian and Michael Spence, "Growth Strategies and Dynamics: Insights from Country Experience," *World Economics*, vol. 9, no. 1, January–March 2008.

12. Key Internal Ingredients of Sustained High-Growth Recipes

1. Basic economic training focuses attention on efficiency in the static sense. (Given technology, how do market systems cause the allocation of resources to be matched to consumer needs and to be reasonably efficient?) There is nothing wrong with this. It is probably the right way to learn microeconomics and price theory. However, for economic performance, the dynamics of competition, innovation, cost reduction, and product differentiation are quantitatively more important in the longer term.

2. The trade surplus is the difference between exports and imports. It can be negative, in which case it is called the trade deficit. The current account surplus is the trade surplus plus interest on foreign assets minus interest payments to foreigners, plus financial aid. When a country's current account surplus is positive, its net international asset holdings are increasing—citizens are buying more foreign assets than foreigners are buying domestic assets. That means there are net capital outflows. The sum of the current and capital account surpluses is always zero.

3. If entities (businesses and households, or even the government) in one country borrow money externally and the debt is denominated in the external currency, then, if the domestic currency falls in value relative to the foreign currency, the debt, valued in the domestic currency, rises. Notice that it is not just foreign borrowing that creates the risk, but that plus having the debt repayment required to be in the foreign currency. That last provision causes the currency risk to be borne by the borrower. This has led developing countries to try to avoid borrowing in this way and to hold reserves so that they have some control over the exchange rate.

4. Sir W. Arthur Lewis is the scholar and Nobel laureate who created the theory of economic growth and development in economies with large supplies of underemployed labor residing in traditional sectors like agriculture. See W. Arthur Lewis, "Economic Development with Unlimited Supplies of Labor," *Manchester School of Economic and Social Studies*, vol. 22, 1954, pp. 139–91. The structural factors that he identified remain an important part of growth dynamics.

5. It is of course crucial that financing for this kind of investment be available. Commonly it is not, and that impedes the development of the agricultural and other traditional sectors. This is a major bottleneck in many developing countries.

14. The Washington Consensus and the Role of Government

1. David Leonhardt, "Bet on Private Sector for Recovery Could Prove Risky," *New York Times*, June 29, 2010.

17. The Political, Leadership, and Governance Underpinnings of Growth

1. David Brady and Michael Spence (editors), *Leadership and Growth*, a volume published by the World Bank Group on behalf of the Commission on Growth and Development, 2010. See, in particular, chapter 1, by Brady and Spence, "Leadership and Politics: A Perspective from the Commission on Growth and Development."

18. Low-Growth Economies in the Developing World

1. *Human Development Report* (HDR 2007/2008), published for the United Nations Development Program (UNDP). Full report can be accessed at the website, hdr.undp.org/en/reports/global/hdr2007-2008.

19. Natural Resource Wealth and Growth

1. The Natural Resource Charter is a work in process. From its website: "The Natural Resource Charter is a global initiative designed to help governments and societies effectively harness the opportunities created by natural resources. Some of the poorest countries in the world have large amounts of natural resources. These can provide a pathway out of poverty. In the past, however, these opportunities have often been missed and resource abundant countries have consequently remained poor." The current version of the charter and related material can be found at the website, www.naturalresourcecharter.org.

21. The Adding-Up Problem

1. The chief authority on the economic analysis of the adding-up problem is William R. Cline. See William R. Cline, "Exports of Manufactures and Economic Growth: The Fallacy of Composition Revisited," Working Paper Number 36, published by the World Bank Group on behalf of the Commission on Growth and Development, 2008. All working papers, volumes, and reports of the commission are accessible at the website, www.growthcommission.org/index.php. In this paper, Cline reviews the experience of the global economy in manufacturing exports since the publication of his important 1982 paper "Can the East Asian Model of Development Be Generalized?" *World Development*, 10(2), 1982, 81–90.

22. Emerging Markets During and After the Global Crisis

1. For a discussion of the impact of the crisis and the lessons learned, from a developing-economy perspective, see *Post-Crisis Growth in the Developing World: A Special Report of the Commission on Growth and Development on the Implications of the 2008 Financial Crisis*, published by the World Bank Group on behalf of the Commission on Growth and Development, 2010. The report can be found on the commission's website, www.growthcommission.org.

2. There are of course many other contributing factors that add to the complexity: incentive and agency problems, unregulated sectors, incomplete information and disclosure requirements, rating-agency issues, challenges for contrarians when the turning point is hard to know, and investors voting with dollars for returns with largely unseen fat-tail risks.

3. China's managed appreciation of the yuan stopped in the summer of 2008 and was pegged to the dollar thereafter. The managed appreciation resumed in June 2010 as China emerged from the crisis with a rapid restoration of growth. When the yuan was pegged to the dollar, it appreciated with respect to most other currencies, including all the developing-country ones, in the first six months of the crisis, because the dollar was appreciating against the euro, the pound, and the developing-country currencies. As of the spring of 2009 this pattern reversed, with the dollar depreciating and along with it the yuan. In some ways for China this is a replay of the '97–'98 crisis, when the Asian currencies depreciated rapidly and China held the peg to the dollar, losing competitiveness and responding with what at the time was a large fiscal stimulus.

4. In East Asia, where there is residual mistrust of the IMF, China provided stabilizing resources during the early stages of the crisis by making its reserves available through swap arrangements with a number of countries. The total of these arrangements, as of June 2009, was about $95 billion. At present the major developing countries are contributing to the expanded IMF resources by buying bonds issued by the IMF. In addition, the IMF is working to reestablish good working relationships with Asian economies. This is important because the Asian economies are a growing part of the global economy and their involvement in maintaining global financial stability is crucial.

5. This control issue does not mean that partial foreign ownership is precluded. Noncontrolling interests in existing institutions or joint ventures with good business models and prospects will remain an attractive option.

6. The McKinsey studies of global capital markets make quite clear that as countries grow and increase their incomes, the financial sector evolves. The share of banking in the total pool of gross assets declines, while the share of traded securities, equity, debt, and securitized assets increases. See *Global Capital Markets: Entering a New Era*, September 2009, published by the McKinsey Global Institute. See also *Mapping Global Capital Markets: Fifth Annual Report*, published by the McKinsey Global Institute, October 2008. MGI publications can be found and downloaded at the website, www.mckinsey.com/mgi.

23. Instability in the Global Economy and Lessons from the Crisis

1. For a fascinating account of the trading activities, the distorted incentives, and the activities of contrarians who were trying to bet against the stability of the system, see Michael Lewis, *The Big Short: Inside the Doomsday Machine*, W. W. Norton & Company, 2010.

2. A power law distribution is one in which the frequency of the occurrence of some variable (say, the size of a city, or the magnitude of an earthquake) declines in such

a way that any percentage increase in the size produces a constant proportional reduction in the frequency. These are surprisingly ubiquitous in science and social science and have been intensively studied.

25. Rebalancing the Global Economy and Its Consequences for Growth

1. I will henceforth refer to the trade deficit. To be perfectly accurate, I should say current account deficit. See above, chapter 12, note 2, on the trade surplus and the current surplus.
2. There are lots of inflows and outflows. The net inflow or outflow is the sum of the inflows and outflows.
3. If incomes rise by 20 percent but the exchange rate depreciates by 20 percent against the dollar, then domestic incomes have not changed in terms of dollar purchasing power. As a result, there is no loss of cost competitiveness in the export sector. The pressure for structural change is removed.

26. The Excess-Savings Challenge in China

1. It isn't really mercantilism. Mercantilism was never a coherent theory but rather a mishmash of conjectures about what produces national wealth. Ingredients that appeared in various versions included hoarding gold, running trade surpluses, blocking imports. Most of the historical writers seem not to have noticed that if you run a trade surplus you are exporting capital. However incoherent the intellectual underpinnings, the term has come to connote trade surpluses, protection, hoarding gold, and adopting policies that don't add up if adopted universally. It is a way to be critical and dismissive without being terribly specific as to why.

29. Periodic Systemic Risk and Investment Behavior

1. For a discussion of making policy decisions in uncertain environments and with incomplete models, the reader may want to look at Mohamed A. El-Erian and Michael Spence, "Growth Strategies and Dynamics: Insights from Country Experiences," *World Economics*, vol. 9, no. 1, 2008.
2. See, for example, Carmen M. Reinhart and Kenneth Rogoff, *This Time Is Different: Eight Centuries of Financial Folly*, Princeton University Press, 2009.
3. The unpredictability of the break point is one of the challenges facing contrarians, be they investors, analysts, or policy makers.
4. Approaching the payout this way is a form of self-insurance against volatility in the income stream. It may or may not be the most efficient way to achieve this result.
5. The ability to do this is clearly affected by the liquidity of the portfolio. I will return to the subject of liquidity in a subsequent section.
6. The arguments are familiar. (E.g., "Why are we spending 4 percent of the endowment when the aggregate annual return, including donations, has been running in the 15–20 percent range for more than a decade?")

7. For a fascinating account of the experience of contrarian investors in the crisis, one should read Michael Lewis, *The Big Short: Inside the Doomsday Machine*, W. W. Norton & Company, 2010.

33. India's Growth, Diversification, and Urbanization

1. As I finishing the writing of the manuscript, the new Terminal 3 at Indira Gandhi International Airport in New Delhi was inaugurated by Prime Minister Dr. Manmohan Singh and UPA (United Progressive Alliance) chairperson Mrs. Sonia Gandhi on July 3, 2010.

35. Energy and Growth

1. Kenneth Rogoff, "Can Good Emerge from the BP Oil Spill?" *Project Syndicate*, July 2, 2010. Project Syndicate essays by distinguished scholars and authors can be found at www.project-syndicate.org.

36. The Challenge of Climate Change and Developing-Country Growth

1. The most recent authoritative estimates of carbon emissions and their impacts can be found in the *Human Development Report, 2007/2008*, published on behalf of the United Nations Development Program. The HDR relies heavily on the reports of the Intergovernmental Panel on Climate Change. This is the body that collects and assesses the scientific evidence on climate change. The *IPCC Fourth Assessment Report of 2007* (its most recent) is available on the IPCC website, www.ipcc.ch. The Fifth Assessment Report is in process and not yet complete.

2. This does not mean that the rest of the developing world can be ignored. These countries will also grow, and they are certainly exposed to potential damage from climate change. In addition, reforestation and afforestation will require the engagement of a much larger group of countries on terms that are understandable and fair.

3. In recent years, much discussion (including in Copenhagen) was devoted setting the long-run targets, either in degrees or CO_2 emissions per capita. This is largely a waste of time. It diverts attention from the task of setting manageable shorter-term goals. In addition, setting longer-term targets is too risky, for both advanced and developing countries. We just don't know at this stage what price we will need to pay or what costs will be incurred to meet those targets. And we won't know that for several decades.

4. See *The Growth Report: Strategies for Sustained Growth and Inclusive Development*, May 2008, at www.growthcommission.org. The section on climate change lays out some of the issues.

5. A useful detailed description of China's green energy programs and energy efficiency strategies can be found in an article in the *McKinsey Quarterly* (May 2009), "China's Green Opportunity," by Martin Joerss, Jonathan R. Woetzel, and Haimeng Zhang. India has implemented a switch to compressed natural gas in high-emissions three-

wheeled vehicles in major cities. Brazil has made major progress in transitioning to an ethanol-based transportation system. There are many other examples.

6. I have tried to describe, in greater detail, the workings of implementation schemes that could go along with a path that accommodates developing-country growth and hits the fifty-year targets. That analysis is in a working paper for the Commission on Growth and Development. "Climate Change, Mitigation, and Developing Country Growth," working paper #64. It is on the Commission on Growth and Development website. It is permanently archived at www.growthcommission.org.

7. I am not suggesting that the UN be relieved of its overall responsibility for global agreements. But setting the priorities and managing the crucial executive support needs to be done in a smaller, more manageable setting.

37. Information Technology and the Integration of the Global Economy

1. Metcalfe's law states that "the value of a telecommunications network is proportional to the square of the number of connected users of the system." Robert Metcalfe is a co-inventor of the Ethernet. This version of the law named after him was articulated by George Gilder.

2. Canada's immigration policy includes a category that it sometimes referred to as the "economic group." Immigrants in this category are admitted according to a point system that is based on age, health, education and skills, and assets. It is designed to ascertain the ease of employability of an applicant. It may also correlate with expected added value of the candidate to the economy.

3. See Paul A. Samuelson, "Where Ricardo and Mill Rebut and Confirm Arguments of Mainstream Economists Supporting Globalization," *Journal of Economic Perspectives*, vol. 18, no. 3, 2004.

40. The G20, the Advanced Countries, and Global Growth

1. David Leonhardt, "Bet on Private Sector Could Prove Risky," *New York Times*, June 29, 2010.

2. Andy Grove, "How America Can Create Jobs," *Bloomberg Businessweek*, July 1, 2010.

3. What worries policy makers in the emerging economies is the apparent desire on the part of the United States to reopen the wide range of issues that were regarded as settled—and to do this without fast-track authority. This would almost certainly cause the process to get bogged down. It may be better to pass a slimmed-down version of the Doha, sometimes called "Doha light," in order to be able to achieve closure and a measure of success and move on. It is clear that something concrete, something that goes beyond words, is needed to make credible the commitments to an open global trading system. That is of extreme importance to the developing countries, as discussed in earlier parts of the book.

Index

Page numbers in *italics* refer to illustrations and graphs.